Knowledge and Certainty

Knowledge and Certainty

Essays and Lectures
by
Norman Malcolm

Prentice-Hall, Inc.   Englewood Cliffs, N. J.

13146

PRENTICE-HALL INTERNATIONAL, INC., *London*

PRENTICE-HALL OF AUSTRALIA, PTY., LTD., *Sydney*

PRENTICE-HALL OF CANADA, LTD., *Toronto*

PRENTICE-HALL FRANCE, S.A.R.L., *Paris*

PRENTICE-HALL OF JAPAN, INC., *Tokyo*

PRENTICE-HALL DE MEXICO, S.A., *Mexico City*

Preface

The following essays and lectures are closely connected in two ways. First, certain philosophical problems about knowledge, perception, verification, certainty, incorrigibility, possibility of error, grounds, proof—concepts that are fundamental to the theory of knowledge—are studied from different angles. Second, the influence of my teachers, friends, and heroes, G. E. Moore and Ludwig Wittgenstein, is evident throughout.

Seven of the essays have been published previously. They are placed here in chronological order. "The Verification Argument" was published in *Philosophical Analysis,* edited by Max Black, Prentice-Hall, Inc., Englewood Cliffs, N.J., 1950. It is published here without revision of the text, but new footnotes have been added. "Knowledge and Belief" was published in *Mind,* Vol. LXI, N. S., No. 242, April, 1952. I have made changes in the text and have added footnotes. "Direct Perception" appeared in *The Philosophical Quarterly,* Vol. III, No. 13, October, 1953. The text has been revised and a number of footnotes added. "Wittgenstein's *Philosophical Investigations*" first appeared in *The Philosophical Review,* Vol. LXIII, No. 4, October, 1954. There is some correction of the text and there are new footnotes. "Knowledge of Other Minds" first appeared in *The Journal of Philosophy,* Vol. LV, No. 23, November 6, 1958. It is published here with scarcely any change. "Anselm's Ontological Arguments" first appeared in

The Philosophical Review, Vol. LXIX, No. 1, January, 1960. Three new footnotes have been added.

"George Edward Moore" was delivered in different versions as a lecture at Cooper Union and at several Scandinavian Universities. It is published here for the first time in English. A somewhat different version of it appeared, in Finnish translation, in *Ajatus,* Vol. XXIV, 1962.

The three lectures on memory were delivered to a colloquium at Princeton University in January, 1962. They have been revised. The first of them, "Memory and the Past," was published in *The Monist,* Vol. 47:2, December, 1962. The second and third are published here for the first time. My thinking about many points in these lectures was greatly benefited by numerous discussions with Professors Jaakko Hintikka and George Henrik von Wright, while I was a Fulbright Research Fellow at the University of Helsinki during the academic year of 1960-1961.

I wish to thank the Editors of *Mind, The Philosophical Quarterly, The Philosophical Review, The Journal of Philosophy, Ajatus,* and *The Monist,* for permission to reprint the articles previously published in those journals.

NORMAN MALCOLM
Ithaca, N.Y., April 1963

Contents

The Verification Argument, 1

Knowledge and Belief, 58

Direct Perception, 73

Wittgenstein's Philosophical Investigations, *96*

Knowledge of Other Minds, 130

Anselm's Ontological Arguments, 141

George Edward Moore, 163

THREE LECTURES ON MEMORY

Memory and the Past, 187

Three Forms of Memory, 203

A Definition of Factual Memory, 222

Knowledge and Certainty

The Verification Argument

A number of arguments have been used by various philosophers to prove that the truth of no empirical statement is absolutely certain. In this paper I wish to examine *one* of these arguments. The argument has, to the best of my knowledge, been stated more forcefully by C. I. Lewis than by any other writer. I will quote from him in order to obtain a strong presentation of the argument.

While engaged in discussing the statement "A piece of white paper is now before me," Lewis says the following:

This judgment will be false if the presentation is illusory; it will be false if what I see is not really paper; false if it is not really white but only looks white. This objective judgment also is one capable of corroboration. As in the other example [the other example, to which Lewis refers, is the statement "There is a flight of granite steps before me"], so here too, any test of the judgment would pretty surely involve some way of acting—*making* the test, as by continuing to look, or turning my eyes, or grasping to tear, etc.—and would be determined by finding or failing to find some expected result in experience. But in this example, if the result of any single test is as expected, it constitutes a partial verification of the judgment only; never one which is absolutely decisive and theoretically complete. This is so because, while the judgment, so far as it is significant, contains nothing which could not be tested, still it has a significance which outruns what any single test, or any limited set of tests, could exhaust. No matter how fully I may have investigated this objective fact, there will remain some theoretical possibility of mistake; there will be further consequences which must be thus and so if the judgment is true, and not all of these will have been determined. The possibility that such further tests, if made, might have a negative result, cannot be altogether precluded; and this possibility marks the judgment as, at the time in question, not fully verified and less than absolutely certain. To quibble about such possible doubts will not, in most cases, be common-sense. But we are not trying to weigh the degree of theoretical dubiety which common-sense practicality should take account of, but to arrive at an accurate analysis of knowledge. This character of being further testable and less than theoretically certain characterizes every judgment of objective fact at all times; every judgment that such and such a real thing exists or has a certain objectively factual property, or that a certain objective event actually occurs, or that any objective state of affairs actually is the case.[1]

The same argument is stated more dramatically by Lewis in *Mind and the World Order*. He says:

Obviously in the statement "This penny is round" I assert implicitly *everything the failure of which would falsify the statement*. The implicit prediction of *all* experience which is essential to its *truth* must be contained in the original judgment. Otherwise, such experience would be irrelevant. All that further experience the failure of which would lead to the repudiation of the apprehension as illusory or mistaken is predicted in the judgment made. Now suppose we ask: How long will it be possible to verify in some manner the fact that this penny is round? What totality of experience would verify it completely beyond the possibility of necessary reconsideration? . . . it seems to be the fact that *no* verification would be absolutely complete; that all verification is partial and a matter of degree. . . . Is it not the case that the simplest statement of objective particular fact implicitly asserts something about possible experience throughout all future time; that theoretically every objective fact is capable of some verification at any later date, and that no totality of such experience is absolutely and completely sufficient to put our knowledge of such particulars beyond all possibility of turning out to be in error?[2]

For the purpose of refuting it, Lewis considers the supposition that at a certain time, designated as t_1, the verification of such a

---

[1] C. I. Lewis, *An Analysis of Knowledge and Valuation* (La Salle, Ill.: Open Court Publishing Co., 1946), p. 180.
[2] *Mind and the World Order* (New York: Charles Scribner's Sons, 1929), pp. 279-281.

statement as "This penny is round" could be complete. He continues the argument:

Now suppose further that at some date, t_2, we put ourselves in position to meet the consequences of this fact, which was accepted as completely established at t_1. And suppose that these consequences fail to appear, or are not what the nature of the accepted fact requires? In that case, will there still be no doubt about the accepted fact? Or will what was supposedly established at t_1 be subject to doubt at t_2? And in the latter case can we suppose it was absolutely verified at time t_1? Since no single experience can be absolutely guaranteed to be veridical, no limited collection or succession of experiences can absolutely guarantee an empirical fact as certain beyond the possibility of reconsideration.[3]

Many other philosophers have made use of this argument.

Carnap, for example, uses it in his paper "Testability and Meaning." [4] He says:

Take for instance the following sentence "There is a white sheet of paper on this table." In order to ascertain whether this thing is paper, we may make a set of simple observations and then, if there still remains some doubt, we may make some physical and chemical experiments. Here . . . we try to examine sentences which we infer from the sentence in question. These inferred sentences are predictions about future observations. The number of such predictions which we can derive from the sentence given is infinite; and therefore the sentence can never be completely verified. To be sure, in many cases we reach a practically sufficient certainty after a small number of positive instances, and then we stop experimenting. But there is always the theoretical possibility of continuing the series of test-observations. Therefore here . . . *no complete verification is possible* but only a process of gradually increasing *confirmation.*[5]

He continues: "For such a simple sentence as e.g. 'There is a white thing on this table' the degree of confirmation, after a few observations have been made, will be so high that we practically

---

[3] *Ibid.*, pp. 281-282.
[4] Rudolf Carnap, "Testability and Meaning," *Philosophy of Science,* III, IV (1936, 1937). This argument is also used by Carnap in *Philosophy and Logical Syntax* (London: Routledge & Kegan Paul, Ltd., 1935), pp. 11-13 and in *Logical Syntax of Language* (New York: Harcourt, Brace & World, Inc., 1937), p. 246; by A. J. Ayer, in *Foundations of Empirical Knowledge* (New York: The Macmillan Company, 1940), pp. 42-45; by K. Popper, in *Logik der Forschung* (Vienna: J. Springer, 1935), pp. 60-62.
[5] *Philosophy of Science,* III (1936), 425.

cannot help accepting the sentence. But even in this case there remains still the theoretical possibility of denying the sentence." [6]

Before proceeding to an analysis of this argument, which I will call "the Verification Argument," I wish to say something about the nature of the conclusion which it is thought to prove. Previously I said that it is thought to prove that no empirical statements are absolutely certain. But this remark is not sufficiently clear because of a haziness in the meaning of the expression "empirical statements." Certainly no philosopher who has used the Verification Argument has intended that the argument should apply to necessary or a priori truths. But there is a class of statements with regard to which philosophers have had difficulty in deciding whether to classify statements of that class as empirical statements; and among those philosophers who have used the Verification Argument there would be disagreement and hesitation about saying whether the argument applies to statements of that class. Statements of the class in question have been called "incorrigible propositions" or "basic propositions" or "expressive statements" or "sense statements." The sentence "It *seems* to me that I hear a scratching sound at the window," when used in such a way as not to imply that there is a scratching sound at the window, would express a statement of this class. The sentence "It *looks* to me as if there are two candles on the table," when used in such a way as not to imply that there are two candles on the table, would express another statement of this class. I will call statements of this class "incorrigible statements," and henceforth I will use the expression "empirical statement" in such a way that the class of empirical statements will be understood to exclude incorrigible statements as well as necessary truths and necessary falsehoods. It is in this sense of "empirical statement" that the conclusion of the Verification Argument will be understood to be the proposition that every empirical statement is "less than absolutely certain."

The class of empirical statements is, of course, enormous. The following are examples of such statements: "There is an ink bottle on that table," "I see a goat in the garden," "We were in Lugano last winter," "I closed the door a moment ago," "There is no milk

[6] *Ibid.*, p. 426.

in the ice box," "Gottlob Frege was not a Spaniard," "Michelangelo designed the dome of St. Peter's," "Water does not flow uphill," "Chickens are hatched from eggs," "This man's neck is broken," "My wife is angry." The Verification Argument is thought to prove that whenever any person has ever asserted that the truth of any one of these statements is absolutely certain his assertion was false or mistaken, and also to prove that if anyone should, in the future, make such an assertion his assertion will be false or mistaken.

It is to be noted that the phrase "It is absolutely certain" is only one of several phrases which are used synonymously in certain contexts. Some of the other synonymous phrases are "It has been completely verified," "It has been established beyond a doubt," "I have made absolutely certain," "I have conclusively established," "I know for certain," "It has been proved beyond any possibility of doubt," "It is perfectly certain." The Verification Argument is thought to prove something with regard to each and every one of these phrases. It is thought to prove that whenever anyone applies one of these phrases to any empirical statement the assertion which he thereby makes is false or mistaken or incorrect or unjustified. It is thought to prove, for example, that if any art historian has ever made the assertion that it is conclusively established that the dome of St. Peter's was designed by Michelangelo, his assertion was false or mistaken or incorrect or unjustified; and if any art historian should, at any time in the future, make this assertion, his assertion will be false or mistaken or incorrect or unjustified. It is thought to prove that if a physician who has just examined a man struck down by a bus should ever assert "I have made absolutely certain that his neck is broken," what he asserts is wrong or improper or unjustified, *no matter how careful his examination has been.*

It is common knowledge that assertions of this sort are *often* mistaken and that it frequently happens that someone asserts that he has made absolutely certain that so-and-so is true, when either so-and-so is not true or else, even if so-and-so is true, he has not made so thorough an investigation as to justify his assertion that he has made absolutely certain that so-and-so is true. The Verification Argument is thought to prove, not simply that many assertions of this sort are mistaken or unjustified, but that *all* such assertions are, *in all cases,* mistaken or unjustified. In short, it is thought to prove that it is not even *possible* that anyone should, in *any* circumstances, make such an assertion without the assertion being false or unjustified or improper or mistaken or incorrect.

In order to state the Verification Argument as clearly as possible I will make use of an example. Let us suppose that a dispute has arisen between a friend and myself as to whether William James used the phrase "the stream of thought" as the title of a chapter in his book *The Principles of Psychology,*[7] my friend contending that James did not use that phrase, but did use the phrase "the stream of consciousness" as the title of a chapter. Whereupon I take from a bookshelf Volume I of James's book, turn the pages until I come to page 224, where I see the title "The Stream of Thought" occurring just under the heading "Chapter IX." Then I say, "You are wrong. Here is a chapter entitled "The Stream of Thought." He says, "Have you made absolutely certain?" I reply, "Yes, I have. Here, look for yourself."

I believe that this example provides a natural usage of the expression "I have made absolutely certain." It is, furthermore, a good example for my purposes because I do wish to maintain that on June 17, 1948, I did make absolutely certain that the phrase "the stream of thought" was, on that day, on page 224 of my copy of Volume I of James's *The Principles of Psychology.* The statement "The phrase 'the stream of thought' was, on June 17, 1948, on page 224 of my copy of Volume I of James's *The Principles of Psychology*" I will call "S." The Verification Argument is thought to prove that I did *not* make absolutely certain that S is true. Let us see whether it does prove this.

The first step in the argument consists in saying that S has "consequences" or "expected results in experience," or that from S one can infer statements which are "predictions about future observations." It seems to me that it is not difficult to see an important thing that is meant by these expressions. If, for example, someone said "Just now a cat went into the closet," and I believed the statement, I should *expect* that if I were to search about in the

---

[7] Two volumes, 1890.

closet I should see or hear or touch a cat. If I did not believe his statement he might naturally say "I assure you that if you look in the closet you will see a cat." And if I did look and did see a cat it would be natural to regard this as *confirming* his first statement "Just now a cat went into the closet." Another way of expressing this matter would be to say that if it is true that a cat went into the closet just now, then it *follows* or is a *consequence* that if I were to search about in the closet I should see or hear or touch a cat. This is a natural use of "follow" and of "consequence." And it is easy to understand what is meant by saying that the conditional statement "If I were to search about in the closet I should see or hear or touch a cat" states a "prediction about future observations." Henceforth I will use the word "consequence" to express these relationships. I will say that it is a "consequence" of the statement "Just now a cat went into the closet" that if I were to search in the closet I should see or hear or touch a cat; and I will say that the conditional statement "If I were to search in the closet I should see or hear or touch a cat" expresses a "consequence" of the former statement. In this use of "consequence" it is a consequence of the statement S that if now, on June 18, 1948, I were to look at page 224 of my copy of Volume I of James's *Principles* I should see the phrase "the stream of thought." I should certainly expect to see that phrase if I were to look at that page now, and I should be greatly astonished if I did not see it.

It may be said that what I have called a "consequence" of S is not a consequence of S alone, but of S conjoined with some other statements. If I thought that since yesterday someone had erased from page 224 of James's book the phrase "the stream of thought," then I should not expect that if I were to look on that page I should see that phrase. Also I should not expect to see it if I knew that my vision was abnormal or that the room was so dark that I could not make out printed words. The statement "If I were to look on that page now I should see that phrase" expresses a consequence, not of S alone, but of the conjunctive statement "The phrase was on that page yesterday, and there is no reason to think that the printing on that page has been altered or has changed since then, and my vision is normal, and the light is good." I cannot see any objection to saying this. I believe that it is a natural way of speaking to say that if S is true then it is a consequence that if I were to look at page 224 now I should see that phrase; and I will continue to speak in that way. But it will be understood that this consequence of S is not a consequence of S alone, but of S conjoined with the other statements mentioned.

A difficult question now arises, namely, what *kind* of statements are the conditional statements that express consequences of S? Consider the statement "If I were to look now at page 224 of my copy of James's book I should see the phrase 'the stream of thought.'" I will call this statement "*c*." *c* is of the form "If *A* then *E*." Now a view has been put forward by Lewis that implies that this consequence of S should really be expressed in these words: "If it were the case that it should *seem* to me that I was looking at page 224 of James's book then it would be the case that I should *seem* to see the phrase 'the stream of thought.'" I will call this statement "*k*." Lewis holds that in a conditional statement which expresses a consequence of an empirical statement, both *A* and *E* (that is, both antecedent and consequent) must be regarded as what I call "incorrigible statements" and what he calls "expressive statements." [8] Lewis calls the statements which express consequences of an empirical statement "predictions"; and so does Carnap. Lewis talks about his believing such a statement as "There is a piece of paper before me." He says that this belief involves numerous predictions, e.g., that if he were to fold it, it would not crack; that if he were to try to tear it, it would tear easily. [9] A moment later, however, he says that he has not expressed himself accurately. He says:

But it was my intention to mention predictions which, though only partial verification of the objective fact I believe in, could themselves be decisively tested. And there I have failed. That the paper, upon trial, would really be torn, will no more be evidenced with perfect certainty than is the presence of real paper before me now. It—provided it takes place—will be a real objective event about which,

---

[8] "The hypothesis '*A*' must here express something which, if made true by adopted action, will be *indubitably* true. . . . And the consequent '*E*' represents an eventuality of *experience*, directly and certainly recognizable in case it accrues, not a resultant objective event, whose factuality could have, and would call for, further verification. Thus both antecedent and consequent of this judgment 'If *A* then *E*,' require to be formulated in expressive language . . ." (*An Analysis of Knowledge and Valuation*, p. 184).

[9] *Ibid.*, p. 175.

theoretically, my momentary experience could deceive me. What I meant to speak of was certain expected experiences—of the *appearance and feeling* of paper being folded; of its *seeming* to be torn.[10]

He is saying that the statement "If I were to try to tear this, it would tear easily" is not a "prediction" and does not express a "consequence," in his use of "prediction" and "consequence," of his belief that there is paper before him. This passage and the one which I quoted from page 184 show that he would regard the statement "If it *seemed* to me that I was trying to tear this, then it would *seem* to me that it was tearing easily" as the sort of statement that is a "prediction" and expresses a "consequence" of his belief and if it were true would partially confirm or verify his belief. Thus it is clear that Lewis's use of "consequence," as this word occurs in his presentation of the Verification Argument, is such that he would say that k is a "consequence" of S, and c is not. There is, of course, an enormous difference between k and c. The difference could be expressed in this way: If I were to look now at page 224 of James's book and were to see there the phrase "the stream of thought," that would *entail* that page 224 of James's book does exist and that the phrase "the stream of thought" is on that page. But if now it were to *seem* to me that I was looking at page 224 of James's book and if it were to *seem* to me that I was seeing there the phrase "the stream of thought," that would *not* entail that page 224 of James's book exists or that that phrase is on any page of any book.

No other philosopher who has used the Verification Argument has, to the best of my knowledge, expressed himself on this point. Carnap, for example, says that when we are trying to verify an empirical statement what we do is to infer from it statements that are "predictions about future observations." [11] But he does not say whether these "predictions" are statements like c or statements like k. Since he does not even allude to the distinction it would be natural to assume that by "predictions" he means statements like c. Whether this is so or not I will henceforth mean by "statements which express consequences of S" statements like c and not like k. I have two reasons for this decision. One is that

[10] *Ibid.*
[11] *Philosophy of Science*, III (1936), 425.

statements like k are awkward and unnatural. The other and more important reason is that I am not sure that there is any natural usage of "confirm" or "verify" according to which the discovery that k is true would confirm or verify that S is true. Suppose that I were in doubt as to whether S is true. If I were to look now at page 224 of James's book and see there the phrase "the stream of thought," that would indeed confirm that the phrase was on that page yesterday. But if it were merely the case that it *seemed* to me now that I was looking at page 224 of James's book and that it *seemed* to me that I was seeing there that phrase, in a sense of the preceding words that is compatible with its being the case that I am dreaming now or having an hallucination and am not seeing any page or any printing at all, then how would this confirm that the printed words "the stream of thought" were on page 224 of James's book yesterday? It is not clear to me that it would in the least confirm S, in any natural sense of "confirm." This is, however, a difficult point and I do not wish to argue it here. I believe that no important part of my treatment of the Verification Argument is affected by the decision to interpret the statements that express consequences of S as statements like c and not like k, and it is open to anyone reading this paper to interpret them in the other way.

There is, however, a fact about the relationship between S and the statements that express consequences of S which should be clearly understood. This is the fact that S does not *entail* any statement that expresses a consequence of S, in whichever of these two ways one interprets these statements. For example, S does not entail c, i.e., the statement "S but not c" is not self-contradictory. It is not self-contradictory to say "The phrase 'the stream of thought' was on page 224 of James's book yesterday but it is not the case that if I were to look on that page now I should see it there." Nor is c entailed by the conjunctive statement "The phrase 'the stream of thought' was on page 224 of James's book yesterday, and there is no reason to think that the printing on that page has changed or been altered since then, and my vision is normal, and the light is good." Even though there is no reason to think that the phrase "the stream of thought" has disappeared from that page since yesterday it *may* have disappeared, and if it has then if I look at that page now I shall not see it there. It should be even clearer that S does not entail k. The whole statement "The phrase 'the stream of thought' was on page 224 of James's book yesterday but it is not true that if it were the case that it should *seem* to me that I was looking at that page it would be the case that I should *seem* to see that phrase" is not self-contradictory. Nor is k entailed by the previously mentioned conjunctive statement of which S is one conjunct. When Carnap says that in order to verify an empirical statement we "infer" or "derive" from it statements that are "predictions about future observations," [12] the words "infer" and "derive" must be understood in a sense in which to say that one infers or derives q from p is *not* to say that p entails q. When Lewis speaks of the "implied consequences" [13] of a belief it is to be understood that to say that a belief "implies" certain consequences is not to say that it entails the statements that express those consequences. Whenever the word "consequence" occurs in my discussion of the Verification Argument it is to be understood that an empirical statement does not entail any statement that expresses a consequence of it. This being understood, I see no reason for not accepting the first step in the Verification Argument. When it is said that S, or any similar statement, has "consequences" or "expected results in experience," or that from S one can infer "predictions about future observations," it seems to me that this has a fairly clear meaning and is also true.

The second step in the argument consists in saying that the number of "consequences" or "expected results in experience" or "predictions about future observations" that can be inferred from S is "infinite" or "unlimited." This step in the argument offers some difficulty, but the following considerations may help to explain it. I said before that it is a consequence of S that if I were to look now at page 224 of this book I should see the phrase "the stream of thought." But it is also a consequence that if I were to look a second from now I should see that phrase, and if I were to look two seconds from now I should see it, and three seconds from now, and so on for an *indefinite* number of seconds. What it means to say that this number of seconds is "indefinite" is that *no* number of seconds from now can be specified such that, after

[12] *Ibid.*
[13] *An Analysis of Knowledge and Valuation,* p. 176.

that number of seconds had elapsed, I should no longer expect that if I were to look at that page I should see that phrase. At some future time that page may be destroyed. But for as long a period of time as it continues to exist and is not injured or tampered with, and provided that during that period my vision remains good, I should expect that if at *any* moment during that period I were to take a good look at that page in a good light I should see that phrase, *however long* that period of time shall be. There is a second consideration: I do not expect merely that if *I* were to look at that page now *I* should see that phrase, but also I expect that if my wife were to look at that page now she would see that phrase, and that if the man who lives on the floor below were to look at that page he would see that phrase, and that, in short, if anyone of an *indefinitely* large number of persons of good vision were to take a good look now at that page he would see that phrase. What is meant by saying that the number of persons in question is "indefinitely" large is that *no* number of persons, however large, can be specified such that I should not expect that if any person of this number were to look at that page he would see that phrase. There is a third consideration that is a combination of the preceding two and may be stated as follows: I should expect that if anyone of an indefinitely large number of persons of good vision were to take a good look at that page either now or at any second of an indefinite number of seconds from now, he would see that phrase, provided that the page had not been injured or tampered with and that he looked at it in good light. I think that the statement that the number of "consequences" or "predictions" or "expected results in experience" that can be inferred from S is "infinite" or "unlimited" or "indefinitely large" means what I have expressed in these three considerations; and if that is so I am prepared to accept the second step in the Verification Argument.

The third step in the argument consists in saying that any of these "consequences" or "expected results in experience" may not turn out as expected and that any of these "predictions about future observations" may prove to be false. What this implies with regard to S, for example, is that if I were to look now at page 224 of James's book I might not see the phrase "the stream of thought," or that if I were to look a second from now I might not see it, or if my wife were to look now she might not see it, and so on. This proposition in the Verification Argument seems to me to require very careful examination, and I shall return to it later.

The fourth step in the Verification Argument consists in saying that if some of these "consequences" or "expected results in experience" or "predictions about future observations" that can be inferred from S should not turn out as expected or should prove to be false, then doubt would be thrown on the truth of S. Lewis expresses this when he says: "And suppose that these consequences fail to appear, or are not what the nature of the accepted fact requires? In that case, will there still be no doubt about the accepted fact?" [14] This fourth proposition in the argument seems to me to express an important truth but one that is difficult to state. If I were to take a good look now at page 224 of James's book and were *not* to see the phrase "the stream of thought," I should not simply conclude that I was mistaken when I asserted previously that it is there, and so dismiss the matter. The truth is that I should at first be too dumbfounded to draw any conclusion! When I had recovered from my astonishment what I should conclude or whether I should conclude anything would depend entirely on the circumstances. Suppose that if I were to look now on that page I should see, or seem to see, the phrase "the stream of *consciousness*" occurring as the title, under the heading "Chapter IX," instead of the phrase "the stream of thought." As I said I should at the first moment be enormously astonished and not know what to say. But suppose that I looked again and again and that I still saw, or seemed to see, the phrase "the stream of consciousness"; that everything else in the room and the things seen through the windows appeared to look the same and to be placed as I remembered them to be the moment before I looked at the page; that I did not feel ill, dizzy, or queer but perfectly normal; that I had assured myself that the book *was* my copy of Volume I of James's *Principles* and that the page *was* page 224; and that there was no reason to believe that the printing on that page had been altered since the last time I had looked at it. If all of these things were to occur, then I must confess that I should begin to feel a doubt as to whether the phrase "the stream of thought" ever

[14] *Mind and the World Order,* p. 282.

was on page 224 of James's book. What is more important is that this would be a *reasonable* doubt. When Lewis asks the rhetorical question, "Will there still be no doubt about the accepted fact?" [15] he means to imply, of course, that there would be a doubt. But, furthermore, he must mean to imply that the doubt that would exist in those circumstances would be a *reasonable* doubt, i.e., that there would be *good* grounds for doubting. For if the doubt were not a reasonable one then the fact that it existed would be no evidence that that which had been accepted as a fact was not a fact. Now when I say that if certain things were to happen I should doubt whether the phrase in question ever did appear on the page in question and that this would be a reasonable doubt, I am accepting the fourth step of the Verification Argument. I am accepting the statement that if certain consequences of S should "fail to appear" then I should have good grounds for believing that I was mistaken when I asserted previously that I had made absolutely certain that S is true. I should have good grounds for believing that the phrase "the stream of thought" was not there on page 224 of James's book, but also for believing that that phrase *never* had been on that page. I do not see any mistake in this fourth step in the Verification Argument.

There is a fifth step in the argument that is also difficult to state. It is implied, I believe, in these remarks by Lewis:

Now suppose . . . that at some date, t_2, we put ourselves in position to meet the consequences of this fact, which was accepted as completely established at t_1. And suppose that these consequences fail to appear, or are not what the nature of the accepted fact requires? In that case, will there still be no doubt about the accepted fact? Or will what was supposedly established at t_1 be subject to doubt at t_2? And in the latter case can we suppose it was absolutely verified at time t_1? [16]

The last two sentences in this quotation express the proposition which I have called "the fifth step" in the argument. This proposition may be stated as follows: If at any time there are good grounds for believing that a given statement p is false then at no previous time was it known with certainty that p is true. This proposition is implied by the rhetorical question, "And in the lat-

---

[15] *Ibid.*
[16] *Ibid.*

ter case can we suppose it was absolutely verified at time t_1?"
The "latter case" referred to is the time t_2 at which there is supposed to exist a reasonable doubt as to whether something that was accepted at t_1 as a fact is really a fact. What the rhetorical question implies is that if there is a reasonable doubt at t_2 as to whether something is a fact then it cannot have been the case that at t_1 it was absolutely verified that that something is a fact. This proposition will, perhaps, be clearer if expressed in the following way: The proposition "There are now good grounds for doubting that p is true" *entails* the proposition "At no previous time was it known with absolute certainty that p is true."

Should we accept this proposition which is the fifth step in the Verification Argument? Let us substitute for p the statement "Hume was the author of *An Abstract of A Treatise of Human Nature.*" Is there any contradiction in supposing that some person, say a publisher, had made absolutely certain in 1740 that Hume was the author of *An Abstract of A Treatise of Human Nature*, but that in 1840 some other person, say a historian, had good grounds for believing that Adam Smith, and not Hume, was the author of it? Is there any contradiction in supposing that some person at one time should possess a body of evidence that conclusively established that so-and-so was the case, but that at a later time another person should possess none of that evidence but should possess *other* evidence on the basis of which it was reasonable to doubt that so-and-so was the case? I cannot see any contradiction in this supposition. Consider this actual example: Some competent Greek scholars are unable to decide whether Plato was the author of the *Lesser Hippias*. They can cite grounds for saying that he was and grounds for saying that he was not. The view that he was the author is subject to a reasonable doubt. But Plato may have been the author. If he was the author then Plato himself, or a contemporary, may have known with certainty that he was the author.[17] Now are the two statements, (*a*) "Someone at some time in the past knew with absolute certainty that Plato was

[17] This statement might be thought to beg the question. It *does* conflict with the conclusion of the Verification Argument. It does *not* beg the question with regard to any premise in the argument. It could do so only if some premise in the argument contained the assertion that no one can know with certainty that any empirical statement is true. But if this were contained in a premise then the Verification Argument itself would beg the question.

the author of the *Lesser Hippias*," and (*b*) "Someone now has good grounds for doubting that Plato was the author of the *Lesser Hippias*," incompatible with one another? They are not at all. The proposition that is the conjunction of (*a*) and (*b*) is not self-contradictory. Nothing is easier to imagine than that it should be the case *both* that Aristotle knew with absolute certainty that Plato was the author of that dialogue *and* that 2400 years later a professor of Greek, not having the evidence which Aristotle had and noticing in the dialogue certain features of style uncharacteristic of Plato, should have a reasonable doubt that Plato was the author. There is no contradiction whatever in this supposition, although it may be false. If this supposition is not self-contradictory, then (*b*) does not entail that (*a*) is false. Therefore, the fifth step in the Verification Argument is an error.

Why should anyone fall into the error of thinking that the proposition "There are now good grounds for believing that *p* is false" entails the proposition "At no previous time was it known with absolute certainty that *p* is true"? I believe that there is something which may explain why this error should be made. What I have in mind is the following: If some person were to make the assertion "Aristotle knew with absolute certainty that Plato was the author of the *Lesser Hippias* but I doubt, and with good reason, that Plato was the author," then his assertion would contain an odd absurdity. The most ordinary use of the phrase "knew with absolute certainty" is such that "*x* knew with absolute certainty that *p* is true" entails "*p* is true." Therefore, the above assertion *entails* the assertion "Plato was the author of the *Lesser Hippias* but I doubt that he was." But if anyone were to assert "Plato was the author of the *Lesser Hippias*" he would *imply*, by his assertion, that he *believed* that Plato was the author of the *Lesser Hippias*. By his assertion "Plato was the author of the *Lesser Hippias* but I doubt that he was" he would *assert* that he doubted something, but also *imply* that he did *not* doubt that something but believed it.[18] The same absurdity would be contained in the assertion "It is raining but I doubt it." If a philosopher had sensed the peculiar absurdity of this sort of assertion he might be led to conclude

---

[18] Moore has called attention to the peculiarity of this sort of statement. Cp. G. E. Moore, "Russell's 'Theory of Descriptions,'" *The Philosophy of Bertrand Russell*, P. A. Schilpp, ed. (Evanston: Northwestern, 1944), p. 204.

that since it would be absurd for anyone to *assert* "At a previous time someone knew with absolute certainty that p is true but I doubt, and with good reason, that p is true," that therefore the proposition "At a previous time someone knew with absolute certainty that p is true and now someone doubts, and with good reason, that p is true" is self-contradictory.

It would be a mistake, however, to draw this conclusion. Although it would be absurd for anyone to assert "It is raining but I doubt, and with good reason, that it is raining," it does not follow that this proposition is self-contradictory. That it is not self-contradictory is shown from the fact that the proposition "It is raining but *he* doubts, and with good reason, that it is raining" is clearly not self-contradictory. Since the latter proposition is not self-contradictory, how can the former one be so? Indeed, I can easily imagine that it should happen *both* that it was raining *and* that, at the same time, I had a reasonable doubt as to whether it was raining. This supposition is certainly not self-contradictory. Thus the proposition "It is raining but I doubt, and with good reason, that it is raining" is not self-contradictory, although it would be an absurdity if I were to *assert* it. If this proposition *were* self-contradictory then "I doubt, and with good reason, that it is raining" *would* entail "It is not raining." But once we see clearly that this proposition is not self-contradictory then, I think, all temptation to believe that this entailment does hold is removed.

It would also be absurd for anyone to assert "Aristotle knew with absolute certainty that Plato was the author of the *Lesser Hippias* but I doubt, and on good grounds, that he was." But it does not follow that the proposition "Aristotle knew with absolute certainty that Plato was the author of the *Lesser Hippias*, but someone now doubts, and on good grounds, that Plato was the author" is self-contradictory. It would be a great mistake to think that the statement "Someone now doubts, and on good grounds, that Plato was the author of the *Lesser Hippias*" entails the statement "It is false that Aristotle knew with absolute certainty that Plato was the author of the *Lesser Hippias*." Lewis makes this mistake, I believe, when he assumes that if something was accepted as a fact at time t_1 but that at time t_2 there arose a reasonable doubt as to whether this something was a fact, then it follows that it was not absolutely verified at t_1 that this something was a fact. With regard to S, which is the statement, "The phrase 'the stream of thought' was on June 17, 1948, on page 224 of my copy of Volume I of James's *The Principles of Psychology*," this fifth step in the Verification Argument claims the following: *If* today, June 18, 1948, those things which I have imagined as happening *should* happen, so that I should have good reason to believe that S is false, then it would follow logically that I did not make absolutely certain yesterday that S is true.

I have tried to show that that claim is false. It is true that it would be an absurdity for me, or anyone, to assert "I made absolutely certain on June 17 that S is true but today, June 18, I doubt, and with good reason, that S is true." This assertion would have the same peculiar absurdity as the assertion "S is true but I doubt that S is true." But it does not follow in the least that the proposition "On June 17 I made absolutely certain that S is true and on June 18 I doubted, and with good reason, that S is true" is self-contradictory. It does not follow at all that the proposition "On June 18 I doubted, and with good reason, that S is true" entails the proposition "It is false that on June 17 I made absolutely certain that S is true." It might be objected that if I had made absolutely certain on June 17 that S is true, then on June 18 I should remember this fact and, therefore, should not be able to doubt that S is true. But it is logically possible that I should not remember on June 18 that on June 17 I had made certain that S is true. There is no logical contradiction whatever in the supposition that on June 18 I should have a reasonable doubt that S is true, although on June 17 I had made absolutely certain that S is true. Thus it seems to me that there is no reason to accept the fifth step in the Verification Argument and that, in fact, it is a definite error.

Can the Verification Argument be restated in such a way as to avoid this error? It seems to me that this can be done by the following two measures. The first measure consists in *strengthening* the fourth step in the argument. The fourth step is the proposition that if certain things were to happen then I should have good grounds for doubting that S is true. This step could be strengthened by substituting the proposition that if a sufficient number of things were to happen I should have *absolutely conclusive* grounds for thinking that S is false. It seems to me that if the fourth step were strengthened in this way it would still be a true proposition. When discussing the fourth step I imagined certain things as happening such that if they *were* to happen I should have grounds for doubting that S is true. But let us imagine that certain additional things should occur. Let us imagine that, being astonished and perplexed at seeing the phrase "the stream of consciousness" on page 224 of James's book, I should ask my wife to look at that page and that she too should see the phrase "the stream of consciousness." Let us suppose that I should examine the manuscript of this paper in order to verify that there was in it the statement that I had made absolutely certain that the phrase "the stream of thought" was on page 224, but that I should find instead that in the manuscript was the statement that I had made absolutely certain that the phrase "the stream of consciousness" was on page 224. Let us imagine that I should then examine other copies of Volume I of *The Principles of Psychology* and see that in each of them the title of Chapter IX was "*The Stream of Consciousness*"; that I should find a number of articles written by psychologists and philosophers which quoted from page 224 of James's book and that each of them quoted the phrase "the stream of consciousness" and that not one quoted the phrase "the stream of thought"; that my wife should declare sincerely that she had read page 224 of my copy of James's book on June 17, 1948, and that she recalled that the phrase "the stream of consciousness" was on that page and not the other phrase; that everyone of several persons who had recently read Chapter IX in other copies should declare sincerely that to his best recollection James had used the phrase "the stream of consciousness" in that chapter and had not used the other phrase. *If* all of these things were to happen then there would be *more* than good grounds for doubting that S is true; there would be, I should say, absolutely conclusive grounds for saying that S is false. In other words, it would be absolutely certain that the phrase "the stream of thought" was not on page 224 of my copy of James's book on June 17, 1948; and it would be absolutely certain that my seemingly vivid recollection of seeing it there was a queer delusion. The fourth step of the Verification Argument could, therefore, be reformulated as saying that *if* a sufficient number of things were to occur then there would be absolutely conclusive grounds for saying that S is false.

The second measure involved in revising the Verification Argument would be to change the fifth step by substituting for the false proposition "If at any time there should be a reasonable doubt that S is true then at no previous time did anyone make absolutely certain that S is true," the true proposition "If at any time there should be absolutely conclusive grounds that S is false then at no previous time did anyone make absolutely certain that S is true." The latter proposition is clearly true. It is a plain tautology. In ordinary discourse the expressions "I made absolutely certain that p is true" and "There are absolutely conclusive grounds that p is false" are used in logical opposition to one another. It would be a contradiction to say "There are absolutely conclusive grounds that p is false but I made absolutely certain that p is true." The statement "I made absolutely certain that p is true" entails "p is true"; and the statement "There are absolutely conclusive grounds that p is false" entails "p is false." Thus the statement "There are absolutely conclusive grounds that p is false but I made absolutely certain that p is true" entails the contradiction "p is false and p is true." Therefore the proposition "If at any time there should be absolutely conclusive grounds that S is false then at no previous time did anyone make absolutely certain that S is true" is a tautology.

If the Verification Argument were revised by strengthening the fourth step and changing the fifth step, in the way that I have suggested, then the argument *would* prove (provided that there were no other error in the argument, which, I think, there is) that on June 17, 1948, I did not make absolutely certain that S is true. But if the argument were revised in this way then it could not be used to prove the *general* proposition that *no* empirical statement can be conclusively established as true, for an obvious reason. In its revised form the argument would contain as a premise the proposition "If at any time there are absolutely conclusive grounds that S is false then at no previous time did anyone make absolutely certain that S is true." Even if the argument could be used as a valid proof that I was mistaken when I asserted that I had made absolutely certain that S is true it could not be used as a valid proof that no empirical statement can be conclusively established as true, *because* one premise of the argument relies on the supposition that a particular statement, the statement "S is false," can be conclusively established as true. The situation with regard to the Verification Argument is, therefore, as follows: When stated in its original form, as presented by Lewis, the fifth step in the argument is a logical error. When the argument is revised so as to avoid this error, then it cannot be used to validly prove the proposition that no empirical statement can be conclusively established as true, which is the conclusion that it was intended to prove.

2

I wish to point out another error in the Verification Argument, an error that I believe to be of very considerable philosophical importance. The whole argument may be stated as follows:

    I. S has consequences.
    II. The number of consequences of S is infinite.
    III. The consequences of S *may* fail to occur.
    IV. *If* some of the consequences of S *were* to fail to occur, then there would be a reasonable doubt that S is true.
    V. If at any time there should be a reasonable doubt that S is true then at no previous time did anyone make absolutely certain that S is true.

    Conclusion: No one did make absolutely certain that S is true.

I will call this the "original" Verification Argument. Before I try to show the second error in the argument I wish to make some remarks. In the first place, I have stated the argument as if it applied only to the statement S. But it is intended, of course, to be a perfectly general argument. There could be substituted for S any other empirical statement. If the argument as stated is sound, then by substituting any other empirical statement for S we could obtain a parallel, sound argument. In this sense the Verification Argument, if it were sound, would prove, with respect to any empirical statement whatever, that no one did make absolutely certain that that statement is true. Indeed, it would prove that no one *can* make absolutely certain that that statement is true, because the argument applies at any *time* whatever. In the second place, I have tried to show that premise V is false. I suggested that this false step could be eliminated by the adoption of these two measures: First, to substitute for IV the proposition, which I will call "IV*a*," "If a sufficient number of the consequences of S were to fail to occur, then it would be absolutely conclusive that S is false"; second, to substitute for V the proposition, which I will call "V*a*," "If at any time it should be absolutely conclusive that S is false then at no previous time did anyone make absolutely certain that S is true." Is seems to me that both IV*a* and V*a* are true. If these substitutions are made then the whole argument may be restated as follows:

I. S has consequences.

II. The consequences of S are infinite in number.

III. The consequences of S may fail to occur.

IV*a*. If a sufficient number of the consequences of S were to fail to occur then it would be absolutely conclusive that S is false.

V*a*. If at any time it should be absolutely conclusive that S is false then at no previous time did anyone make absolutely certain that S is true.

Conclusion: No one did make absolutely certain that S is true.

This second statement of the argument I will call the "revised" Verification Argument. The revised argument is different from the original argument in two respects. First, premise V of the original argument is false but the corresponding premise of the revised argument is true. Second, premise IV*a* of the revised argument contains the assumption that an empirical statement "S is false" can be conclusively established as true. If we substituted for S in the revised argument any other empirical statement *p* then IV*a* would contain the assumption that it can be conclusively established that the contradictory of *p* is true. No premise of the original argument, however, contains the assumption that any empirical statement can be conclusively established as true. This difference between the two arguments might be expressed in this way: If all of its premises were true the original argument would prove, with regard to any empirical statement that was substituted for S, that that statement cannot be conclusively established; and no premise of the argument assumes that any empirical statement can be conclusively established; therefore it could properly be said that if all of its premises were true the original argument would prove the general proposition that *no* empirical statement can be conclusively established. If all of its premises were true the revised argument would also prove, with regard to any empirical statement that was substituted for S, that that statement cannot be conclusively established; but since one premise assumes that an empirical statement can be conclusively established, it would be wrong to say that the revised argument, if its premises were all true, would prove the general proposition that *no* empirical statement can be conclusively established. No matter what statement was substituted for S, premise IV*a* would assume that the contradictory of that statement can be conclusively established. The revised argument has this peculiar logical character, that if all of its premises were true it would prove, with regard to *any* empirical statement, that that statement cannot be completely verified, but it would not prove that *no* empirical statement can be completely verified.[19]

[19] [I was mistaken in this assessment of the revised argument. Peter Geach pointed out to me that a proponent of the Verification Argument does not have to assume *categorically* that an empirical statement can be conclusively established. He might assume it *hypothetically* in order to prove that any given empirical statement (for example, S) is not conclusively established. Let us substitute for IV*a* the following proposition (call it "IV*b*"): "*If* any empirical statement can be conclusively established as true or false, then if a sufficient number of the consequences of S were to fail to occur, it would be absolutely conclusive that S is false." With this alteration, the revised argument would still be deductively valid. And it would not be the case that any premise of the argument assumes categorically that some empirical statement can be conclusively established. Nothing in the *form* of the argument, therefore, prevents a proponent of it from concluding that *no* empirical statement can be conclusively established.

My criticism of premise III is not affected by this amendment.

In an interesting study of my essay, Harry G. Frankfurt suggests another way of amending the "original" argument ("Philosophical Certainty," *The Philosophical Review*, LXXI, No. 3, July 1962, 303-327). He proposes to retain IV without change and to substitute for V the following proposition (called "V*b*"): "If at any time t_2 there should be a reasonable doubt that S is true, then at no previous time t_1 did anyone make absolutely certain

The revised argument, however, does *seem* to prove, with regard to my statement S, that no one can make absolutely certain that S is true. If it does prove this then it follows that I was mistaken when I asserted that on June 17, 1948 I made absolutely certain that S is true. I have previously accepted premises I, II, IV*a* and V*a*. This leaves premise III. I believe that III contains a serious mistake. I expressed III in this way: "The consequences of S *may* fail to occur." Lewis makes use of III in the following passage:

No matter how fully I may have investigated this objective fact, there will remain some theoretical possibility of mistake; there will be further consequences which must be thus and so if the judgment is true, and not all of these will have been determined. The possibility that such further tests, if made, might have a negative result, cannot be altogether precluded; and this possibility marks the judgment as, at the time in question, not fully verified and less than absolutely certain.[20]

When Lewis says, "The possibility that such further tests, if made, might have a negative result, cannot be altogether precluded," he is asserting the proposition which I have called "III." Carnap, in discussing the statement "There is a white thing on this table," says that "the degree of confirmation, after a few observations have been made, will be so high that we practically cannot help accepting the sentence." When he adds, "But even in this case there remains still the theoretical possibility of denying the sentence"[21] he is, I believe, making use of III. It is unlikely that he is merely saying that it is possible that someone should deny the statement to be true, because the fact that someone had denied the statement to be true would in no way tend to show that the

---

that S is true, *provided that the evidence possessed at t_2 includes all the evidence possessed at t_1*" (*ibid.*, p. 306). As far as I can see, Frankfurt is right in saying that his reformulation of V "is an accurate expression of what is intended by proponents of the Verification Argument" (*ibid.*, p. 305), and he is also right in saying that his revised argument is deductively valid (*ibid.*, p. 307). Furthermore, his version of the argument does not even appear to possess the "peculiar logical character" that I attributed (mistakenly) to the "revised" argument.]

New footnotes, which have been added to the original text of the previously published essays, are enclosed in brackets.

[20] *An Analysis of Knowledge and Valuation,* p. 180.
[21] "Testability and Meaning," *Philosophy of Science,* III (1936), 426.

statement cannot be completely verified. It is likely that what he is asserting is that there "remains still the theoretical possibility" that some of the statements, which are "predictions about future observations" and which can be inferred from the statement in question, should turn out to be false. If this is a correct interpretation of his remarks then he is asserting III.

In order that we shall be clear about the meaning of III let us remind ourselves of what are some of the "consequences" or "expected results in experience" or "predictions about future observations" that can be inferred from S. If S is true then one consequence is that if I were to look now at page 224 of James's book I should see the phrase "the stream of thought." Another consequence is that if I were to look again two seconds later I should again see it; another is that if my wife were to look a second later at that page she would see that phrase; and so on. What proposition III says is that it is *possible* that some or all of these things should fail to occur, that it is *possible*, for example, that if I were to look at page 224 now I should *not* see that phrase. Although it may appear obvious to some philosophers what is meant by saying that such a thing is "possible," it does not appear at all obvious to me, and I wish to scrutinize proposition III.

In order for the Verification Argument to be a valid deductive argument (i.e., an argument in which the premises entail the conclusion) III must be understood in such a way that it implies the following proposition, which I will call "IIIa": "It is not certain that the consequences of S will occur." Why must III be understood in this way? For this reason, that someone might agree that it is *possible* that some or all the consequences of S should fail to occur but at the same time maintain that it is *certain* that they will occur. I might agree, for example, that it is *possible*, in some sense of "possible" that if I were to look at page 224 of James's book now I should not see the phrase "the stream of thought," but maintain, nevertheless, that it is certain that if I were to look at that page now I should see that phrase. The assertion of proposition IIIa is, therefore, a required step in the argument. If III is understood in such a way that it implies IIIa then the revised argument is a valid deductive argument. This will be seen if we substitute IIIa for III and write down the whole argument, which I will call the "finished" Verification Argument:

I. S has consequences.

II. The consequences of S are infinite in number.

III*a*. It is not certain that the consequences of S will occur.

IV*a*. If a sufficient number of the consequences of S should fail to occur then it would be absolutely conclusive that S is false.

V*a*. If at any time it should be absolutely conclusive that S is false then at no previous time did anyone make absolutely certain that S is true.

Conclusion: No one did make absolutely certain that S is true.

It seems to me that the conclusion does follow logically from the premises. To put the argument more briefly: If it is the case that were certain things to happen then it would be conclusively established that S is false, and if it is not certain that those things will not happen, then it follows that no one has made certain that S is true. I have accepted premises I, II, IV*a*, and V*a*. I have admitted that the conjunction composed of these premises and of III*a* entails the conclusion. Therefore, if I were to accept III*a* I should be agreeing that the finished argument is sound and that its conclusion is proved. I should have to admit that I was mistaken when I asserted that I had made absolutely certain that S is true. I do not see, however, any good reason for accepting III*a*. I believe that it has seemed obvious to the proponents of the Verification Argument both that III is true and that III implies III*a*. I wish to show that this is a mistake. I wish to show that III may be understood in several senses, that in some of these senses III it true and that in some it is false, and that only in the senses in which III is false does III imply III*a*.

I expressed proposition III in the words "The consequences of S *may* fail to occur." I could have expressed III in several other ways. I could have expressed it by saying "It is *possible* that the consequences of S will not occur," or by saying "The consequences of S *might* not occur" or by saying "*Perhaps* the consequences of S will not occur," or by saying "It *may be* that the consequences of S will not occur," or by saying "The consequences of S *could* fail to occur." The words "may," "possible," 'might," "perhaps," "may be," "could," "can" are related to one another in such a way that for any statement that uses one of these words there may be substituted an equivalent statement that uses another of them. But whichever one of this class of statements we employ to express III, its meaning will be open to several different interpretations.

Let us consider some of the different things which might be meant by the proposition "It is possible that the consequences of S will not occur." One thing which might be meant is that the statement "The consequences of S will not occur" is not self-contradictory. Frequently in philosophical discourse and sometimes in ordinary discourse when it is said "It is possible that so-and-so will happen" or "So-and-so may happen," what is meant is that the statement "So-and-so will happen" is not self-contradictory. If, for example, I were to say that it is possible that beginning tomorrow the temperatures of physical objects will vary with their colors, or that it is possible that in one minute the desk on which I am writing will vanish from sight, one thing which I should mean is that the statements "Beginning tomorrow the temperatures of physical objects will vary with their colors" and "In one minute this desk will vanish from sight" are not self-contradictory. When III is interpreted in this way what it says is that it is not the case that the contradictory of any statement which expresses a consequence of S is self-contradictory. It says, for example, that the statement "If I were to look now at page 224 of James's book I should *not* see the phrase 'the stream of thought'" is not self-contradictory. This interpretation of III I will call "III$_1$."

Another thing which might be meant by III is that no statement that states the *grounds* for holding that any consequence of S will occur *entails* that it will occur. Let me make this clearer by an example. If someone were to ask me why I am sure that if I were to look now at page 224 of James's book I should see the phrase "the stream of thought," I might reply "I saw it there yesterday and there is no reason to believe that the page has changed or been altered since then and my vision is normal and the light is good." But what I offer as reasons or grounds for saying that if I were to look at that page now I should see that phrase, does not *entail* that if I were to look at that page now I should see that phrase. In the sense of "possible" which is used in III$_1$, it is possible that the following statement is true: "I saw the phrase on that page yesterday and there is no reason to believe that the printing on that page has changed or been altered since then and my vision is normal and the light is good, *but* if I were to look on that page now I should *not* see that phrase." This statement is not self-contradictory. I have called the following statement, "c": "If I were to look now at page 224 of James's book I should see the phrase 'the stream of thought.'" c expresses one of the consequences of S. Let us call the statement that I have just used to state the reasons for holding c to be true, "R." The proposition "R but not c" is not self-contradictory. In other words, R does not entail c. It is possible, in the sense of "possible" that is used in III_1, that c is false even though R is true. It is possible, in this sense, that the phrase "the stream of thought" has vanished from page 224 even though there is no reason to think that it has; and if it had vanished I should not see it there. It is not self-contradictory to suppose that it has vanished although there is no reason to think that it has. It seems to me, that with regard to any statement p that expresses a consequence of S, it is the case that it is not entailed by any statement q that states the grounds for saying that p is true. This is one natural interpretation of the meaning of III. I will call it "III_2." It must not be supposed that III_1 and III_2 are equivalent. With regard to c, for example, III_1 says that the phrase "not c" or "c is false" is not self-contradictory. What III_2 says, with regard to c, is that the statement "R but not c" is not self-contradictory. III_1 says that the negative of c is not, by itself, self-contradictory. III_2 says that the conjunction of R and the negative of c is not self-contradictory, or, in other words, that R does not entail c. III_1 and III_2 are entirely different propositions and both of them seem to me to be clearly true. The conjunction of III_1 and III_2 is, I believe, what would ordinarily be meant by the statement "It is *logically* possible that the consequences of S will not occur."

I wish now to point out other uses of "possible" and the correlative words that are of quite a different *kind* than the two so far mentioned. When it is said in ordinary life that "It is possible that so and so will happen," what is very frequently meant is that *there is some reason to believe* that so-and-so will happen. Suppose that my wife were to say, "It's possible that Mr. Jones will come to see us this evening." If I were to ask "Why do you think so?" she might naturally reply "He said to me this morning that he would come if he did not have to work." In this example the reply consists in stating a piece of *evidence* in favor of saying that he will come. Suppose that a friend, who looks to be in perfect health, should say "I may be extremely ill tomorrow." To my question "Why do you say that?" he might reply "Because I ate scallops for lunch and they have always made me very ill." Here again the reply offers a *reason*, some *grounds* for saying that he will be ill. This usage of "possible," "may," "might," and their correlatives is enormously frequent in ordinary discourse, and it is strikingly different from the usages noted in III$_1$ and III$_2$. When my friend replied to my question "Why do you say that you may be ill tomorrow?" his reply did not consist in pointing out the logical truth that the statement "I shall be ill tomorrow" is not self-contradictory; nor did it consist in pointing out the logical truth that no statement which expressed grounds for saying that he will not be ill tomorrow would entail that he will not be ill tomorrow. It did consist in giving some reason, or evidence, or grounds, for believing that he will be ill tomorrow. My question "Why do you think so?" or "Why do you say that?" would be naturally understood as a request for the reason for believing that he will be ill tomorrow. It would be quite absurd for him to reply to my question by saying, "Because the statement 'I shall be ill tomorrow' is not self-contradictory" or by saying, "Because it does follow logically from the fact that my health is excellent and that I feel perfectly well that I shall *not* be ill tomorrow." If he were to reply in this way it would be regarded as a joke. If a Greek scholar were to remark "It's possible that Plato was not the author of *The Republic*" we should ask "Why do you say so?" and it would be only a joke if he were to reply "The statement 'Plato was not the author of *The Republic*' is not self-contradictory," or to reply "The evidence we have for saying that Plato was the author does not *entail* that he was the author." We should naturally interpret his first remark to mean "There is evidence that Plato was not the author of *The Republic*"; and our question "Why do you say so?" would be naturally understood as a request for him to say what the evidence was. His reply gave no evidence. He failed to show that it is *possible* that Plato was not the author of *The Republic*, in the sense of "possible" which was appropriate to the context.

A radical difference between the use of "possible" that I am now describing and its uses in III₁ and III₂ consists in the fact that the kind of "possibility" now being described admits of *degree,* whereas those other kinds do not. The ordinary expressions "There is some possibility," "It is barely possible," "There is a slight possibility," "There is a considerable possibility," "There is a greater possibility that so-and-so than that such and such," "It is very possible," "There is a strong possibility," all belong to the use of "possible" now being described and not to its uses in III₁ and III₂. If the man who says "It is possible that I shall be ill tomorrow" supports his statement by saying that he had just eaten scallops and scallops had always made him ill, then he could have correctly expressed his statement by the words "It is *very* possible that I shall be ill tomorrow" or "There is a *strong* possibility that I shall be ill tomorrow." But if he supports his statement by saying that "I shall be ill tomorrow" is not self-contradictory, or by saying that the fact that he is in excellent health does not entail that he will not be ill tomorrow, then he could *not* have correctly expressed his statement by the words "It is *very* possible that I shall be ill tomorrow" or "There is a *considerable* possibility that I shall be ill tomorrow." The expressions "There is some possibility," "There is a considerable possibility," "There is a greater possibility that so-and-so than that such and such" mean roughly the same as the expressions "There is some evidence," "There is a fair amount of evidence," "There is more evidence that so-and-so than that such and such." The expressions of both types are expressions of *degree.* If the man who says "It is possible that Plato was not the author of *The Republic*" means that the statement "Plato was not the author of *The Republic*" is not self-contradictory, then he is not using "possible" in a sense that admits of degree. There can be more or less evidence for a statement, the reasons for believing it can be more or less strong, but a statement cannot be more or less self-contradictory. The statement "There is a slight possibility that the Smiths are in Paris this week but a greater possibility that they are in Rome" illustrates a use of "possibility" which is totally different from *logical* possibility. The statement obviously does not mean that "The Smiths are in Rome" is *less* self-contradictory than "The

Smiths are in Paris." It does not make sense to say that one statement is "less" self-contradictory than another. And it obviously does not mean that the evidence as to the whereabouts of the Smiths entails "The Smiths are in Rome" *more* than it entails "The Smiths are in Paris." It does not make sense to say "*p* entails *q* more than it entails *r*." The statement obviously means that there is some reason to think that the Smiths are in Paris but greater reason to think that they are in Rome.

I hope that I have made it sufficiently clear that there is a common use of the word "possible" and of the correlative words, according to which the statement "It is possible that so-and-so" means "There is some reason to believe that so-and-so." When proposition III is interpreted in this sense it is equivalent to the proposition "There is some reason to believe that the consequences of S will not occur." I will call this interpretation of III, "III$_3$."

There are other common uses of "possible" closely analogous to its use in III$_3$. Suppose that the members of a committee are to meet together. All of the committee, save one, turn up at the appointed time and place. Someone asks "Does K. (the missing member) know that there is a meeting?" Inquiry reveals that no one recalls having notified K. of the meeting. It is also pointed out that, although an announcement of the meeting appeared in the local newspaper, K. frequently does not read the newspaper. A member of the committee sums up the situation by saying, "Then it is possible K. does not know about the meeting." This latter statement means that *there is no reason* to think that K. does know about the meeting; and this seems to me to be a very common usage of the word "possible" and its correlatives. The proposition "It is possible that the consequences of S will not occur," which is proposition III, if interpreted in the sense just described, would mean "There is no reason to think that the consequences of S will occur." This interpretation of III, I will call "III$_4$."

Suppose that the question arises as to whether M. was in a certain theater at the time when a murder was committed there. It is known that he left a bar only fifteen minutes before and that it would be extremely difficult for any man to go from the bar to the theater in fifteen minutes. The situation might be summed up by saying "It is unlikely that M. was at the theater at the time of the murder but it is *possible* that he was." This statement means that there is good reason to believe that *M.* was not at the theater but that the reason is not absolutely conclusive. It is a very common use of "possible" to say that although there are strong grounds for believing that so-and-so is the case, it is still *possible* that so-and-so is not the case, where this is equivalent to saying that although the grounds for saying that so-and-so is true are strong, they are not absolutely conclusive. If III were interpreted in this way it would mean "The grounds for saying that the consequences of S will occur are not absolutely conclusive." This interpretation of III, I will call "III$_5$."

I have wished to show that sentences of the sort "It is possible that so-and-so," "It may be that so-and-so," "Perhaps so-and-so," have several different uses. The very same sentence has, in different contexts, quite different meanings. I do not know that there are not still other uses of those sentences; but if there are I cannot think of them. The third premise of the Verification Argument is expressed by a sentence of this sort. When it is said "It is possible that the consequences of S will not occur," the question arises, therefore, in which of these different ways is this sentence being used? When Lewis says "The possibility that such further tests, if made, might have a negative result, cannot be altogether precluded" his statement is equivalent to "It is possible that further 'tests,' if made, will have negative results." How are we to understand the use of "possible" in this important premise of the argument? In what sense of "It is possible that so-and-so" is it possible that if I were to look now at page 224 of James's book I should not see the phrase "the stream of thought"? A proponent of the Verification Argument cannot reply that it is possible in the *ordinary* meaning of "It is possible." There is not such a thing as *the* ordinary meaning of that phrase. A sentence of the sort "It is possible that so-and-so" does not have just *one* meaning that is the same in all contexts. The only course open to us is to examine each of the several different interpretations of the third premise in order to see whether there is any interpretation of it which will make the "revised" Verification Argument a sound argument.

III is the proposition "It is possible that the consequences of the statement S will not occur." III*a* is the proposition "It is not known that the consequences of S will occur." I pointed out previously that in order for the revised argument to be a valid deductive argument III must be understood in such a way that it implies III*a*. In order for the revised argument to be a *sound* argument it must also be the case that III is true. (I am using the phrase "a sound argument" in such a way that a deductive argument is a sound argument if and only if it is both the case that it is a valid deductive argument and that all of its premises are true.) Is there an interpretation of III in accordance with which III implies III*a and* III is true? The following are the different interpretations of III which arose from the description of the several meanings of sentences of the sort "It is possible that so-and-so":

III$_1$. The statement "The consequences of S will not occur" is not self-contradictory.

III$_2$. No statement p which expresses a consequence of S is entailed by any statement q which states the grounds for holding that p is true.

III$_3$. There is some reason to believe that the consequences of S will not occur.

III$_4$. There is no reason to think that the consequences of S will occur.

III$_5$. The grounds for holding that the consequences of S will occur are not absolutely conclusive.

With regard to these propositions I think that the following is the case: III$_1$ and III$_2$ are true. But neither of them implies III*a*. III$_3$, III$_4$, and III$_5$ each implies III*a*. But each of them is false. I wish to defend these statements, and I will do so by discussing each of these interpretations of III.

(III$_1$) It is clearly not self-contradictory to say either that all or that some of the consequences of S will not occur. It is possible, in one sense of "It is possible," that they will not occur. But it does not follow in the least that it is not absolutely certain that they will occur. Here is a source of philosophical confusion. With regard to any contingent statement, it is the case that "p is false" is not self-contradictory. A natural way to express this logical truth about p is to say "It is possible that p is false." This provides the temptation to say "Since it is possible that p is false, therefore it is not certain that p is true." But this is a confusion. From the sense of "It is possible that p is false" in which this means that "p is false" is not self-contradictory, it does not follow either that there is some reason to believe that p is false, or that there is no reason to believe that p is true, or that the reason for holding that p is true is not conclusive. The fact that it is possible that p is false, in this sense, *has nothing to do with the question of whether p is false*. In this sense of "It is possible that p is false" it is not self-contradictory to say "It is certain that p is true although it is possible that p is false." In the senses of "It is possible that p is false" that are expressed by III_4 and III_5, it *is* self-contradictory to say "It is certain that p is true although it is possible that p is false." In the sense of "It is possible that p is false" that is expressed by III_3, it is not self-contradictory to say "It is certain that p is true although it is possible that p is false," for the reason that I gave in discussing proposition V. But in the sense of III_3 to say "It is possible that p is false" *is* to say something that counts *against* saying "It is certain that p is true."

It is easy to be misled by these different uses of "It is possible" and to conclude that from the fact that it is possible that p is false, when this means that "p is false" is not self-contradictory, that therefore it is not certain that p is true. But in the use of "It is possible" that is expressed by III_1, "It is possible that p is false" only tells us what *kind* of statement p is. It only tells us that p is a contingent statement and not a necessary truth or a necessary falsehood. It tells us *nothing* about the state of the evidence with respect to p. In the uses of "It is possible" that are expressed by III_3, III_4, and III_5, the statement "It is possible that p is false" does tell us something about the state of the evidence. It tells us that there is some evidence for believing that p is false, or that there is no evidence for believing that p is true, or that the evidence for p, although strong, is not conclusive. In these latter uses the statement "It is possible that p is false" says something *against* its being certain that p is true. The statement "'p is false' is not self-contradictory" says nothing whatever against its being certain that p is true. That statement is *neutral* with regard to the question of whether p is true or of whether it is certain that p is true. To say that "'p is false' is not self-contradictory" entails "It is not certain that p is true" amounts to saying that "p is a contingent statement" entails "It is not certain that p is true." But to say the latter would be to say something false. It is not self-contradictory to say "There are many contingent statements which I know with certainty to be true." c is the statement "If I were to look now at page 224 of James's book I should see the phrase 'the stream of thought.'" c is a contingent statement, which entails that "c is false" is not self-contradictory. It is correct to express this logical fact about c by saying "It is *possible* that if I were to look now at page 224 I should *not* see the phrase 'the stream of thought.'" But although this statement expresses a truth it is not a truth which is even *relevant* to the question of whether it is certain that if I were to look now at that page I should see that phrase.

(III$_2$) Previously I said that the grounds for saying that c is true are expressed by the statement "I saw the phrase when I looked there yesterday, there is no reason to believe that the printing on that page has changed or been altered since then, my vision is normal, and the light is good." I said that this statement R does not entail c. A natural way of expressing this fact about the logical relationship of R to c is to say "Even though R is true it is *possible* that c is false." This expresses the fact that the inference from R to c is not a deductive or demonstrative inference. But it provides another great source of philosophical confusion. There is a temptation to conclude from the fact that it is possible, in this sense, that c is false even though R is true that, therefore, it is not *certain* that c is true. It does not, however, follow from the fact that R does not entail c either that it is not certain that c is true or that R does not state the grounds on the basis of which it is certain that c is true. The temptation arises from the fact that there are several uses of "It is possible that p is false" and that frequently these words mean that there is some reason to believe that p is false, or that there is no reason to believe that p is true, or that it is not absolutely conclusive that p is true. When one says "Although R is true c may be false" and expresses by this the fact that "R and not c" is not self-contradictory, it is easy to be misled by the variety of uses of "possible" and "may be" into supposing that one has said something that counts against its being certain that c is true. But the statement that R does not entail c, i.e., that "R and not c" is not self-contradictory, says nothing that counts either for or against its being certain that c is true. Whether it is certain that c is true depends upon the state of the evidence with regard to c. The statement "R does not entail c" says no more about the state of the evidence with regard to c than does the statement " 'c is false' is not self-contradictory." Both statements are irrelevant to that matter. The statement "The fact that R is true makes it absolutely certain that c is true" is in no way contradicted by the statement "R does not entail c." The two statements are perfectly compatible with one another. One statement describes the evidence concerning c. The other describes a logical relationship between R and c of which one could be aware even though one knew nothing whatever about the state of the evidence concerning c.[22] The fact that R

[22] [Frankfurt ("Philosophical Certainty," *The Philosophical Review,* LXXI, 309) disagrees with me here. He says that the statement that R does not entail c "is obviously about the evidence for c." But as Frankfurt acknowledges, it is irrelevant to the question of *how much* evidence there is for c, and in this sense it has nothing to do with the state of the evidence for c. In what sense *is* it about the evidence for c? In supposing that it "obviously" is, Frankfurt would appear to be thinking that if R does not *entail* c, then it is not certain that c is true. He goes on to indicate, however, that he is not sure about this point and that I may be right in my view of the matter (*ibid.,* p. 310). But he says that I have offered "surprisingly little" support for my view (*ibid.,* p. 309). The only support I know how to give is examples—that is, cases in which we should *say* that something is "perfectly certain" or "conclusive," and yet in which it is clear to us that the evidence does not entail the thing in question. In the essay I do this. I go on to mention, for example, the fact that if the printed words "the stream of thought" were on page 224 of James's book yesterday, "then it is perfectly certain that they have been there as long as the book has existed" (see p. 38). This *is* perfectly certain: and it is also perfectly obvious that there is no entailment. Countless other examples lie at hand. (It is perfectly certain that Harry G. Frankfurt is the author of an article entitled "Philosophical Certainty," but my evidence that he wrote it does not *entail* that he wrote it.) The aim of the examples is to bring out the fact that our use of the locutions "certain," "perfectly certain," "conclusive," "absolutely conclusive," and so on, as applied to empirical propositions in everyday life, is not tied up with the question of whether the evidence for the propositions *entails* the propositions. This latter question is generally *irrelevant.* (It is not always irrelevant because sometimes an empirical proposition is based on a calculation, e.g., "I spent a total of $12.42 at the grocer's.") Why is it so difficult to see this? Why are we so strongly inclined to think that III₂ entails IIIa? Partly because of the ambiguity of III. Partly (I am now inclined to think) because the verb "entails" incorporates *one* use of the verb "follows," and in ordinary speech we have another more frequent use of it, in which

does not entail c provides no ground for doubting that c is true. It is a mistake to suppose that because it is possible that c is false even though R is true, in the sense of III_2, that therefore "It is possible that c is false," where these latter words imply that it is not quite certain that c is true. What I have said about c applies equally to every other statement which expresses a consequence of S.

(III_3) III_1 and III_2 provide no basis whatever for accepting $IIIa$. The same thing cannot be said of III_3. If there is some reason for believing that any consequence of S will not occur, this counts in favor of holding that it is not certain that it will occur. But is III_3 true? Is there some reason or ground or evidence for thinking that any consequence of S will not occur; for thinking, for example, that if I were to look now at page 224 of James's book I should *not* see there the phrase "the stream of thought"? There is none whatever. Let us consider what *would* be a reason for thinking that any consequence of S will not occur. If some person of normal vision had carefully looked for that phrase on that page a few minutes ago and had not found it there, then that would be a reason, and a powerful one, for thinking that if I were to look now I should not see it there. Or if my copy of James's book possessed the peculiar characteristic that sometimes the printing on the pages underwent spontaneous changes, that printed words were suddenly replaced by different printed words without external cause, then that would be a reason for doubting that if I were to look now at that page I should see that phrase. But there is no reason to think that any person has looked for that phrase and has not found it there, or to think that my copy of James's book does possess that peculiar characteristic.

It might be objected that although there is no reason to think that these things are true nevertheless they *may* be true. In which of the several senses of "may be" is it that these things *may* be true? If it is in the senses of III_1 and III_2 then it does not follow

to say such a thing as "It does not follow from the evidence you offer that p" just *means* that the evidence is not good enough, is not conclusive, does not make it certain that p. In our philosophical thinking about empirical certainty, it is easy for us to confuse these different uses of "follows." (The topics of certainty and entailment are discussed, in a special connection, in my review of Wittgenstein's *Investigations*, pp. 113-117.)]

that it is not certain that they are false. It cannot be said that they may be true in the sense that there is some reason to think that they are true, for we are supposing it to be admitted that there is no reason. May they be true in the sense that there is no reason to think that they are false, or in the sense that the grounds for saying they are false are not conclusive? But there *is* reason to think that they are false. There is reason to think that no one has tried and failed to find that phrase on that page. The reason is that I did make certain that the phrase was there yesterday, and if those printed words were there yesterday then it is perfectly certain that they have been there as long as the book has existed. This is not only a reason but is what would ordinarily be regarded as a conclusive reason for saying that no one of normal vision who has carefully looked for that phrase on that page in good light has failed to see it there. The reason is obvious for saying that my copy of James's book does not have the characteristic that its print undergoes spontaneous changes. I have read millions of printed words on many thousands of printed pages. I have not encountered a single instance of a printed word vanishing from a page or being replaced by another printed word, suddenly and without external cause. Nor have I heard of any other person who had such an encounter. There is overwhelming evidence that printed words do not behave in that way. It is just as conclusive as the evidence that houses do not turn into flowers—that is to say, absolutely conclusive evidence.

It cannot be maintained that there is any particular evidence for thinking that the consequences of S will not occur. It might be held, however, that there is a *general* reason for doubting whether they will occur. The reason is that the consequences of *some* statements *do* fail to occur. It might be argued that, since sometimes people are disappointed in expecting the consequences of a certain statement to occur, therefore I may be disappointed in expecting the consequences of S to occur. This would be similar to arguing that since people are sometimes mistaken when they declare a statement to be true therefore I may be mistaken when I declare S to be true, or that since people sometimes suffer from hallucinations therefore I may have been suffering from an hallucination when I thought that I was making certain that S is true.

There is undoubtedly a temptation to argue this way. The following remarks by Russell are but one example of it. "Lunatics hear voices which other people do not hear; instead of crediting them with abnormally acute hearing, we lock them up. But if we sometimes hear sentences which have not proceeded from a body, why should this not always be the case? Perhaps our imagination has conjured up all the things that we think others have said to us." [23] Here Russell is arguing that since sometimes people imagine voices, therefore in every case when one "hears a voice" one may have imagined the voice. I cannot undertake to examine in this paper all of the sources of the temptation to argue in this way. They lie in some serious difficulties surrounding the philosophical question, "How do I know that I am not dreaming or having an hallucination?" To investigate them would lead us away from the Verification Argument.

I do want to point out that this sort of arguing is, on the face of it, entirely invalid. To argue that since people sometimes make mistakes therefore I may be mistaken when I say that S is true is like arguing that Francis Bacon may not have been an Englishman because some men are not Englishmen, or that Bismarck may not have been a statesman because some men are not statesmen, or that I may be blind because some men are blind. This is a travesty of correct reasoning. There are *some* circumstances in which reasoning of that sort is acceptable. If the door to the adjoining office is closed and we are wondering what the man in there is doing and someone says that surely he is sitting at his desk, one of us might reply "He may not be sitting at his desk because sometimes he sits on the floor." In these circumstances the fact that sometimes he sits on the floor *does* count against saying that it is surely the case that he is sitting at his desk. But if we were to open the door and see him sitting at his desk then it would be absurd for anyone to say "He may not be sitting at his desk because sometimes he sits on the floor." This sort of reasoning is acceptable in those circumstances where one has not yet investigated the question at issue, where one is not in a position to know the answer, where one can only make conjectures. If there is an unexamined chair in the closet and someone assumes that it is wooden, we might reply "It may be metal because some chairs

[23] Bertrand Russell, *An Outline of Philosophy* (W. W. Norton & Company, Inc., 1927), p. 9.

are metal." But once we have looked at it, felt it, and scratched some splinters from it then it would be only amusing to say "It may be metal because some chairs are metal." Here is a type of reasoning that is appropriate in some circumstances but not in all circumstances. There might be circumstances in which it would be reasonable to say "I may be having an hallucination because people do have hallucinations" or to say "I may have imagined that I heard a voice because sometimes I do imagine that I hear voices"; but it is an error to suppose that this is a reasonable thing to say in *all* circumstances.

These remarks apply to what we were considering as a general reason for doubting that the consequences of S will occur. The suggestion was that the consequences of S may fail to occur because the consequences of some statements do fail to occur, that since sometimes people make false statements and are disappointed when they expect their consequences to occur, that therefore when I asserted S I may have made a false statement and may be disappointed in expecting its consequences to occur. There are circumstances in which it is highly reasonable to temper the confidence with which I assert something, by reminding myself that sometimes other people and myself make erroneous assertions. But it is a mistake to suppose this to be reasonable in *all* circumstances, to suppose, for example, that it is reasonable to conclude that, since sometimes I am mistaken, therefore when I say that I am more than ten years old I may be mistaken and that it is not quite certain that I am more than ten. Thus the suggestion that there is a general reason for believing that the statements that express consequences of S are false, and that the reason is that *some* statements that people expect to be true turn out to be false, is completely in error and presents nothing more than a caricature of good reasoning. It would be a caricature of good reasoning if a member of a society of Greek scholars were to declare to the society that there is reason to believe that Plato was not the author of *The Republic* and when asked for the reason were to reply that people often believe propositions which are false.

I conclude that III₃ is false. It asserts that the consequences of S may fail to occur in the sense that there is some reason for thinking that they will not occur. But there is no reason at all, neither any particular reason nor any general reason, for thinking that any of the consequences of S will not occur.

(III₄) Proposition III₄, which expresses another common usage of "It is possible," says that there is *no* reason to believe that the consequences of S *will* occur. III₄ is false because there is a very good reason for saying that the consequences of S will occur. The reason is that S is true. What better reason could there be? Two objections might be made to this. First, it might be said that no empirical statement, p, is evidence for another empirical statement, q, unless p entails q: S does not entail any statement that expresses a consequence of S (e.g., S does not entail c); therefore the fact that S is true is no evidence that any statement is true that expresses a consequence of S. This objection, however, cannot be made use of by a proponent of the Verification Argument. The fourth premise in that argument says that if some of the consequences of S were not to occur then there would be some reason to think that S is false. But the contradictory of a statement which expresses a consequence of S does not entail that S is false (e.g., "c is false" does not entail "S is false"). Therefore, one step in the Verification Argument assumes what is clearly correct, that a statement, p, can be evidence for a statement, q, even though p does not entail q. The second objection that might be made is that if S is true then there is good reason to think that the consequences of S will occur, but that it is not absolutely certain that S is true. If a person made this objection it would be necessary to ask him what his reason is for saying that it is not absolutely certain that S is true. Is his reason that he has looked at that page of James's book and failed to find that phrase there? In other words is he saying that there are particular grounds for thinking that it is not certain that S is true? But there are no such grounds. Is his reason the general philosophical proposition that no empirical statement is absolutely certain? But that is the very proposition that the Verification Argument is meant to prove and so that proposition cannot be used as a step in the argument. There is no way in which it can be consistently upheld, within the context of the Verification Argument, that there is no reason to believe that the consequences of S will occur. III₄ cannot be accepted as an interpretation of proposition III in the argument, because not only is

III$_4$ false but also its use as a premise would lead either to an inconsistency or to a circular argument.

(III$_5$) It is unlikely that any philosopher who has used the Verification Argument would wish to maintain either that there is some reason to believe that the consequences of S will not occur or that there is no reason to believe that they will occur. But undoubtedly he would wish to maintain that the grounds for saying that they will occur are not absolutely conclusive. The statements that express consequences of S are empirical statements and the Verification Argument is intended to prove that the grounds for no empirical statement are absolutely conclusive. If the conclusion of the argument is true then III$_5$ is true, and it would be inconsistent to accept the conclusion and not to accept III$_5$. But we are now regarding III$_5$ as a *premise* in the argument intended to prove that conclusion. Within the context of the Verification Argument the proposition that is the conclusion of it cannot be offered in support of premise III$_5$, because the argument would then be circular. What is to be offered in support of III$_5$?

The Verification Argument is subject to a serious logical difficulty. It cannot be a valid deductive argument unless it contains the premise that it is not certain that the consequences of S will occur. The fact that this premise is required is obscured by the ambiguity of proposition III, which is the proposition "It is possible that the consequences of S will not occur." The meaning of III is open to several interpretations. Only if III is interpreted in such a way that it implies IIIa is the argument valid. III$_5$ is one natural interpretation of III, and III$_5$ implies IIIa. In fact, III$_5$ and IIIa are logically equivalent propositions. III$_5$ entails IIIa and IIIa entails III$_5$. But IIIa (or III$_5$) is a proposition which requires *proof*. Proposition IIIa is extremely similar to the proposition which is the general conclusion of the Verification Argument. The conclusion says something about every member of the entire class of empirical statements—it says that the truth of not one of those statements is completely certain. Proposition IIIa says the same thing about every member of a certain subclass of empirical statements, namely, the class of conditional statements which express consequences of S. S was but one example of an empirical statement, picked at random, and could be replaced by any other empirical statement. Whatever statement may be substituted for

S, proposition III*a* would say that it is not certain that the conditional statements that express consequences of *that* statement are true. In effect, therefore, proposition III*a* says that the truth of not one of an enormous class of statements—namely, all conditional statements which express consequences of any empirical statement—is completely certain. This sweeping and paradoxical claim requires to be justified as much as does the general conclusion of the Verification Argument. Every one of us in ordinary life frequently makes assertions of the following sort: "It is absolutely certain that if you look through these binoculars you will see a canoe on the lake," "We know for certain that if you pour that acid into this solution you will see a red precipitate form," "It is perfectly certain that if you were to touch that wire you would receive a shock." That is to say, every one of us frequently asserts of some conditional, empirical statement that its truth is entirely certain and beyond question. Shall it be said that the conditional, empirical statements which express consequences of S, or of any statement substituted for S, are not certainly true because *no* conditional, empirical statement is certainly true? What is the justification for the latter proposition? What is the justification for saying that every time anyone has made an assertion of the preceding sort his assertion has been false or mistaken or unjustified?

Here is a gap in the Verification Argument and the Verification Argument itself cannot be used to fill that gap. What is to fill it? Some other philosophical argument? Hume produced an argument that, if it were sound, would prove that it is not certain that any of the conditional statements that express consequences of S are true. But Hume's argument could not be used by a proponent of the Verification Argument to prove premise III*a*. Hume's argument was intended to prove that no inferences about matters of fact are "founded on reasoning." [24] He meant that there can be no reason to accept any inference about matters of fact—that there can be no reasonable inferences about matters of fact. But premise IV of the original Verification Argument asserts that if some of the consequences of S were not to occur then there would be reason to think that S is false. That premise implies that there can

[24] David Hume, *An Enquiry Concerning Human Understanding*, Part II, sec. 4.

be reasonable inferences about matters of fact. Thus Hume's argument is incompatible with the Verification Argument. Perhaps there is some other philosophical argument that could be offered in support of III*a*; but until it has been presented we cannot determine whether it is sound or whether it is compatible with the Verification Argument.

The Verification Argument does not stand on its own feet. Proposition III*a*, a required premise, makes a claim which is of the *same nature* as the general conclusion of the argument and only slightly less grandiose. The philosophers who have used the argument have tended to tacitly assume III*a*. They have not clearly seen that III*a* needs to be set down as a premise and to be *supported*. The explanation for this, I believe, is that these philosophers have been confused by the variety of uses of the phrases "It is possible," "It may be," and their equivalents. When they have said that "It is possible that further tests will have a negative result" or that "The predictions about future observations may prove to be false," they have thought that they were saying something that is so obviously true that it does not require support *and* that shows that it is not certain that those further "tests" will have a "positive result" or that those "predictions" will prove to be true. The fact is, however, that although there are natural interpretations of III according to which III is obviously true, none of those interpretations show that III*a* is true; and although there are natural interpretations of III which, if true, would show that III*a* is true, there is no reason to think that III is true in any of those interpretations. The result of this confusion is that III*a*, although a required premise, is an unsupported premise.

There is one passage in his exposition of the Verification Argument in which it is clear that Lewis is asserting a proposition corresponding to III$_5$ and, therefore, to III*a*. He is discussing his "belief" that there is a piece of paper before him. He says:

And my belief must imply as probable, anything the failure of which I should accept as tending to discredit this belief. Also it is the case that such future contingencies implied by the belief are not such that failure of them can be absolutely precluded in the light of prior empirical corroborations of what is believed. However improbable, it remains thinkable that such later tests could have a negative result. Though truth of the belief itself implies a positive result of such later tests, the evidence to date does not imply this as more than probable, even though the difference of this probability from theoretical certainty should be so slight that practically it would be foolish to hesitate over it. Indeed we could be too deprecatory about this difference: if we interrogate experience we shall find plenty of occasions when we have felt quite sure of an objective fact perceived but later circumstance has shocked us out of our assurance and obliged us to retract or modify our belief.[25]

When he says "The evidence to date does not imply this as more than probable" ("this" refers to "a positive result of such later tests") it is clear that Lewis is asserting that the evidence for any statement that expresses a consequence of his belief is not absolutely conclusive. (If the evidence for a statement is not absolutely conclusive then it follows that it is not certain that the statement is true, i.e., III_5 entails $IIIa$.) What is his reason for saying that there is no absolutely conclusive evidence that later "tests" will not have a "negative result"? I think that part of his reason lies in the statement "However improbable, it remains *thinkable* that such later tests could have a negative result." It is clear that he is using "thinkable" as equivalent to "conceivable." The phrase "It is conceivable" is used in ordinary language in exactly the same way as are the phrases "It is possible" and "It may be." The expression "It is conceivable that so-and-so" is open to the same variety of interpretations as is the expression "It is possible that so-and-so." How shall we understand the statement "However improbable, it remains conceivable that later tests will have a negative result"? If it means that it is not self-contradictory to suppose that later "tests" will have a "negative result," or that the evidence for saying that later "tests" will have a "positive result" does not *entail* that they will, then this statement is true; but it provides no ground for denying that the evidence is absolutely conclusive that later "tests" will have a "positive result." If the statement means that there is *some evidence* that later "tests" will have a "negative result," then the statement is false. With regard to c, it is not true that there is some evidence that if I were to look at page 224 of James's book I should *not* see the phrase "the stream of thought." The statement does not mean that there is *no* evidence that later "tests" will have a "positive result"; for Lewis clearly holds that it may be probable or even highly

[25] *An Analysis of Knowledge and Valuation,* p. 176.

probable that later "tests" will have a "positive result." The only thing left for the statement to mean, so far as I can see, is that the evidence, although strong, is not absolutely conclusive that later "tests" will have a "positive result." But if the statement "However improbable, it remains conceivable that later tests will have a negative result" has this meaning, then it provides no justification at all for the statement that "the evidence to date does not imply as more than probable that later tests will have a positive result." The two statements are then *identical* in meaning and the former statement can provide no justification for the assertion of the latter statement. Both statements are equally in need of support.

I believe that there is something else in the paragraph just quoted from Lewis that he may have regarded as supporting his claim that "the evidence to date does not imply this as more than probable, even though the difference of this probability from theoretical certainty should be so slight that practically it would be foolish to hesitate about it." He continues: "Indeed we could be too deprecatory about this difference: if we interrogate experience we shall find plenty of occasions when we have felt quite sure of an objective fact perceived but later circumstance has shocked us out of our assurance and obliged us to retract or modify our belief." In terms of my statement S, I understand Lewis to be saying the following: It is no more than probable that the consequences of S will occur; but it may be so highly probable that there is no "practical difference" between this high probability and "theoretical certainty." It may be so highly probable that it would be foolish to hesitate over this difference and to feel any doubt that the consequences of S will occur. But then, he warns, perhaps we are deprecating this difference too much. ("Indeed we could be too deprecatory about this difference.") I understand him to be saying that we should remember that it is not certain that the consequences of S will occur and that perhaps we should hesitate a little, i.e., feel a slight doubt that they will occur. Why? *Because* there have been numerous occasions when we felt sure of something and then discovered later that we were mistaken. If I understand Lewis correctly, he is using the latter fact both to reinforce his claim that it is not conclusive that the consequence of S will occur and as a ground for suggesting that perhaps it would be reasonable to feel a slight doubt that they will occur. But if he is doing this then he is making a mistake that I mentioned in my discussion of proposition III₃. That mistake consists in thinking that there is a *general* reason for doubting any particular statement that we believe to be true, the reason being that it has frequently happened that what we believed to be true turned out to be false. I am not entirely confident that Lewis is arguing in that way; but if he is then enough was said in our discussion of III₃ to show that this alleged general reason for doubt is no good reason at all for doubting that the consequences of S will occur and that to argue in this way is to commit a travesty of correct thinking.

The passage that I have just quoted contains the clearest assertion of proposition III₅ that I can find in Lewis' writing or in the writing of any other proponent of the Verification Argument. In this passage no good grounds are offered in defense of III₅ and the assertion of it seems to obtain its plausibility from the ambiguity of the expression "It is conceivable" ("thinkable"), which has the same ambiguity as the expression "It is possible." Almost anyone who reflects on these matters will, indeed, feel an inclination to say that III₅ is true. What is the source of this strong inclination? I believe that it lies exactly in that ambiguity. Consider *c*, which is the statement "If I were to look now at page 224 of James's book I should see there the phrase 'the stream of thought,'" and which expresses a consequence of S. One feels compelled to say that it is possible that *c* is false. And this is correct. It *is* possible that *c* is false *in the sense* that "*c* is false" is not self-contradictory, and *in the sense* that the grounds for affirming *c* do not entail *c*. Now feeling assured that the statement "It is possible that *c* is false" is undeniably true, one wants to conclude "Therefore it is not *certain* that *c* is true." And from the latter statement one correctly concludes "Therefore the grounds for affirming *c* are not conclusive." Reasoning in this way leads one to accept III₅. But this reasoning is fallacious. The error lies in the step from "It is possible that *c* is false" to "Therefore it is not certain that *c* is true." In the senses of "It is possible" in which it is undeniably true that it is possible that *c* is false, the fact that it is possible is irrelevant to the question of whether or not it is certain that *c* is true. The fact that, in those senses, it is possible that *c* is false is entirely compatible with the fact that the grounds for affirming *c* are perfectly conclusive and that it is perfectly certain that *c* is true. The grounds I should give for affirming *c* are that I saw the phrase "the stream of thought" when I looked at page 224 of James's book yesterday and that there is no reason to believe that the printing on the page has changed or been altered since then, and that my vision is normal, and that the light is good. These grounds would be accepted as absolutely conclusive by everyone in ordinary life. In what way do they fail to be conclusive?

It will be said "It is possible that you had an hallucination yesterday and did not see the page of a book at all." As I said before, there are connected with this statement problems of great importance which cannot be studied in this paper. I will limit myself to these remarks: The meaning of the statement is not that there is *some reason* to think that *I* had an hallucination yesterday. The philosopher who makes this statement does not intend to claim that by virtue of a particular knowledge of me and of my circumstances yesterday he has evidence that I suffered from an hallucination. This statement is intended to make the general claim that *every time anyone* has believed that he did perceive a certain thing it is possible that he did not perceive that thing at all and that he had an hallucination instead. Furthermore this statement does not claim merely that whenever anyone has believed that he perceived a certain thing it is possible that he was having an *hallucination*. It is intended to claim that it is *also* possible that he was *dreaming* or that he had an *optical illusion*, or, in short, that he suffered from *an error of some sort*. The philosophical statement "Whenever anyone has made a perceptual judgment it is possible that he was suffering from hallucination" is a disguised way of claiming "Whenever anyone has made a perceptual judgment it is possible that his judgment was in error," or of claiming "It is possible that every perceptual statement is false."

Now is it possible that every perceptual statement is false in any sense of "It is possible" from which it follows that it is not *certain* that any perceptual statement is true? Let us review the uses of "It is possible" that we have described. Any perceptual statement may be false in the sense that the contradictory of any perceptual statement is not self-contradictory; but it does not fol-

THE VERIFICATION ARGUMENT 49

low that it is not certain that any perceptual statement is true (III$_1$). It is true, I believe, that the evidence that one could offer in behalf of any perceptual statement does not *entail* that the statement is true; but, again, it does not follow that it is not certain that any perceptual statement is true (III$_2$). It cannot be maintained that with respect to each perceptual statement there is some particular evidence that that statement is false; e.g., there is no evidence at all that my statement that I saw a page of a book yesterday is false (III$_3$). To argue that since some perceptual statements are false therefore it is not certain that any particular perceptual statement is true is unsound reasoning (III$_3$). It would be absurd to contend that there is no reason to accept any perceptual statement (III$_4$).

Nothing remains to be meant by the statement "It is possible that every perceptual statement is false" except the claim that the grounds for accepting any perceptual statement are never conclusive (III$_5$). As I said, I believe that the grounds which one could offer in behalf of any perceptual statement do not *entail* that the statement is true. It does not follow in the least, however, that the grounds are not perfectly conclusive. I can produce enormously good grounds for accepting my perceptual statement that I saw the phrase "the stream of thought" on page 224 of James's book yesterday. The best way to show that those grounds are not conclusive would be to offer *some evidence* for saying that I did not see that phrase yesterday. But no philosopher is prepared to do this. Therefore, the philosophical claim that those grounds are not conclusive does not rest on *evidence*. On what does it rest? On a confusion, I believe. One is inclined to argue "It is not conclusive that that perceptual statement is true because it is possible that it is false." But examination of this statement shows that the words "It is possible that it is false" do not mean that there is *evidence* that it is false. They mean that it is *logically* possible that it is false. But the fact that it is logically possible that it is false does not tend to show in any way that it is not conclusive that it is true.

The inclination to contend that it is possible that every perception is hallucinatory rests, in part at least, upon the same confusion which lies at the root of the Verification Argument, a confusion over the usage of the expression "It is possible." One can construct an argument intended to prove that it is not certain that I did not have an hallucination yesterday, which closely resembles, in an important respect, the Verification Argument. This argument may be stated as follows:

If certain things were to happen there would be good reason to believe that I had an hallucination yesterday.

It is possible that those things will happen.

Therefore, it is not certain that I did not have an hallucination yesterday.

The second premise of this argument corresponds to premise III of the Verification Argument. In order that the conclusion should follow, this second premise must be understood in such a way that it implies the proposition "It is not certain that those things will not happen." I contend that there is no natural interpretation of this premise in which it is both the case that the premise is true and that it implies that proposition.

I have tried to show that there is no sense of the expression "It is possible," and the correlative expressions, in which the statement "It is possible that the consequences of S will not occur" *both* is true *and* implies the statement "It is not certain that the consequences of S will occur." To show this is to expose the most important error in the Verification Argument. The Verification Argument is a very tempting argument. From the propositions that S has an infinite number of consequences and that it is *possible* that these consequences will not occur and that if a sufficient number of them did not occur it would be conclusive that S is false and that if it were conclusive that S is false then no one previously made certain that S is true, it *seems* to follow that I did not make certain yesterday that S is true. The proposition that it is *possible* that these consequences will not occur is the premise of central importance. When one first meets the argument one feels that this premise cannot be questioned. It seems so obviously true that there is scarcely need to state it. This apparently invulnerable premise conceals a serious fallacy. This premise must be understood in such a way that it implies that it is not certain that the consequences of S will occur. Anyone who undertakes to examine carefully the several ordinary usages of "It is possible" should see that in the usages expressed by III_1 and III_2 this premise does not imply in the least that it is not certain that the consequences of S will occur. He should see that in the usages expressed by III$_3$ and III$_4$ this premise is clearly false. He should see that in the usage expressed by III$_5$ this premise stands in need of support and that the proponents of the Verification Argument have offered nothing valid in support of it and that if it were to be supported by philosophical argument it could not, without circularity, be supported by the Verification Argument itself. The persuasiveness of the Verification Argument arises from the failure to distinguish several usages of "It is possible" that occur in different contexts in ordinary discourse. The result of this failure is that in the philosophical context of the argument one tries to make that phrase straddle several different ordinary usages all at once. In the usages expressed by III$_1$ and III$_2$ the proposition "It is possible that the consequences of S will not occur" is an obvious logical truth. In the usages expressed by III$_3$, III$_4$, and III$_5$ this proposition expresses a *doubt*, implies an *uncertainty*. Through neglecting to distinguish these two sets of usages one is led to think *both* that the proposition "It is possible that the consequences of S will not occur" is an obvious truth *and* that it implies that it is not certain that the consequences of S will occur.

The proponents of the Verification Argument have emphasized their proposition that the consequences of an empirical statement are *infinite* in number. They have exerted themselves mainly in arguing for that premise of their argument, while they have said hardly anything at all about proposition III*a*. If, however, III*a* is true then it does not matter, in a sense, whether II is true or not. If S has only *one* consequence and if that consequence is such that if it failed to occur S would be refuted and if it is not certain that the consequence will occur, then it follows both that it is not certain that S is true and that I did not make certain yesterday that S is true. It will be replied, of course, that if S had only one consequence then we could put that one consequence to the test. If *c*, for example, expressed the only consequence of S then we could find out whether *c* is true by my performing the action of looking now at page 224 of James's book. If we knew that *c* is true and if *c* expressed the only consequence of S, then we should know with certainty that S is true. But S has not just one or several consequences, but an infinite number. We cannot put an infinite number of consequences to the test. Therefore we cannot know with certainty that S is true.

This argument makes an important assumption. The assumption is that I cannot know that any consequence *will* occur. I can know that it *is* occurring and, perhaps, that it *has* occurred, but not that it *will* occur. It assumes that I cannot know that c is true *until* I perform the action of looking at page 224 of James's book. *This assumption is identical with proposition IIIa.* Why should we accept this assumption? The philosophers who use the Verification Argument have given us no reason at all. This assumption goes against our ordinary ways of thinking and speaking. I should say, for example, that it is certain that if I were to look now at page 224 of my copy of James's book I should see there the phrase "the stream of thought." My grounds for saying this are that I saw the phrase there yesterday, that there is no reason to think that the printing on that page has changed or been altered since then, that my vision is normal, and that the light is good. These are not merely "very good" grounds; they would ordinarily be regarded as absolutely conclusive. What grounds do those philosophers have for saying that it is not certain that if I were to look now at that page I should see that phrase? None at all! There is nothing whatever which prevents me from knowing now that c is true. *I do not have to perform the act of looking now in order to know that if I did perform it now I should see that phrase.* I should also say that it is certain that if my wife were to look at that page now she would see that phrase and that it is certain that if my neighbor were to look now he would see it and so on for an indefinite number of persons. If I can know now that c is true I can also know now that *any* number of other statements, which express consequences of S, are true. That this number of statements is infinite or unlimited or indefinitely large does not prevent me from knowing that they are all true. I cannot perform an infinite number of actions of looking; but it does not follow in the least that I cannot know what the results would be *if* any of an infinite number of possible actions of looking were performed. With regard to any one of an infinite number of statements which express consequences of S, I can give grounds for saying that it is certain that that statement is true and the grounds are what would ordinarily be regarded as perfectly conclusive.

The philosophers who use the Verification Argument have put their emphasis in the wrong place. The critical step in the argument is not the proposition that an empirical statement has an infinite number of consequences; it is the unjustified assumption that it cannot be certain that those consequences will occur.

3

Our attention has been concentrated on the fallacies contained in propositions III and V of the original argument. There are, however, other errors involved in the thinking that surrounds the argument. One of these errors consists in a misunderstanding of the ordinary usage of expressions such as "verify," "establish," "make certain," "find out." The proponents of the argument say that if I want to find out whether a certain proposition is true I make a few "tests" or "observations." These few tests may be enough "for practical purposes" but, they say, I can go on making tests forever. "But there is always the theoretical possibility of continuing the series of test-observations. Therefore here also *no complete verification is possible* but only a process of gradually increasing *confirmation*." [26]

Let us take an example. Suppose that I think that *Paradise Lost* begins with the words "Of Man's first disobedience," but that I am not sure and wish to verify it. I take from the shelf a book entitled *Milton's Poetical Works.* I turn to the first page of verse and under the heading *Paradise Lost, Book I,* I see that the first four words of the first line of verse are "Of Man's first disobedience." It would ordinarily be said that I had verified it. The proponents of the Verification Argument would say that I had not "completely" verified it. They would say that I had not even "completely" verified the fact that the first four words of verse on *the page before me* are the words "Of Man's first disobedience." What shall I do to *further* verify this latter fact? Shall I look again? Suppose that I do and that I see the same thing. Shall I ask someone else to look? Suppose that he looks and that he sees the same thing. According to this philosophical theory it is still not "completely" verified. How shall I further verify it? Would it

---

[26] Carnap, "Testability and Meaning," *Philosophy of Science,* III (1936), 425.

be "further verification" if I were to look *again* and *again* at this page and have more and more other people look again and again? Not at all! We should not describe it so! Having looked once carefully, if I then continued to look at the page we should not say that I was "further verifying" or "trying to further verify" that the first four words of verse on that page are "Of Man's first disobedience." Carnap declares that although it might be foolish or impractical to continue "the series of test-observations" still one could do so "theoretically." He implies that *no matter what the circumstances* we should describe certain actions as "further verifying" or "further confirming" this fact. That is a mistake. Suppose that I continued to look steadily at the page and someone wondered why I was behaving in that way. If someone else were to say "He is trying to further verify that those are the first four words," this would be an absurd and humorous remark. And this description would be equally absurd if my actions consisted in showing the book to one person after another. In those circumstances there is nothing which we should *call* "further verification." To suppose that the "process of verification" can continue "without end" is simply to ignore the ordinary usage of the word "verify." It is false that "there is always the theoretical possibility of continuing the series of test-observations." It *is* possible that I should continue *to look at the page*. It is *not* possible that I should continue the verification of that fact because, in those circumstances, we should not describe *anything* as "further verification" of it. The verification *comes to an end*.

Carnap would say that the statement "The first four words of verse on this page are 'Of Man's first disobedience'" is not "completely" verified because "there remains still the theoretical possibility of denying the sentence." [27] What does he mean by "there remains still the theoretical possibility of denying the sentence"? Does he mean that it is logically possible that someone should *deny* that statement? This is true, but irrelevant to the question of whether it has been established that the statement is true. Does he mean that the contradictory of the above statement is not self-contradictory? This is also true and also irrelevant. Does he mean that there is *some reason* for thinking that the statement is false,

[27] *Ibid.*, p. 426.

or that there is *no reason* for thinking it true? But there is the best of reasons for saying it is true, namely, that I looked carefully at the page a moment ago and saw that those were the first four words; and there is no reason whatever for saying that it is false. Does he mean that the fact that I looked at the page and saw that those were the first four words of verse does not "completely" establish that the statement is true? In what way does it fail to establish it "completely"? Shall we repeat that it does not "completely" establish it because "there remains still the theoretical possibility of denying the statement"? But this is circular reasoning. Carnap's statement "There remains still the theoretical possibility of denying the sentence" embodies the same confusion that surrounds premise III of the Verification Argument, the confusion produced by the failure to distinguish the several different usages of the expression "It is possible."

Some philosophers have thought that, when it is said in ordinary discourse that it is absolutely certain that so-and-so, what this means is that it is *practically* certain that so-and-so. This is clearly a mistake. The ordinary usage of "practically certain" is quite different from the ordinary usage of "absolutely certain." It is "practically certain" normally means "It is almost certain." To say that it is practically certain that so-and-so implies that it is *not* absolutely certain. "It is practically certain that p is true" implies that it is reasonable to have a slight doubt that p is true and implies that the evidence that p is true is not absolutely conclusive. "It is absolutely certain that p is true" implies, on the contrary, that the evidence that p is true is absolutely conclusive and implies that in the light of the evidence it would be unreasonable to have the slightest doubt that p is true.

Lewis and Carnap do not, of course, make the mistake of identifying absolute certainty with practical certainty. They make a different mistake. They identify absolute certainty with "theoretical certainty." Lewis, for example, uses the expressions "absolutely certain" and "theoretically certain" interchangeably.[28] Both he and Carnap say that the truth of an empirical statement can be practically certain but not "theoretically certain." How are they using the expression "theoretical certainty"? What state of affairs,

---

[28] Cp. *An Analysis of Knowledge and Valuation*, p. 180.

if it could be realized, would they call "theoretical certainty"? In what circumstances, supposing that such circumstances could exist, would it be "theoretically certain" that a given statement is true? The answer is clear from the context of their arguments. It would be "theoretically certain" that a given statement is true only if an *infinite* number of "tests" or "acts of verification" had been performed. It is, of course, a *contradiction* to say that an infinite number of "tests" or acts of any sort have been performed by anyone. It is not that it is merely impossible in practice for anyone to perform an infinite number of acts. It is impossible *in theory*. Therefore these philosophers *misuse* the expression "theoretically certain." What they call "theoretical certainty" cannot be attained even *in theory*. But this misusage of an expression is in itself of slight importance. What is very important is that they identify what they mean by "theoretically certain" with what is ordinarily meant by "absolutely certain." If this identification were correct then the ordinary meaning of "absolutely certain" would be contradictory. The proposition that it is absolutely certain that a given statement is true would *entail* the proposition that someone had performed an infinite number of acts. Therefore, it would be a *contradiction* to say, for example, "It is absolutely certain that Socrates had a wife." Statements of this sort are often false, or they are often unjustified on the strength of the evidence at hand. But to say that such statements are one and all *self-contradictory* is perfectly absurd. A philosophical theory that has such a consequence is plainly false.[29]

---

[29] [Frankfurt very properly raises the question as to what certainty, and the highest degree of certainty, *is*. He complains that I have not "ever attempted seriously and precisely to say what certainty is and what its general criteria are" ("Philosophical Certainty," *The Philosophical Review*, LXXI, 317). I do not do this in the present essay, but I do attempt it in "Knowledge and Belief." I try to describe what I call "the strong sense of 'know,'" and I make the conjecture that it is what various philosophers have had in mind when they have spoken of "strict," "perfect," or "metaphysical" certainty (see p. 70). I return to the subject in "Direct Perception" (see p. 90). Frankfurt himself tries to characterize the notion of certainty by drawing a connection between a person's regarding a statement as certain and his being "willing to take the risks associated with the statement if there is nothing to be gained by refusing to do so" (*The Philosophical Review, op. cit.*, p. 319). He goes on to say that "a statement *is* certain only if it would be reasonable for anyone possessing the evidence available for it to regard the statement as certain" (*ibid.*). Finally, he characterizes the *highest* degree of certainty,

which he calls "philosophical certainty," as follows: "A statement enjoys the highest degree of certainty only if it is supported by evidence which justifies a willingness to risk the greatest possible penalty on the truth of the statement. For a person to regard a statement as being certain in the highest degree, he must be willing to risk *anything* on its truth" (*ibid.*, p. 323).

There appears to be *some* sort of connection between certainty and risk taking. "How much will you bet?" is often a good question to ask when someone has claimed that something is certain. But it is doubtful that Frankfurt has stated any *necessary conditions* of certainty. For one thing, it is a dubious assumption that whenever it is certain that a statement is true it is "supported by evidence." (If this were so, philosophical certainty would not apply to "protocol statements," as Frankfurt thinks: *ibid.*, p. 323.) For another thing, the notion that there should be *any* statement at all (whether empirical, protocol, or a priori) with respect to which it would be *reasonable* for a person to risk *"anything"* (disgrace, torture, eternal hell-fire?) on its being true, does not seem intelligible to me. Finally, Frankfurt appears to assume that whenever a person is entitled to assert that something is certain, there is a *risk* ("the risks associated with the statement") of his being *mistaken*. This must mean that the person *could be mistaken*. But it is precisely the *impossibility of being mistaken* that is fundamental to the concept of certainty. And we are most inclined to speak of "perfect," "metaphysical," or "philosophical" certainty, or of certainty in "the highest degree," in those cases where there is a *conceptual absurdity* in the suggestion that one could be mistaken. Furthermore, there are *different kinds* of that sort of conceptual absurdity. Some of these kinds are discussed in "Knowledge and Belief," "Direct Perception," and in Part IV of "Memory and the Past." For a report of some remarks of Wittgenstein about certainty "in the highest degree," see my *Ludwig Wittgenstein: A Memoir* (New York: Oxford University Press, 1958), pp. 87-92.]

Knowledge and Belief

"We must recognize that when we know something we either do, or by reflecting, can know that our condition is one of knowing that thing, while when we believe something, we either do or can know that our condition is one of believing and not of knowing: so that we cannot mistake belief for knowledge or vice versa." [1]

This remark is worthy of investigation. Can I discover *in myself* whether I know something or merely believe it?

Let us begin by studying the ordinary usage of "know" and "believe." Suppose, for example, that several of us intend to go for a walk and that you propose that we walk in Cascadilla Gorge. I protest that I should like to walk beside a flowing stream and that at this season the gorge is probably dry. Consider the following cases:

(1) You say "I believe that it won't be dry although I have no particular reason for thinking so." If we went to the gorge and found a flowing stream we should not say that you *knew* that there would be water but that you thought so and were right.

(2) You say "I believe that it won't be dry because

[1] H. A. Prichard, *Knowledge and Perception* (Oxford: The Clarendon Press, 1950), p. 88.

it rained only three days ago and usually water flows in the gorge for at least that long after a rain." If we found water we should be inclined to say that you knew that there would be water. It would be quite natural for you to say "I knew that it wouldn't be dry"; and we should tolerate your remark. This case differs from the previous one in that here you had a *reason*.

(3) You say "I know that it won't be dry" and give the same reason as in (2). If we found water we should have very little hesitation in saying that you knew. Not only had you a reason, but you *said* "I know" instead of "I believe." It may seem to us that the latter should not make a difference—but it does.

(4) You say "I know that it won't be dry" and give a stronger reason, e.g., "I saw a lot of water flowing in the gorge when I passed it this morning." If we went and found water, there would be no hesitation at all in saying that you knew. If, for example, we later met someone who said "Weren't you surprised to see water in the gorge this afternoon?" you would reply "No, I *knew* that there would be water; I had been there earlier in the day." We should have no objection to this statement.

(5) Everything happens as in (4), except that upon going to the gorge we find it to be dry. We should not say that you knew, but that you *believed* that there would be water. And this is true even though you declared that you knew, and even though your evidence was the same as it was in case (4) in which you did know.

I wish to make some comments on the usage of "know," "knew," "believe," and "believed," as illustrated in the preceding cases:

(*a*) Whether we should say that you knew, depends in part on whether you had grounds for your assertion and on the strength of those grounds. There would certainly be less hesitation to say that you knew in case (4) than in case (3), and this can be due only to the difference in the strength of the grounds.

(*b*) Whether we should say that you knew, depends in part on how *confident* you were. In case (2), if you had said "It rained only three days ago and usually water flows in the gorge for at least that long after a rain; but, of course, I don't feel absolutely sure that there will be water," then we should *not* have said that you knew that there would be water. If you lack confidence that

p is true then others do not say that you know that p is true, even though *they* know that p is true. Being confident is a necessary condition for knowing.

(c) Prichard says that if we reflect we cannot mistake belief for knowledge. In case (4) you knew that there would be water, and in case (5) you merely believed it. Was there any way that you could have discovered by reflection, in case (5), that you did not know? It would have been useless to have reconsidered your grounds for saying that there would be water, because in case (4), where you *did* know, your grounds were identical. They could be at fault in (5) only if they were at fault in (4), and they were not at fault in (4). Cases (4) and (5) differ in only one respect—namely, that in one case you did subsequently find water and in the other you did not. Prichard says that we can determine by reflection whether we know something or merely believe it. But where, in these cases, is the material that reflection would strike upon? There is none.

There is only one way that Prichard could defend his position. He would have to say that in case (4) you did *not* know that there would be water. And it is obvious that he would have said this. But this is false. It is an enormously common usage of language to say, in commenting upon just such an incident as (4), "He knew that the gorge would be dry because he had seen water flowing there that morning." It is a usage that all of us are familiar with. We so employ "know" and "knew" every day of our lives. We do not think of our usage as being loose or incorrect —and it is not. As philosophers we may be surprised to observe that it *can* be that the knowledge that p is true should differ from the belief that p is true *only* in the respect that in one case p is true and in the other false. But that is the fact.

There is an argument that one is inclined to use as a proof that you did not know that there would be water. The argument is the following: It could have turned out that you found no water; if it had so turned out you would have been mistaken in saying that you would find water; therefore you could have been mistaken; but if you could have been mistaken then you did not know.

Now it certainly *could* have turned out that the gorge was quite dry when you went there, even though you saw lots of water flowing through it only a few hours before. This does not show, however, that you did not know that there would be water. What it shows is that *although you knew you could have been mistaken.*[2] This would seem to be a contradictory result; but it is not. It seems so because our minds are fixed upon another usage of "know" and "knew"; one in which "It could have turned out that I was mistaken," implies "I did not know."

When is "know" used in this sense? I believe that Prichard uses it in this sense when he says that when we go through the proof of the proposition that the angles of a triangle are equal to two right angles we *know* that the proposition is true (p. 89). He says that if we put to ourselves the question: Is our condition one of knowing this, or is it only one of being convinced of it? then "We can only answer 'Whatever may be our state on other occasions, here we are knowing this.' And this statement is an expression of our *knowing* that we are knowing; for we do not *believe* that we are knowing this, we know that we are" (p. 89). He goes on to say that if someone were to object that we might be making a mistake "because for all we know we can later on discover some fact which is incompatible with a triangle's having angles that are equal to two right angles, we can answer that we *know* that there can be no such fact, for in knowing that a triangle must have such angles we also know that nothing can exist which is incompatible with this fact" (p. 90).

It is easy to imagine a non-philosophical context in which it would have been natural for Prichard to have said "I know that the angles of a triangle are equal to two right angles." Suppose that a young man just beginning the study of geometry was in doubt as to whether that proposition is true, and had even constructed an ingenious argument that appeared to prove it false. Suppose that Prichard was unable to find any error in the argument. He might have said to the young man: "There must be an

[2] [Some readers seem to have thought that I was denying here that "I knew that *p*" entails "that *p*." That was not my intention, and my words do not have that implication. If I had said *"although you knew you were mistaken,"* I should have denied the above entailment and, also, I should have misused "knew." The difference between the strong and weak senses of "know" (and "knew") is not that this entailment holds for the strong but not for the weak sense. It holds for both. If it is false that *p*, then one does not (and did not) know that *p*.]

error in it. I know that the angles of a triangle are equal to two right angles."

When Prichard says that "nothing can exist which is incompatible with" the truth of that proposition, is he prophesying that no one will ever have the ingenuity to construct a flawless-looking argument against it? I believe not. When Prichard says that "we" *know* (and implies that *he* knows) that the proposition is true and *know* that nothing can exist that is incompatible with its being true, he is not making any *prediction* as to what the future will bring in the way of arguments or measurements. On the contrary, he is asserting that *nothing* that the future might bring could ever count as evidence against the proposition. He is implying that he would not *call* anything "evidence" against it. He is using "know" in what I shall call its "strong" sense. "Know" is used in this sense when a person's statement "I know that *p* is true" implies that the person who makes the statement would look upon nothing whatever as evidence that *p* is false.

It must not be assumed that whenever "know" is used in connection with mathematical propositions it is used in the strong sense. A great many people have *heard* of various theorems of geometry, e.g., the Pythagorean. These theorems are a part of "common knowledge." If a schoolboy doing his geometry assignment felt a doubt about the Pythagorean theorem, and said to an adult "Are you *sure* that it is true?" the latter might reply "Yes, I know that it is." He might make this reply even though he could not give proof of it and even though he had never gone through a proof of it. If subsequently he was presented with a "demonstration" that the theorem is false, or if various persons reputed to have a knowledge of geometry soberly assured him that it is false, he might be filled with doubt or even be convinced that he was mistaken. When he said "Yes, I know that it is true," he did not pledge himself to hold to the theorem through thick and thin. He did not absolutely exclude the possibility that something could prove it to be false. I shall say that he used "know" in the "weak" sense.

Consider another example from mathematics of the difference between the strong and weak senses of "know." I have just now rapidly calculated that 92 times 16 is 1472. If I had done this in the commerce of daily life where a practical problem was at stake, and if someone had asked "Are you sure that $92 \times 16 = 1472$?" I might have answered "I *know* that it is; I have just now calculated it." But also I might have answered "I know that it is; but I will calculate it again to *make sure*." And here my language points to a distinction. I say that I *know* that $92 \times 16 = 1472$. Yet I am willing to *confirm* it—that is, there is something that I should *call* "making sure"; and, likewise, there is something that I should *call* "finding out that it is false." If I were to do this calculation again and obtain the result that $92 \times 16 = 1372$, and if I were to carefully check this latter calculation without finding any error, I should be disposed to say that I was previously mistaken when I declared that $92 \times 16 = 1472$. Thus when I say that I know that $92 \times 16 = 1472$, I allow for the possibility of a *refutation*; and so I am using "know" in its weak sense.

Now consider propositions like $2 + 2 = 4$ and $7 + 5 = 12$. It is hard to think of circumstances in which it would be natural for me to say that I know that $2 + 2 = 4$, because no one ever questions it. Let us try to suppose, however, that someone whose intelligence I respect argues that certain developments in arithmetic have shown that $2 + 2$ does not equal 4. He writes out a proof of this in which I can find no flaw. Suppose that his demeanor showed me that he was in earnest. Suppose that several persons of normal intelligence became persuaded that his proof was correct and that $2 + 2$ does not equal 4. What would be my reaction? I should say "I can't see what is wrong with your proof; but it *is* wrong, because I *know* that $2 + 2 = 4$." Here I should be using "know" in its strong sense. I should not admit that any argument or any future development in mathematics could show that it is false that $2 + 2 = 4$.

The propositions $2 + 2 = 4$ and $92 \times 16 = 1472$ do not have the same status. There *can* be a demonstration that $2 + 2 = 4$. But a demonstration would be for me (and for any average person) only a curious exercise, a sort of *game*. We have no serious interest in proving that proposition.[3] It does not *need* a proof. It

---

[3] Some logicians and philosophers have taken an interest in proving that $2 + 2 = 4$ (e.g., Leibniz, *New Essays on the Understanding*, Bk. IV, ch.

stands without one, and would not fall if a proof went against it. The case is different with the proposition that $92 \times 16 = 1472$. We take an interest in the demonstration (calculation) because that proposition *depends* upon its demonstration. A calculation may lead me to reject it as false. But $2 + 2 = 4$ does *not* depend on its demonstration. It does not depend on anything! And in the calculation that proves that $92 \times 16 = 1472$, there are steps that do not depend on any calculation (e.g., $2 \times 6 = 12$; $5 + 2 = 7$; $5 + 9 = 14$).

There is a correspondence between this dualism in the logical status of mathematical propositions and the two senses of "know." When I use "know" in the weak sense I am prepared to let an investigation (demonstration, calculation) determine whether the something that I claim to know is true or false. When I use "know" in the strong sense I am not prepared to look upon anything as an *investigation*; I do not concede that anything whatsoever could prove me mistaken; I do not regard the matter as open to any *question*; I do not admit that my proposition could turn out to be false, that any future investigation *could* refute it or cast doubt on it.[4]

We have been considering the strong sense of "know" in its application to mathematical propositions. Does it have application anywhere in the realm of *empirical* propositions—for example, to propositions that assert or imply that certain physical things exist? Descartes said that we have a "moral assurance" of the truth of some of the latter propositions but that we lack a "metaphysical certainty."[5] Locke said that the perception of the existence of physical things is not "so certain as our intuitive

7, sec. 10; Frege, *The Foundations of Arithmetic*, sec. 6). They have wished to show that it can be deduced from certain premises, and to determine what premises and rules of inference are required in the deduction. Their interest has not been in the *outcome* of the deduction.

[4] Compare these remarks about the strong sense of "know" with some of Locke's statements about "intuitive knowledge": ". . . in this the mind is at no pains of proving or examining. . . ." "This part of knowledge . . . leaves no room for hesitation, doubt, or examination. . . ."

"It is on this intuition that depends all the certainty and evidence of all our knowledge; which certainly every one finds to be so great, that he cannot imagine, and therefore not require a greater. . . ." Locke, *Essay*, Bk. IV, ch. 2, sec. 1.

[5] Descartes, *Discourse on the Method*, Part IV.

knowledge, or the deductions of our reason" although "it is an assurance that deserves the name of knowledge." [6] Some philosophers have held that when we make judgments of perception such as that there are peonies in the garden, cows in the field, or dishes in the cupboard, we are "taking for granted" that the peonies, cows, and dishes exist, but not knowing it in the "strict" sense. Others have held that all empirical propositions, including judgments of perception, are merely hypotheses.[7] The thought behind this exaggerated mode of expression is that any empirical proposition whatever *could* be refuted by future experience— that is, it *could* turn out to be false. Are these philosophers right?

Consider the following propositions:

(i) The sun is about ninety million miles from the earth.
(ii) There is a heart in my body.
(iii) Here is an ink-bottle.

In various circumstances I should be willing to assert of each of these propositions that I know it to be true. Yet they differ strikingly. This I see when, with each, I try to imagine the possibility that it is false.

(i) If in ordinary conversation someone said to me "The sun is about twenty million miles from the earth, isn't it?" I should reply "No, it is about ninety million miles from us." If he said "I think that you are confusing the sun with Polaris," I should reply, "I *know* that ninety million miles is roughly the sun's distance from the earth." I might invite him to verify the figure in an encyclopedia. A third person who overheard our conversation could quite correctly report that I knew the distance to the sun, whereas the other man did not. But this knowledge of mine is little better than hearsay. I have seen that figure mentioned in a few books. I know nothing about the observations and calculations that led astronomers to accept it. If tomorrow a group of eminent astronomers announced that a great error had been made and that the correct figure is twenty million miles, I should not

---

[6] Locke, *Essay*, Book IV, ch. 11, sec. 3.
[7] E.g., ". . . no proposition, other than a tautology, can possibly be anything more than a probable hypothesis." A. J. Ayer, *Language, Truth and Logic*, second ed. (New York: Dover Publications, Inc., 1951), p. 38.

insist that they were wrong. It would surprise me that such an enormous mistake could have been made. But I should no longer be willing to say that I *know* that ninety million is the correct figure. Although I should *now* claim that I know the distance to be about ninety million miles, it is easy for me to envisage the possibility that some future investigation will prove this to be false.

(ii) Suppose that after a routine medical examination the excited doctor reports to me that the X-ray photographs show that I have no heart. I should tell him to get a new machine. I should be inclined to say that the fact that I have a heart is one of the few things that I can count on as absolutely certain. I can feel it beat. I know it's there. Furthermore, how could my blood circulate if I didn't have one? Suppose that later on I suffer a chest injury and undergo a surgical operation. Afterwards the astonished surgeons solemnly declare that they searched my chest cavity and found no heart, and that they made incisions and looked about in other likely places but found it not. They are convinced that I am without a heart. They are unable to understand how circulation can occur or what accounts for the thumping in my chest. But they are in agreement and obviously sincere, and they have clear photographs of my interior spaces. What would be my attitude? Would it be to insist that they were all mistaken? I think not. I believe that I should eventually accept their testimony and the evidence of the photographs. I should consider to be false what I now regard as an absolute certainty.

(iii) Suppose that as I write this paper someone in the next room were to call out to me "I can't find an ink-bottle; is there one in the house?" I should reply "Here is an ink-bottle." If he said in a doubtful tone "Are you sure? I looked there before," I should reply "Yes, I know there is; come and get it."

Now could it turn out to be false that there is an ink-bottle directly in front of me on this desk? Many philosophers have thought so. They would say that many things could happen of such a nature that if they did happen it would be proved that I am deceived. I agree that many extraordinary things could happen, in the sense that there is no logical absurdity in the supposition. It could happen that when I next reach for this ink-bottle my hand should seem to pass *through* it and I should not feel the contact of any object. It could happen that in the next moment the ink-bottle will suddenly vanish from sight; or that I should find myself under a tree in the garden with no ink-bottle about; or that one or more persons should enter this room and declare with apparent sincerity that they see no ink-bottle on this desk; or that a photograph taken now of the top of the desk should clearly show all of the objects on it except the ink-bottle. Having admitted that these things *could happen*,[8] am I compelled to admit that if they did happen then it would be proved that there is no ink-bottle here *now*? Not at all! I could say that when my hand seemed to pass through the ink-bottle I should *then* be suffering from hallucination; that if the ink-bottle suddenly vanished it would have miraculously ceased to exist; that the other persons were conspiring to drive me mad, or were themselves victims of remarkable concurrent hallucinations; that the camera possessed some strange flaw or that there was trickery in developing the negative. I admit that in the next moment I could find myself under a tree or in the bathtub. But this is not to admit that it could be revealed in the next moment that I am now dreaming. For what I admit is that I might be instantaneously transported to the garden, but not that in the next moment I might *wake up* in the garden. There is nothing that could happen to me in the next moment that I should call "waking up"; and therefore nothing that could happen to me in the next moment would be accepted by me now as proof that I now dream.

Not only do I not *have* to admit that those extraordinary occurrences would be evidence that there is no ink-bottle here; the fact is that I *do not* admit it. There is nothing whatever that could happen in the next moment or the next year that would by me be called *evidence* that there is not an ink-bottle here now. No

[8] [My viewpoint is somewhat different here from what it is in "The Verification Argument." There I am concerned with bringing out the different ways in which such a remark as "these things *could* happen" can be taken. I wish to show, furthermore, that from none of the senses in which the remark is *true* does it follow that it is *not certain* that the things in question will *not* happen. Finally, I hold there, that it is perfectly certain that they will not happen. Here, I am not disagreeing with any of those points, but I am adding the further point that my admission that, in some sense, the things *could happen,* does not require me to admit that *if* they were to happen, that would be evidence that there is no ink-bottle here now.]

future experience or investigation could prove to me that I am mistaken. Therefore, if I were to say "I know that there is an ink-bottle here," I should be using "know" in the strong sense.

It will appear to some that I have adopted an *unreasonable* attitude toward that statement. There is, however, nothing unreasonable about it. It seems so because one thinks that the statement that here is an ink-bottle *must* have the same status as the statements that the sun is ninety million miles away and that I have a heart and that there will be water in the gorge this afternoon. But this is a *prejudice*.

In saying that I should regard nothing as evidence that there is no ink-bottle here now, I am not *predicting* what I should do if various astonishing things happened. If other members of my family entered this room and, while looking at the top of this desk, declared with apparent sincerity that they see no ink-bottle, I might fall into a swoon or become mad. I *might* even come to believe that there is not and has not been an ink-bottle here. I cannot foretell with certainty how I should react. But if it is *not* a prediction, what is the meaning of my assertion that I should regard nothing as evidence that there is no ink-bottle here?

That assertion describes my *present* attitude towards the statement that here is an ink-bottle. It does not prophesy what my attitude *would* be if various things happened. My present attitude toward that statement is radically different from my present attitude toward those other statements (e.g., that I have a heart).[9] I do *now* admit that certain future occurrences would disprove the latter. Whereas no imaginable future occurrence would be considered by me *now* as proving that there is not an ink-bottle here.

These remarks are not meant to be autobiographical. They are meant to throw light on the common concepts of evidence, proof, and disproof. Every one of us upon innumerable occasions of

[9] [The word "attitude" is not very satisfactory, but I cannot think of another noun that would do the trick. By "my attitude" I mean, here, *what I should say and think* if various things were to happen. By "my *present* attitude" I mean what I should say and think now, when I imagine those things as happening, in contrast with what I should say and think at some future time if those things actually did happen at that time. It is this distinction that shows that my description of "my present attitude" is not a *prophecy*.]

daily life takes this same attitude towards various statements about physical things, e.g., that here is a torn page, that this dish is broken, that the thermometer reads 70, that no rug is on the floor. Furthermore, the concepts of proof, disproof, doubt, and conjecture *require* us to take this attitude. In order for it to be possible that any statements about physical things should *turn out to be false* it is necessary that some statements about physical things *cannot* turn out to be false.

This will be made clear if we ask ourselves the question, When do we *say* that something turned out to be false? When do we use those words? Someone asks you for a dollar. You say "There is one in this drawer." You open the drawer and look, but it is perfectly empty. Your statement turned out to be false. This can be said because you *discovered* an empty drawer. It could not be said if it were only probable that the drawer is empty or were still open to question. Would it make sense to say "I had better make sure that it is empty; perhaps there is a dollar in it after all?" Sometimes; but not always. Not if the drawer lies open before your eyes. That remark is the prelude to a search. What search can there be when the emptiness of the drawer confronts you? In certain circumstances there is nothing that you would call "making sure" that the drawer is empty; and likewise nothing that you would call "its turning out to be false" that the drawer is empty. You *made* sure that the drawer is empty. One statement about physical things *turned out to be false* only because you *made sure* of another statement about physical things. The two concepts cannot exist apart. Therefore it is impossible that *every* statement about physical things *could* turn out to be false.

In a certain important respect some a priori statements and some empirical statements possess the same logical character. The statements that $5 \times 5 = 25$ and that here is an ink-bottle, both lie beyond the reach of doubt. On both, my judgment and reasoning *rests*. If you could somehow undermine my confidence in either, you would not teach me *caution*. You would fill my mind with chaos! I could not even make *conjectures* if you took away those fixed points of certainty; just as a man cannot *try* to climb whose body has no support. A conjecture implies an understanding of what certainty would be. If it is not a certainty that $5 \times 5 = 25$ and that here is an ink-bottle, then I do not understand what it is. You cannot make me doubt either of these statements or treat them as hypotheses. You cannot persuade me that future experience could refute them. With both of them it is perfectly unintelligible to me to speak of a "possibility" that they are false. This is to say that I know both of them to be true, in the strong sense of "know." And I am inclined to think that the strong sense of "know" is what various philosophers have had in mind when they have spoken of "perfect," "metaphysical," or "strict certainty." [10]

It will be thought that I have confused a statement about my "sensations," or my "sense-data," or about the way something *looks* or *appears* to me, with a statement about physical things. It will be thought that the things that I have said about the statement "Here is an ink-bottle" could be true only if that statement is interpreted to mean something like "There appears to me to be an ink-bottle here," i.e., interpreted so as not to assert or imply that any physical thing exists. I wish to make it clear that my statement "Here is an ink-bottle" is *not* to be interpreted in that way. It would be utterly fantastic for me in my present circumstances to say "There appears to me to be an ink-bottle here."

If someone were to call me on the telephone and say that he urgently needed an ink-bottle I should invite him to come here and get this one. If he said that it was extremely urgent that he should obtain one immediately and that he could not afford to waste time going to a place where there might not be one, I should tell him that it is an absolute certainty that there is one here, that nothing could be more certain, that it is something I absolutely guarantee. But if my statement "There is an ink-bottle here" were a statement about my "sensations" or "sense-data," or if it meant that there *appears* to me to be an ink-bottle here or that something here *looks* to me like an ink-bottle, and if that is

---

[10] Descartes, for example, apparently took as his criterion for something's being "entirely certain" that he could not *imagine* in it the least ground of doubt: ". . . je pensai qu'il fallait . . . que je retasse comme absolument faux tout ce en quoi je pourrais imaginer le moindre doute, afin de voir s'il ne me resterait point après cela quelque chose en ma creánce qui fut entière-ment indubitable" (*Discourse*, Part IV). And Locke (as previously noted) said of "intuitive knowledge" that one *cannot imagine* a greater certainty, and that it "leaves no room for hesitation, doubt, or examination." *Essay*, Bk. IV, ch. 2, sec. 1.

all that I meant by it—then I should react quite differently to his urgent request. I should say that there is probably an ink-bottle here but that I could not *guarantee* it, and that if he needs one very desperately and at once then he had better look elsewhere. In short, I wish to make it clear that my statement "Here is an ink-bottle" is strictly about physical things and not about "sensations," "sense-data," or "appearances." [11]

Let us go back to Prichard's remark that we can determine by reflection whether we know something or merely believe it. Prichard would think that "knowledge in the weak sense" is mere belief and not knowledge. This is wrong. But if we let ourselves speak this way, we can then see some justification for Prichard's remark. For then he would be asserting, among other things, that we can determine by reflection whether we know something in the strong sense or in the weak sense. This is not literally true; however, there is this truth in it—that reflection can make us realize that we are *using* "I know it" in the strong (or weak) sense in a particular case. Prichard says that reflection can show us that "our condition is one of knowing" a certain thing, or instead that "our condition is one of believing and not of knowing" that thing. I do not understand what could be meant here by "our condition." The way I should put it is that reflection on *what we should think* if certain things were to happen may make us realize that we should (or should not) call those things "proof" or "evidence" that what we claim to know is not so. I have tried to show that the distinction between strong and weak knowledge does not run parallel to the distinction between a priori and empirical knowledge but cuts across it, i.e., these two kinds of knowledge may be distinguished *within* a priori knowledge and *within* empirical knowledge.

Reflection can make me realize that I am using "know" in the strong sense; but can reflection show me that I *know* something in the strong sense (or in the weak)? It is not easy to state the

[11] [The remainder of the essay is newly written. The original conclusion was wrongly stated. The reader is referred to the following exchange between Richard Taylor and myself, in respect to the original paper: Taylor, "A Note on Knowledge and Belief," *Analysis*, XIII, June 1953; Malcolm, "On Knowledge and Belief," *Analysis*, XIV, March 1954; Taylor, "Rejoinder to Mr. Malcolm," *ibid.*]

logical facts here. On the one hand, if I make an assertion of the form "I know that *p*" it does not follow that *p*, whether or not I am using "know" in the strong sense. If I have said to someone outside my room "Of course, I know that Freddie is in here," and I am speaking in the strong sense, it does not *follow* that Freddie is where I claim he is. This logical fact would not be altered even if I *realized* that I was using "know" in the strong sense. My reflection on what I should say if . . . , cannot show me that I *know* something. From the fact that I should not call anything "evidence" that Freddie is not here, it does not follow that he *is* here; therefore, it does not follow that I *know* he is here.

On the other hand, in an actual case of my using "know" in the strong sense, I cannot envisage a possibility that what I say to be true should turn out to be not true. If I were speaking of *another person's* assertion about something, I *could* think both that he is using "know" in the strong sense and that nonetheless what he claims he knows to be so might turn out to be not so. But *in my own case* I cannot have this conjunction of thoughts, and this is a logical and not a psychological fact. When *I* say that I know something to be so, using "know" in the strong sense, it is unintelligible *to me* (although perhaps not to others) to suppose that anything could prove that it is not so and, therefore, that I do not know it.[12]

---

[12] This is the best summary I can give of what is wrong and right in Prichard's claim that one can determine by reflection whether one knows something or merely believes it. A good part of the ideas in this essay were provoked by conversations with Wittgenstein. A brief and rough account of those talks is to be found in my *Ludwig Wittgenstein: A Memoir* (New York: Oxford University Press, 1958), pp. 87-92. Jaakko Hintikka provides an acute treatment of the topic of "knowing that one knows," with special reference to Prichard's claim. See his *Knowledge and Belief* (Ithaca: Cornell University Press, 1962), ch. 5.

Direct Perception

I

I wish to discuss the curious inclination of Professor G. E. Moore to consciously hold two apparently contradictory views about perception. One is the view that "we do constantly *see directly* parts of the surfaces of physical objects."[1] The other is the view that we *cannot* directly see any physical surface. Moore says: "I am strongly inclined to take both of these incompatible views. I am completely puzzled about the matter, and only wish I could see any way of settling it."[2] I believe that an examination of this conflict in Moore's thought will yield an insight into a major problem of the philosophy of perception.

Moore has a highly interesting way of explaining his own philosophical use of the expression "directly see." He calls attention to that ordinary use of the word "see" in which a person who has an after-image when his eyes are closed may be said to see the after-image. This use of "see," Moore calls "directly see." He thinks that there are analogous uses of "hear," "smell," "taste." Directly seeing, directly smelling, etc., are varieties of "directly apprehending." He so uses the expression "sense-datum" that

[1] "A Reply to My Critics," *The Philosophy of G. E. Moore*, P. A. Schilpp, ed. (Evanston: Northwestern, 1942), pp. 649-650.
[2] *Ibid.*, p. 659.

from the fact that something is directly apprehended it follows that it is a sense-datum. Thus an after-image is a sense-datum. Moore also says that "a tooth-ache which you feel, is necessarily a 'sense-datum.'"[3]

Moore expresses his inclination to think that no physical surface can be directly apprehended as follows: "I am inclined to think that it is as impossible that . . . *anything whatever which is directly apprehended,* any *sense-datum,* that is, should exist unperceived, as it is that a headache should exist unfelt. If this is so, it would follow at once, that *no* sense-datum can be identical with any physical surface [Moore is confident that the supposition that a physical surface might exist unperceived is free from contradiction] which is the same thing as to say that no physical surface can be directly apprehended: that it is a contradiction to say that any is."[4] He offers, so far as I know, no sort of argument or explanation in support of his opposite inclination to think that physical surfaces can be directly apprehended.

Philosophers discussing problems of perception have frequently used the expressions "direct perception," "direct apprehension," "immediate awareness," and their cognates. But these expressions have no familiar use in ordinary life, and those philosophers usually have given either no explanation, or an obscure one, of their intended philosophical use. Moore's directions as to his use of "directly seeing" (the "visual variety" of "directly apprehending") are the most lucid that exist in the literature of perception.[5] To see an after-image with eyes closed is to *directly see* it; and to see *anything, x,* in that same sense of "see" in which one may see an after-image with eyes closed, is to *directly see x.*[6]

Unfortunately, when we begin to think about the notion of seeing an after-image, we find that it is full of philosophical difficulties. These may prevent us from correctly understanding the

[3] *Ibid.,* p. 643.
[4] *Ibid.,* p. 658.
[5] For Moore's directions, *ibid.,* pp. 629-631.
[6] Moore's reference to Macbeth's use of the sentence "Is this a dagger which I see before me?" as another example of "see" being used to mean "directly see," has considerably less merit than his appeal to the use of "see" with after-images; for it is not obvious just *how* Macbeth is supposed to have been using his sentence, and there is no way of finding out.

important conceptions of "seeing directly" and "immediately apprehending," that this notion is meant to elucidate. By studying the use of statements about after-images, I intend to examine the concept of seeing an after-image, and to compare it with the concept of seeing a physical reality. I should say that it does not appear to me that the distinction between seeing after-images with open eyes and seeing them with closed eyes has any importance for this inquiry. My main aim is to clarify the philosophical concept of direct perception. A secondary aim is to provide a conclusive proof that a physical surface *cannot* be "directly seen," in Moore's explicit sense of this expression.

Let us begin by noting a remark that Moore made a few years before—namely, that "there is an absurdity in supposing that any one of the after-images which I saw could also have been seen by any one else: in supposing that two different people can ever see the *very same* after-image." [7] Agreeing that this is an absurdity, I want to know what *sort* of absurdity it is. Suppose that two persons, A and B, performed the following experiment: Each of them gazed steadily at a piece of white paper cut in the shape of a four-pointed star and placed on a black ground, and then turned his eyes to a sheet of white paper, and both of them looked at the very same white sheet. Suppose that each of them saw a gray patch on the white ground, the gray patch having roughly the shape of a four-pointed star. Suppose that each of them traced with a finger the location of his after-image on the white ground, and each traced the very same path. Should we say that the after-image that A saw is the very same one that B saw; or should we say that A's after-image was exactly similar to B's and was seen in the same place, but that A's was numerically different from B's? What further experiment could we make in order to answer this question? What investigation should we carry out? To what criterion should we appeal? The answer is that we do not have the faintest idea as to what would be an investigation of this matter. It is not the case that we have a conception of an investigation but are prevented by practical obstacles from carrying it out. Rather, the word "investigation" has no

[7] "Proof of an External World," *Proceedings of the British Academy*, XXV, 9.

usage in this connection. We do not understand the sentence "It turned out that A and B saw numerically the same image." Nor do we understand the sentence "It turned out that A's image was *not* numerically identical with B's image." Neither sentence, to be sure, expresses a contradiction. Nonetheless, neither sentence has any meaning, in the sense that no one has the least notion as to what the circumstances should be in which we should *say* the one sentence as opposed to the other. One way to state this fact would be to say that the concepts of numerical identity and numerical difference do not *apply* to after-images.

If I have painted two circles of the same color, area, and shape on the wall of a room, and have placed A and B together in the room, with the instruction to describe what they see, then I, standing outside the room and hearing their identical descriptions, may be in doubt as to whether the area that A describes is exactly similar to but not identical with the area that B describes, or whether it is identical with it. This doubt I can quickly resolve by entering the room and observing that A and B do or do not look and point at the very same part of the wall. I can have a doubt as to whether the hat that A wears in the morning is exactly similar to the one that B wears in the afternoon. I can discover that it is or is not. Having discovered that it is I can wonder whether it is the very same hat. Perhaps I cannot find out, because A and B share an apartment to which no other person is ever admitted. But there is something that you and I would *call* "finding out"—e.g., watching from the closet and observing whether the very same hat that is on A's head when he returns from his morning walk is transferred to B's head. The concept of numerical identity applies to hats and painted circles but not to after-images.

Moore's remark that there is an "absurdity" in supposing that two people can see the very same after-image must not be understood, if taken as true, as implying that they see different after-images; but as implying that questions of identity or difference simply do not belong to our discourse about after-images. It is as absurd to suppose that the after-image that I see is *not* identical with the one that you see as to suppose that it is. A's after-image may be different from B's in the sense of being *unlike* it. But when we are speaking of after-images, "x is *unlike* y" does not entail "x is numerically different from y." [8]

If from the fact that A has an after-image and B also has one we "conclude" that "at least two after-images exist," this would only be a bizarre way of saying that each of two people sees an after-image. To "infer" from the fact that I have seen after-images three times in my life, that "at least three after-images have existed" would be an eccentric way of announcing that on at least three occasions someone has seen an after-image. It would be idle to raise a further question as to whether the after-image seen at one of those times was or was not numerically identical with one seen at another time.

Consider another question about after-images. Would it be possible for A to have made a mistake about the gray star, e.g., to have got the number of points wrong, there being actually five instead of four? What would determine that this was or was not so? Would B's report that he, B, saw four points, be evidence that A saw four? One could not think so except by making the senseless supposition that A and B saw *the very same thing*. I say "senseless" advisedly, because it is a supposition that one can no more *deny* than affirm.

It is tempting to suppose that A might look more carefully at the gray patch and discover *for himself* that it had five points instead of four. But can he *look at* the gray patch? If one can look at something then one can also look *away* from it. And if I can look away from something, that implies that it can continue to exist when I no longer see it. Would it have meaning to think that A's after-image existed after he saw it? We may note that the sentences "A has an after-image" and "A sees an after-image" are synonymous in their ordinary usage and that, therefore, it would be a contradiction to say that A has an after-image that he does not see. Nor could it be said that someone other than A

---

[8] [This remark makes me uncomfortable. One certainly has a strong inclination to deduce numerical difference from qualitative difference. It would perhaps be better to accept this as a rule for after-images (as well as other things). But in the case of after-images, if x and y are qualitatively the same, it makes no sense to raise a *further* question as to whether they are *numerically* the same.]

has or does not have that "very same" after-image of A's when A does not see it; for questions of numerical identity cannot be raised with regard to after-images.

That there is no sense in supposing that my after-image might exist when I do not see it will seem obvious to many. It is connected with a point that will not seem obvious—namely, that there is no sense in saying that I might look *away* from my after-image and, therefore, no sense in saying that I look *at* it. If I cannot look at it then I cannot look at it again, nor examine it more carefully.

The reason that one cannot look away from an after-image is not that it will *follow* one's line of sight. It might or might not. If upon turning one's head, one found that one no longer saw the after-image, one *could* call this "looking away" from the after-image. But it would not mean the same as looking away from a mirror image. One could raise an intelligible question as to whether a mirror image continued to exist while one's head was turned—intelligible in the sense that one can conceive of evidence for or against.[9] There is no parallel intelligible question concerning the after-image. We have no idea what should be considered as evidence that my after-image did, or did not, exist after I looked away from it.

"Looking away" from an after-image may *feel* like looking away from a shadow or a reflection. The difference between the two is *conceptual*, not a difference in experience. We are dealing with questions that *cannot* be settled by producing an after-image and noting what happens.

Can one fail to notice certain features of one's after-image? It is an ordinary use of language to say "I didn't notice" in response to various questions put by another about one's recent after-image, e.g., "Was it red in the center?" But this use of that expression is quite unlike its use when it is said in reply to the question, "Did the man whom you saw in the garage yesterday wear shoes?" In the latter case the reply, "I didn't notice," suggests a need for further inquiry. In the former case it *ends* inquiry.

If I say "I didn't notice whether it was red in the center," that

[9] [But of course a mirror image is a *reflection*. It would not be a mirror image if one's face "appeared" in a mirror when it was *not* reflected in it. I have no idea what we should call it.]

statement is properly regarded as *belonging to my description* of my after-image. It is equivalent to saying that my after-image was in that respect *indefinite*. If the description of an after-image is fragmentary it does not follow that the description is incomplete.

Descriptions of after-images differ in their logical status depending upon their degree of contiguity in time with the after-images they describe. If several days after seeing an after-image I declare that I did not notice its color at the center, one can suppose that I did notice but have forgotten. This supposition has sense *because* there could have been a previous report of mine that supplied this detail. But if in a description that is contemporaneous or nearly contemporaneous with the after-image I declare that I did not notice some detail, then it is absurd to think that I have forgotten. That description is not "more likely" to be accurate than the description that I give from memory a month later. It is not "better evidence." It is your *criterion* for determining the character of my after-image.

Thus there is such a thing as not noticing a feature of one's after-image; but it is not *failing* to notice. If it happens that while I have my after-image I report that "I cannot tell" whether it is red in the center, or immediately after say that "I did not notice" whether it was, then it would be foolish for you to argue that the center of it either was red or was not red, and to conclude that I had failed to notice which it was. What would be your authority for saying that either it was or was not red in the center? Are you appealing to an a priori principle? But what reason is there to think that whatever is an a priori principle of our discourse about physical surfaces is also an a priori principle of our discourse about after-images? "I did not notice whether it was red in the center" has the same *finality,* in an after-image report, as "It was shaped like a star." If I do not know what its color in the center was this "not knowing" is not ignorance.

You find out about my after-image by hearing that report of mine that is contemporaneous or nearly contemporaneous with the after-image. *I* do not find out about my present or just past after-image, in this way or in any other. I could find out about it a year later, by consulting a record of my original report. But the accuracy of that *original* report cannot be questioned by either of us. It is tempting to think that we have the concept of its being in error, but that *you* cannot determine whether it is, and only *I* can. This is entirely wrong. Suppose that while I have an after-image I report that it is star-shaped. Then, while I still have it, can I observe it and compare my report with it? How can I observe it? "Observing" it could not even imply *looking at it*, as I have previously pointed out. Normally, by "observing," and also by "comparing," we mean something that can be done accurately or inaccurately. If I declare "Yes, it is star-shaped," what would it mean to say that I have accurately observed it? I can try to observe more accurately the shape of a shadow by changing my position so as to obtain a better view of it. What would it mean to get a *better view* of my after-image? Nothing at all. I cannot even *try* to "observe" an after-image "more accurately." Nor would my second report "Yes, it is star-shaped" *confirm* my first report that it was star-shaped. For if it would, then the report "No, it isn't star-shaped" would *dis*confirm the first report. But this is not how we should interpret such a sequence of reports. Normally, the latter sequence would be understood as meaning that previously I saw a star-shaped after-image but *no longer* do. If my second report was "No, it isn't star-shaped *and* my after-image has not changed," we should not take even this as refuting the first report. Instead, we should regard that whole sequence of discourse as *unintelligible*. In this sense the subsequent report can *discredit* the previous report. But it does not show it to be *inaccurate*.

I can see a star-shaped after-image and a star-shaped shadow. In either case I can *count* the number of points. Is it the same sense of "count"? Suppose that, with eyes open, I see an after-image on a surface of white paper. Suppose that I determine that it has seven points by counting in succession from one to seven, pointing my fingers at a different point of the after-image each time I utter a numeral. Might not I count the points of a shadow in *the same way*?

It is true that my movements and utterances would be the same in both cases; and there might be no difference in my experience —but the logic of the two cases is very different. It is sensible for me, and for you, to wonder whether, unwittingly, I had placed my finger twice on one point of the shadow. There might be various proofs that I had done so and that, therefore, my count was a miscount. Could there ever be a reason to think that I had mis-counted the points of my after-image? It appears so. If I were to exclaim "It has six points, not seven; I miscounted," then would not you have reason to say that I had miscounted—the reason being my own assertion?

I do not doubt that it would be a natural occurrence for a per-son reporting on his after-image to correct himself in this way; nor do I doubt that anyone else would naturally conclude that the former had miscounted. I do not doubt, therefore, that there is a natural use of "miscount" in this connection. But what *is* that use? What is the status of my assertion that I miscounted? Could I be mistaken about *that*; is it perhaps the case that *seven* is the right count after all? The question trails off into emptiness. We are trying to lay upon *this* notion of "miscounting" a burden that it cannot support. My assertion that I miscounted has for you the same sort of unquestionable validity as does my assertion that the after-image is star-shaped or that the pain in my shoulder is a dull pain. All of these assertions might be called "self-confirm-ing," implying by this that really they have *no* confirmation.

If I report that the number of pages in a manuscript is seven, I may say later, "I miscounted; six is the correct number." You can discover that, contrary to my belief, my former count was *not* a miscount. You cannot discover, "contrary to my belief," that my first count of the points of my after-image was not a miscount. My assertion that it was a miscount is not *responsible* to any investigation, not even my own. For shall I count again? Does not "counting again" pose a difficulty similar to that of "looking again"? Counting involves shifting one's attention successively along the series of items counted. One might ask: "Isn't it possible that the constitution of an after-image is affected by alterations in the degree of one's attention to its parts?" The question is silly, in the sense that it points nowhere. We do not know what to look for to answer it. "Counting again" does not have a clear sense with after-images. This shows that the notion of miscounting that applies to after-images is only a shadow of the notion of miscount-ing that applies to physical realities. It lacks that body of implica-tions that belongs to the latter.

There could be other reasons for thinking that a man's declara-tion that his after-image is seven-pointed results from a miscount.

Suppose that he commonly miscounts physical realities such as eggs and onions. This might suggest the possibility that his counting with respect to the after-images is in error. Or suppose that many others have been subjected to the same physical stimulation and that every one of them has reported seeing a six-pointed after-image. This might suggest that it is probable that he miscounted. But if he sincerely reassures us that seven is the correct number, that decisively refutes our conjectures. These "possibilities" and "probabilities" collapse before his confident reassertion that he counted correctly. This brings out the respect in which the latter assertion is "self-confirming." It shows also how *flimsy* is the "possibility" that he miscounted. There is a possibility that he made a mistake only insofar as there is a possibility that *he* will *say* that he made a mistake. The possibility that he is mistaken about his after-image is only a weak imitation of that full-fledged sense in which it is possible that he made a mistake in counting the forks and spoons. For the latter has clear meaning *in spite of* his sincere denial that he miscounted. With regard to anyone's description of his own after-image, there is no clear difference in meaning between his assertion that *he made a mistake* and his assertion that *he expressed himself incorrectly*.

A report on one's own after-image is an odd sort of discourse, in which each statement is unimpeachable, unless amended or cancelled by a subsequent statement in that report. And there can be only a *minimum* of correcting, beyond which we should hesitate to call it a genuine report on an after-image.

Suppose that a man traces upon the wall the outline of an after-image that he sees against it, and traces only six points although he says that he *sees* seven. Do we have evidence that he miscounted? If he sees seven points then he is not tracing correctly and if he is tracing correctly then he does not see seven points. He says *both* that his after-image has seven points *and* that he has traced it accurately. Which statement is true? We can shrug our shoulders at this conflict in his description—and nothing more! Any preference for one statement over the other would be entirely arbitrary. If someone's description of a physical reality is self-contradictory, it is sensible to speak of trying to find out whether this one or that one of the contradicting statements is true; and this makes it meaningful to assert "Either this one or that one must be true." When the contradictory statements belong to an after-image description the latter assertion is devoid of meaning; for that description is our criterion of what the after-image is like, and consulting it exhausts our inquiry. If *it* is self-contradictory then it defeats us in a way that a self-contradictory description of a physical reality does not. We are prevented from drawing *any* conclusion (for example, that the man miscounted) except the conclusion that we do not know what to make of this piece of discourse that started out as a description of an after-image.

I will mark the difference between after-image descriptions and reports, and descriptions and reports of physical realities, by saying that the former are "incorrigible" and the latter are not.[10] I want to warn, however, against some misunderstandings that may be caused by the use of this technical term. When I say that the former are "incorrigible" I do not imply, of course, that a man cannot correct his own after-image description by telling us that he misspoke (e.g., that he said "a reddish circle blue in the center" when he should have said "a bluish circle red in the center"), or by amending or withdrawing a previous statement in his description. Nor do I imply that anything whatever that is offered as a description of an after-image should be accepted without question. If it were self-contradictory we should not regard it as a perfectly good, although unusual, description of an after-image. If we found that someone constantly misused certain color adjectives in his descriptions of physical realities, then we should not accept at face value his after-image descriptions containing those adjectives. If there was any language at all whose use in relation to physical realities he had not mastered, then we should disallow his use of it in an alleged after-image report.

Furthermore, there is a sense in which a person can be mistaken even in reporting that he sees an after-image. An after-image

---

[10] [J. L. Austin criticizes "incorrigibility" in his *Sense and Sensibilia* (New York: Oxford University Press, Inc., 1962), pp. 110-115. He is attacking a number of views formerly held by A. J. Ayer, and it is not easy to determine how much, if any, of what he says goes against the position I take here. He says: "There isn't, there couldn't be, any kind of sentence which as such is incapable, once uttered, of being subsequently amended or retracted" (*ibid.*, p. 112). I imagine so, but that is not how I expound the notion of incorrigibility. (A discussion centered on this notion also occurs in "Wittgenstein's *Philosophical Investigations*," see pp. 110 and 127.)]

(called an "after-sensation" by some psychologists) is "the impression of a vivid sensation, retained after the external cause is withdrawn" (*Oxford English Dictionary*). If a man in a room looks at the window through which the light pours it may be that, when he shifts his glance to the dark wall or closes his eyes, he will see an image of the window with its bright panes and darker sashes (or the bright and dark may be reversed). He will then be seeing an after-image. If he continued to look at the window and to see it as distinctly as before, and if he has not previously looked at an even brighter area, and if there neither is nor seems to him to be any decrease in the intensity of the window light, then he cannot be seeing an after-image because there has been no cessation or diminution of sensations. One cannot see an after-image in just *any* circumstances, this being a matter of definition and not an experimental fact. A man might not know that certain special conditions must be fulfilled before it is correct to say that he sees an after-image. Or he might know this but think that they were fulfilled when they were not. In either case, his assertion that he sees an after-image could be said to embody an "error of use." If a person, A, placed in circumstances so markedly inappropriate for seeing an after-image that it would be *a misuse of language* to say "A sees an after-image," were to say "I see an after-image," then it would be quite correct to say that A is mistaken.

On the other hand, if A had been properly instructed in the use of the expression "after-image," and if he had previously used it correctly, and if he were placed in circumstances such that it would *not* be a misuse of language to say "A sees an after-image," *then* if A said "I see an after-image," it would be entirely senseless for us to suppose that A was mistaken. This feature of after-image statements sharply differentiates them from statements about purported physical realities. If A had long ago learned to use correctly the words "I see flames" and had never shown any tendency to misuse them, and if his circumstances were such that it would not be a misuse of language to say "A sees flames," then if A reported "I see flames," it would *still* be sensible for us to suppose that A is mistaken. We could suppose, for example, that what appear to be flames on the horizon will turn out to be billowing colors in the sky.

Thus in saying that after-image reports are "incorrigible" I do not deny that there *is* a sense in which someone can be mistaken when he asserts that he sees an after-image. He can properly be said to be mistaken if it would be a misuse of language to say that he sees an after-image. But there is also *a* sense in which a person's report that he sees an after-image *cannot* be mistaken; and it is this sense that I intend when I say that his report is "incorrigible." If he has correctly used the words "I see an after-image" on numerous occasions and has never misused them, and if his circumstances are such that it would not be a misuse of language to say of him that he sees an after-image (e.g., he has just looked steadily at a bright light and then closed his eyes) then there cannot be a *question* of his being in error when he says "I see an after-image." There cannot be a *question* of whether he "takes" something to be an after-image that is really not one. There can be a question as to whether what he says is *true*; but it is identical with the question of whether he is fibbing.

Not only is there a sense in which a person cannot be mistaken in reporting that he sees an after-image; there is also *a* sense in which he cannot be mistaken as to the color, shape, or other sensible characteristics of his after-image. To be sure, if in his discourse about physical realities he constantly misused the word "blue," this would be a sufficient condition for saying that he describes his after-image incorrectly when he says to us, "It is blue." Furthermore, it is a sufficient condition for saying that a part of his description is mistaken that, while he still sees the after-image, he honestly says that it is mistaken; but here there is no clear distinction in meaning between "making a mistake" and "expressing oneself incorrectly." If, however, his use of the word "blue" in his talk about physical realities is perfectly normal, and if he has not only said but earnestly reaffirmed that his after-image is blue, then the supposition that he might be mistaken as to the color of it is entirely without meaning. This differs remarkably from a case in which he is called upon to describe the color and shape of a part of the surface of a wall. Perhaps he is too far from it or the light is poor or it is partly concealed by a curtain. It is plain enough what steps would be in order for removing those possible causes of error. In contrast, think how ludicrous it would be to suggest that he ought to come closer to his after-image or to look at it in a better light in order to improve his view of it; or to suggest that perhaps part of it is concealed from him. I will formulate the difference between after-image descriptions and descriptions of physical realities by saying that the former, like the latter, can embody *errors of use and of expression,* but that, unlike the latter, they cannot embody *errors of perception.*

II

Let us bring the preceding observations to bear on the question of whether physical realities can be "directly perceived" or "directly apprehended," in the sense that Moore explicitly gave to those expressions. It is easily seen that they cannot be. It is quite impossible, for example, that anyone should "directly see" a physical surface. To directly see something is to see it in "that sense of see" in which one may see an after-image. The latter use of "see" cannot be set forth except by describing the logical features of those statements in which it occurs, i.e., reports and descriptions of after-images. The two statements "The piece of cloth that I see is round, bluish and red in the center" and "The after-image that I see is round, bluish and red in the center" differ in a most important feature and can, with propriety, be said to illustrate different senses of "see." [11] There is a kind of error—namely, an error of perception—in regard to which the suggestion is meaningful that perhaps I am in error in thinking that I really see a cloth of that description; and in regard to which the suggestion is *not* meaningful that perhaps I am in error in "thinking" that I see an after-image of that description.

Therefore, it is a consequence of Moore's explanation of his own use of "directly apprehend" that physical realities cannot be directly apprehended. My argument to prove this is a justification

[11] [One is not forced to say this, and it may be more plausible to think that the differences in implication between the sentences "I see an after-image" and "I see a wall" come from the nouns "wall" and "after-image." The insistence that "see" is used in different senses here obscures the important point. For my present purposes, it does not matter whether the different implications come from the verb or the nouns. The marked difference, in respect to possibility of error, between seeing an after-image and seeing a wall (or a piece of cloth, a shadow, or any other "physical reality") is sufficient to show that if the former is "direct perception" the latter is not —at least not in the same sense.]

of Moore's inclination to think that they cannot be. Indeed, it shows that "inclination" is too modest a word.

But why does Moore have an inclination to think that physical realities *can* be directly apprehended? What is the nature of the confusion from which this contrary inclination springs? I have an hypothesis to offer; but I wish to emphasize that it is extremely *tentative*.

Let us first note an important feature of the use of the expressions "direct apprehension," "direct perception," "immediate awareness," and their cognates, that has prevailed among philosophers. The latter have commonly thought of *direct* perception as something that is not open to the possibility of error. Berkeley, discussing errors of perception (e.g., mistaking a square tower, seen at a distance, to be round), remarked of the person in error: "His mistake lies not in what he perceives immediately and at present (it being a manifest contradiction to suppose that he should err in respect of that), but in the wrong judgment he makes concerning the ideas he apprehends to be connected with those immediately perceived. . . ." [12] Here Berkeley says that it is a contradiction to suppose that a man could be mistaken about what he perceives immediately; and this remark may be taken as stipulating a necessary condition for the use of the expressions "immediate perception" or "direct perception." We should further note that Moore says that "directly see" is "the visual variety of what Berkeley called '*direct* perception.'" [13] Thus Moore thinks that his use of "direct perception" conforms to Berkeley's.

It may appear that notions other than the impossibility of error have been included in the standard philosophical conception of direct perception. For example, it has been implied that if one directly perceives something one cannot *doubt* that one perceives it.[14] I do not believe, however, that this is really a different idea. It is unlikely that it is intended as a psychological observation. More probably it expresses the thought that, in a common use of "doubt," a person cannot have a doubt that he perceives something unless it makes sense to suppose that he is mistaken in

[12] *Third Dialogue between Hylas and Philonous.*

[13] "Reply," *op. cit.*, p. 629.

[14] E.g., H. H. Price, *Perception*, second ed. (London: Methuen & Co., Ltd., 1950), p. 3.

thinking that he perceives it, and that whenever this does not make sense neither does a "doubt."

It is said also that perception is immediate only if it contains no *inference*.[15] What shall be the criterion for determining whether a given perception "contains an element of inference"? An appeal to the ordinary use of "inference" will not be very helpful, because the philosophical use is different. The following quotation from J. S. Mill is an example of the latter:

> I affirm, for example, that I hear a man's voice. This would pass, in common language, for a direct perception. All, however, which is really perception, is that I hear a sound. That the sound is a voice, and that voice the voice of a man, are not perceptions but inferences. I affirm, again, that I saw my brother at a certain hour this morning. If any proposition concerning a matter of fact would commonly be said to be known by the direct testimony of the senses, this surely would be so. The truth, however, is far otherwise. I only saw a certain coloured surface; or rather I had the kind of visual sensations which are usually produced by a coloured surface; and from these as marks, known to be such by previous experience, I concluded that I saw my brother. I might have had sensations precisely similar when my brother was not there. I might have seen some other person so nearly resembling him in appearance as, at the distance, and with the degree of attention which I bestowed, to be mistaken for him. I might have been asleep, and dreamed that I saw him; or in a nervous state of disorder, which brought his image before me in a waking hallucination. In all these modes, many have been led to believe that they saw persons well known to them, who were dead or far distant. If any of these suppositions had been true, the affirmation that I saw my brother would have been erroneous; but whatever was matter of direct perception, namely, the visual sensations, would have been real. The inference only would have been ill grounded; I should have ascribed those sensations to a wrong cause.[16]

In Mill's philosophical terminology, a perception involved "inference" and, therefore, was not "direct," if it "might have been erroneous."

Some philosophers who make little or no use of the phrase "direct perception" express the same idea by speaking of "the given" in perception. Commonly they contrast that which is

---

[15] ". . . in truth the senses perceive nothing which they do not perceive immediately: for they make no inferences" (Berkeley, *First Dialogue*).

[16] *A System of Logic*, Bk. IV, ch. 1, sec. 2 (New York: Longmans, Green & Co., Inc., 1884).

"given" with that which is the result of "interpretation." For example, C. I. Lewis says "Perceptual knowledge has two aspects or phrases; the givenness of something given, and the interpretation which, in the light of past experience, we put upon it." [17] What is the criterion for distinguishing these two aspects? The following: Subtract from a perceptual experience *all that conceivably could be mistaken*; the remainder is the given content of the experience. . . ." [18]

I think, in short, that "impossibility of error" is the main feature of the standard philosophical conception of direct perception. I take the liberty of making this explicit by constructing a definition of "direct perception" in terms of it, as follows: "A *directly* perceives x if and only if A's assertion that he perceives x could not be mistaken; and A *directly* perceives that x has the property F, if and only if A's assertion that he perceives that x is F could not be mistaken." I will later point out a respect in which the definition is ambiguous.

The next step in putting forward my hypothesis about Moore's contrary inclination will be to remind you of Moore's disposition to assert, in the course of a philosophical argument, that not only does he perceive some physical object (e.g., a hand or a tree) but, furthermore, that he could not be mistaken about it. Consider the following remarks:

I am not, therefore, afraid to say that I do now perceive that that is a door, and that that is a finger . . . some philosophers seem to me to have denied that we ever do in fact know such things as these, and others not only that we ever know them but also that they are ever true. And, if, in fact, I never do know such a thing, or if it is never true, it will, of course, follow that I never perceive such a thing; since I certainly cannot, in this sense, perceive anything whatever, unless I both know it and it is true. But it seems to me a sufficient refutation of such views as these, simply to point out cases in which we do know such things. This, after all, you know, really is a finger; there is no doubt about it: I know it, and you all know it.[19]

And recall his assertion, at one point in his British Academy

[17] *An Analysis of Knowledge and Valuation* (La Salle, Ill.: Open Court Publishing Co., 1946), p. 188.

[18] *Ibid.*, p. 183.

[19] Moore, *Philosophical Studies* (New York: Harcourt, Brace & World, Inc., 1922), pp. 227-228.

lecture, that he *knew,* a few moments before, that he perceived two hands:

> How absurd it would be to suggest that I did not know it, but only believed it, and that perhaps it was not the case! You might as well suggest that I do not know that I am now standing up and talking— that perhaps after all I'm not, and that it's not quite certain that I am![20]

Moore thinks that sometimes, but not always, when he says "I see a door" he *knows* that there is a door there. I believe that he uses "know," in this connection, in what I have called its "strong" sense.[21] I think that what he is trying to express when he says, in his emphatic way, such a thing as "I *know* that that is a door," is that nothing would be *evidence* that there is no door there, that it could not *turn out* that there was none, that he could not be *shown* to be in error. And these remarks would not reveal an attitude of prejudice or dogmatism. They would not be a denial that anything whatever could happen. Instead, they would reveal an important feature of his (and our) ordinary use of the expressions "evidence," "turning out to be false," "shown to be in error" —namely, that in the particular case in question, there is nothing that Moore would *call* "evidence" that there is no door before him; that he does not understand what it would be like for it to "turn out" that there is no door, nor what discovery could "show" it. When he says "there is no doubt about it," he is not making the psychological assertion that he and others *feel* no doubt, but the logical assertion that for him (and others similarly placed) a *doubt* that there is a door there would be a senseless thing, because it would have no reference to any inquiry. Whenever Moore is placed in circumstances that are *the best possible* for examining the sort of object that a door is, then he cannot be in doubt as to whether it is a door, in that sense of "being in doubt" that implies that he who is in doubt has some conception of what is lacking and what to look for.

Thus Moore is disposed to hold that sometimes when he and others perceive a door or a tree, they *know* that there is a door or a tree before them. The sense in which they know this might

---

[20] "Proof of an External World," *Proceedings of the British Academy,* XXV, 26.

[21] See p. 62.

quite naturally be expressed by saying that they "could not be mistaken" about it. What this ambiguous phrase would mean in this use of it is not that they have strong or even conclusive evidence, but rather that nothing could show or tend to show that they were mistaken.

In accordance with the definition of "direct perception" that I proposed, we may say that Moore's view is that sometimes he and others directly perceive physical objects and physical surfaces, since he holds that on some occasions he and others cannot be mistaken when they assert that they perceive physical surfaces. Of course, I have not presented, nor could present, anything like *conclusive* evidence to show that Moore's inclination has this origin.

III

Leaving aside the question of whether the preceding considerations do account, in part at least, for Moore's inclination to think that sometimes physical surfaces are directly perceived, I want to ask whether it is a *blunder* to hold that sometimes when a person asserts that he perceives some physical reality, it is impossible that he should be mistaken. Clearly it would be a blunder to hold that the latter is so *in the very same sense* in which it is impossible that he should be mistaken when he asserts that he sees an after-image. The respect in which after-image reports cannot be in error (their "incorrigibility") was elucidated by numerous contrasts between them and reports about physical realities. To maintain that sometimes the latter are incorrigible would be to destroy the whole distinction.[22]

---

[22] [Austin tries to destroy it. He says: "Once one drops the idea that there is a special *kind of sentence* which is *as such* incorrigible, one might as well admit (what is plainly true anyway) that *many* kinds of sentences may be uttered in making statements which are *in fact* incorrigible—in the sense that, when they are made, the circumstances are such that they are quite certainly, definitely, and unretractably *true*" (*Sense and Sensibilia, op. cit.*, pp. 114-115). If I have put myself, he says, into "the very best possible position" for making the statement "That's a pig," then it too "will be 'incorrigible,' nothing could be produced that would show that I had made a mistake" (*ibid.*). I agree entirely. But it appears that Austin did not notice the ambiguity of "nothing could be produced that would show that I had made a mistake." I am trying to prove that this characterization, which is sometimes true of statements about physical realities as well as of statements

Is it a tenable position to contend that reports of physical reali ties, although corrigible, sometimes cannot be in error? It is if we can make out a sense of "cannot be in error" and "could not be mistaken" that is other than the sense of those phrases in which they apply to after-image statements, yet is a sense in which they sometimes apply to statements about physical realities. Inciden tally, if we do this we shall have revealed an ambiguity in my definition of "direct perception" and shall have, as a result, pro vided *two* senses for this expression.

Let us consider an example of a "perceptual statement" (a type of physical object statement) trying to see, first, the respect in which it cannot be in error and, second, the respect in which it is nevertheless, not incorrigible. Suppose that you and I are search ing for a missing dinner plate. I think that I spot it under the bed If it is pretty dark under there I can perfectly well understand the suggestion that perhaps what I see is not a plate, but only a shadow or perhaps a rug. Then I fetch it out and *make sure* that it is a plate. If you inquired, from another room, whether I see a dinner plate I could reply that I do. Now if you came up, and having a full, close view of it, said "Perhaps it isn't a plate but only a shadow, or maybe a rug," then I should not *understand* your remark! I do understand the *normal* use of your sentence My failing to understand it, in this case, is not like my failing to understand the sentence "Donkeys hibernate bismuth," which has *no* normal use. Indeed, it is a *consequence* of my familiarity with the normal use of your sentence that I should be bewildered by your saying it in this case. Your remark would strike me as a fool ish "expression of doubt" because, in this situation, neither of us has any conception of what would be a *better* proof that it is a plate. We did have a moment before, when it was under the bed *Then*, I understood the possibility that I might be mistaken; *now*

---

about after-images, does not have the same *meaning* in these two applica tions. It can indeed be true that when I make a particular statement about some physical reality, nothing could prove to me that I had made a mistake yet my statement is "corrigible." The sense in which I "could not be mis taken" is not the same as it is when I report on an after-image. It is un doubtedly confusing to say of a particular statement of mine that it is cor rigible and yet that "nothing could be produced that would show that I had made a mistake." But the distinction is real. The basic source of confusion is not the technical terms "corrigible" and "incorrigible," but the variety of cases covered by the ordinary expression "could not be mistaken."]

do not. It will be thought that at least I must conceive the possibility that I have an hallucination. But this is not so. The situation might be such that at that time I could conceive of no future happening that would show, or tend to show, that I was having an hallucination.

Does this mean that the statement "I see a plate," that I might utter at that first moment when I saw beyond question that what I held was a plate, would be incorrigible *in those circumstances*? [23] Not if we use the term "incorrigible," as I do, to include the whole logic of after-image statements. For it is not difficult to see several points of difference. I will mention two. First of all, any person who does not see the plate in my hand can understand the supposition that perhaps my statement that I see a plate is in error: for example, he can understand that *he* might look at my hand and see nothing in it at all, i.e., he can understand the supposition (although *I* cannot) that I may be having an hallucination. In contrast: if I announce that I see an after-image, *neither I nor anyone else* attaches meaning to the suggestion that I may be making an error, *other* than an error of use or of expression. In the second place, to any other person who does not have a good view of the plate and who voices a doubt that I really see one, I could say, "I will *prove* it to you; come here and look at it yourself." A similar invitation to one who doubts that I see an after-image would be without meaning.

It is noteworthy that it is only in a *qualified* sense that the concept of a possible error of perception fails to apply to the perceptual statement, i.e., only the person who utters the statement (and any other person who has an equally privileged view of the object) cannot conceive that he is making an error of perception; and all others can. Whereas it is in an *unqualified* sense that the concept of a possible error of perception fails to apply to the after-image statement, i.e., no one *at all* can conceive that the person who utters it is making an error of perception.

IV

Let us return to our starting point—namely, Moore's opposite inclinations. So long as we adhere strictly to Moore's explicit

[23] [Note Austin's remarks quoted in the immediately preceding footnote.]

directions as to his intended use of the expression "direct perception" (actually of its synonym "direct apprehension") then it mus
be admitted that it is an error to think that physical realities cai
ever be directly perceived. But we remarked that in the history o
theorizing about perception an important condition for the use o
the phrase "*direct* perception" has been the idea that one coulc
not be mistaken about what he directly perceives. This phrase
"could not be mistaken," is a natural and apt phrase for summariz
ing the peculiar logic of after-image statements. It is also a natura
and apt phrase for summarizing the partly similar and also widel
different logic of perceptual statements uttered in circumstance
that are *the best possible* for perceiving the physical realitie
claimed to be perceived. If the influence of this natural phrasi
tended to control one's use of the philosophical expression "direc
perception," one would be led to confuse *two*, resembling bu
distinct, concepts of direct perception. One would be disposed t
hold that *both* after-images and physical realities can be directl
perceived; and might partly see and partly fail to see that differ
ent ideas of "direct perception" are involved. It is my surmise tha
this is the explanation of Moore's being torn between opposing
inclinations.[24]

There is one difficulty with this explanation which I must men
tion briefly. If it were correct one would expect Moore to be in
clined to hold that *bodies* are sometimes directly seen, and no
solely *surfaces* of bodies. But Moore maintains that bodies (a
least, opaque ones) cannot be directly seen. "You certainly do no
see *your hand* in that same sense in which you see *that part of it
surface* which is turned toward you; and it is only the latter sens
of 'see'—that in which you are seeing a particular part of its sur
face, and *not* seeing other parts—which can possibly be identica
with that sense of 'see' in which you see an after-image with close
eyes." [25] In his short paper "Visual Sense-Data," [26] Moore says tha
in the case of a transparent body, "like a drop of clear water," i
seems possible that one can "see the whole object at once," [27] bu

[24] [The remainder of this essay is newly written.]
[25] "Reply," *op. cit.*, p. 632.
[26] C. A. Mace, ed., *British Philosophy in the Mid-Century* (New York
The Macmillan Company, 1957), pp. 205-211.
[27] *Ibid.*, p. 205.

that when you see an opaque body you do not see "all parts of its surface nor its inside." [28] It is evident that, for Moore, a necessary condition of seeing something directly is that you should see every bit of it at once! It is worth noting that this condition is met when you see an after-image. If we added this condition to the condition expressed in my definition of the standard philosophical conception of direct perception,[29] we should obtain the following definition of "directly see": "A directly sees x, if and only if A could not be mistaken in asserting that he sees x *and* there is not a bit of x which he does not see." The second condition could not be satisfied in the case of an opaque body. There could be circumstances in which both conditions were satisfied in respect to part of the surface of a body. In such a case Moore would be inclined to say that that part of the surface was directly seen. Why should it be merely an *inclination*, and why should he have a contrary inclination? My suggestion is that he felt, without being distinctly aware of, the ambiguity of the first condition. The language of this condition can express either the notion of "incorrigibility," which does not apply to the seeing of physical surfaces, or the notion of "knowing in the strong sense" that one sees something, which does apply to the seeing of physical surfaces. Whether or not I have succeeded in diagnosing Moore's hesitations, this ambiguity seems to me to be an important source of confusion for the philosophy of perception.[30]

[28] *Ibid.*, p. 206.
[29] See p. 89.
[30] [It is worth noting that Moore, in his "Visual Sense-Data" (*op. cit.*, pp. 210-211), published four years after the present essay, finally came to the conclusion, which I hold to be correct, that one *cannot* "directly" see a part of the surface of a body.]

Wittgenstein's
Philosophical Investigations[1]

*Ein Buch ist ein Spiegel; wenn ein Affe hinein-
guckt, so kann freilich kein Apostel heraussehen.*

LICHTENBERG

An attempt to summarize the *Investigations* would be neither successful nor useful. Wittgenstein compressed his thoughts to the point where further compression is impossible. What is needed is that they be unfolded and the connections between them traced out. A likely first reaction to the book will be to regard it as a puzzling collection of reflections that are sometimes individually brilliant, but possess no unity, present no system of ideas. In truth the unity is there, but it cannot be perceived without strenuous exertion. Within the scope of a review the connectedness can best be brought out, I think, by concentrating on some single topic—in spite of the fact that there are no separate topics, for each of the investigations in the book criss-crosses again and again with every other one. In the following I center my attention on Wittgenstein's treatment of the problem of how language is related to inner experiences—to sensations,

---

[1] Ludwig Wittgenstein, *Philosophical Investigations*, German and English on facing pages. Tr. by G. E. M. Anscombe (New York: The Macmillan Company, 1953).

feelings, and moods. This is one of the main inquiries of the book and perhaps the most difficult to understand. I am sufficiently aware of the fact that my presentation of this subject will certainly fail to portray the subtlety, elegance, and force of Wittgenstein's thinking and will probably, in addition, contain positive mistakes.

References to Part I will be by paragraph numbers, e.g. (207), and to Part II by page numbers, e.g. (p. 207). Quotations will be placed within double quotation marks.

Private language. Let us see something of how Wittgenstein attacks what he calls "the idea of a private language." By a "private" language is meant one that not merely is not but *cannot* be understood by anyone other than the speaker. The reason for this is that the words of this language are supposed to "refer to what can only be known to the person speaking; to his immediate private sensations" (243). What is supposed is that I "*associate* words with sensations and use these names in descriptions" (256). I fix my attention on a sensation and establish a connection between a word and the sensation (258).

It is worth mentioning that the conception that it is possible and even necessary for one to have a private language is not eccentric. Rather it is the view that comes most naturally to anyone who philosophizes on the subject of the relation of words to experiences. The idea of a private language is presupposed by every program of inferring or constructing the 'external world' and 'other minds.' It is contained in the philosophy of Descartes and in the theory of ideas of classical British empiricism, as well as in recent and contemporary phenomenalism and sense-datum theory. At bottom it is the idea that there is only a contingent and not an *essential* connection between a sensation and its outward expression—an idea that appeals to us all. Such thoughts as these are typical expressions of the idea of a private language: that I know only from my *own* case what the word 'pain' means (293, 295); that I can only *believe* that someone else is in pain, but I *know* it if I am (303); that another person cannot have *my* pains (253); that I can undertake to call *this* (pointing inward) 'pain' in the future (263); that when I say 'I am in pain' I am at any rate justified *before myself* (289).

In order to appreciate the depth and power of Wittgenstein's assault upon this idea you must partly be its captive. You must feel the strong grip of it. The passionate intensity of Wittgenstein's treatment of it is due to the fact that he lets this idea take possession of him, drawing out of himself the thoughts and imagery by which it is expressed and defended—and then subjecting those thoughts and pictures to fiercest scrutiny. What is written down represents both a logical investigation and a great philosopher's struggle with his own thoughts. The logical investigation will be understood only by those who duplicate the struggle in themselves.

One consequence to be drawn from the view that I know only from my *own* case what, say, 'tickling' means is that "I know only what *I* call that, not what anyone else does" (347). I have not *learned* what 'tickling' means, I have only called something by that name. Perhaps others use the name differently. This is a regrettable difficulty; but, one may think, the word will still work for me as a name, provided that I apply it consistently to a certain sensation. But how about 'sensation'? Don't I know only from my *own* case what *that* word means? Perhaps what I call a "sensation" others call by another name? It will not help, says Wittgenstein, to say that although it may be that what I have is not what others call a "sensation," at least I have *something*. For don't I know only from my own case what "having something" is? Perhaps my use of *those* words is contrary to common use. In trying to explain how I gave 'tickling' its meaning, I discover that I do not have the right to use any of the relevant words of our common language. "So in the end when one is doing philosophy one gets to the point where one would like just to emit an inarticulate sound" (261).

Let us suppose that I did fix my attention on a pain as I pronounced the word 'pain' to myself. I think that thereby I established a connection between the word and the sensation. But I did not establish a connection if subsequently I applied that word to sensations other than pain or to things other than sensations, e.g., emotions. My private definition was a success only if it led me to use the word correctly in the future. In the present case, 'correctly' would mean 'consistently with my own definition'; for the question of whether my use agrees with that of others has been given up as a bad job. Now how is it to be decided whether I have used the word consistently? What will be the difference between my having used it consistently and its *seeming* to me that I have? Or has this distinction vanished? "Whatever is going to seem right to me is right. And that only means that here we can't talk about 'right'" (258). If the distinction between 'correct' and 'seems correct' has disappeared, then so has the concept *correct*. It follows that the 'rules' of my private language are only *impressions* of rules (259). My impression that I follow a rule does not confirm that I follow the rule, unless there can be something that will prove my impression correct. And the something cannot be another impression—for this would be "as if someone were to buy several copies of the morning paper to assure himself that what it said was true" (265). The proof that I am following a rule must appeal to something *independent* of my impression that I am. If in the nature of the case there cannot be such an appeal, then my private language does not have *rules*, for the concept of a rule requires that there be a difference between 'He is following a rule' and 'He is under the impression that he is following a rule'—just as the concept of understanding a word requires that there be a difference between 'He understands this word' and 'He thinks that he understands this word' (cf. 269).

'Even if I cannot prove and cannot know that I am correctly following the rules of my private language,' it might be said, 'still it *may* be that I am. It has *meaning* to say that I am. The supposition makes sense: you and I *understand* it.' Wittgenstein has a reply to this (348-353). We are inclined to think that we know what it means to say 'It is five o'clock on the sun' or 'This congenital deaf-mute talks to himself inwardly in a vocal language' or 'The stove is in pain.' These sentences produce pictures in our minds, and it *seems* to us that the pictures tell us how to *apply* them—that is, tell us what we have to look for, what we have to do, in order to determine whether what is pictured is the case. But we make a mistake in thinking that the picture contains in itself the instructions as to how we are to apply it. Think of the picture of blindness as a darkness in the soul or in the head of the blind man (424). There is nothing wrong with it *as a picture*. "But *what* is its application?" What shall count for or against its being said that this or that man is blind, that the picture applies to him?

The *picture* doesn't say. If you think that you understand the sentence 'I follow the rule that *this* is to be called "pain" ' (a rule of your private language), what you have perhaps is a picture of yourself checking off various feelings of yours as either being *this* or not. The picture appears to solve the problem of how you determine whether you have done the 'checking' right. Actually it doesn't give you even a hint in that direction; no more than the picture of blindness provides so much as a hint of *how* it is to be determined that this or that man is blind (348-353, 422-426, p. 184).

One will be inclined to say here that one can simply *remember* this sensation and by remembering it will know that one is making a consistent application of its name. But will it also be possible to have a *false* memory impression? On the private-language hypothesis, what would *show* that your memory impression is false —or true? Another memory impression? Would this imply that memory is a court from which there is no appeal? But, as a matter of fact, that is *not* our concept of memory.

Imagine that you were supposed to paint a particular colour "C," which was the colour that appeared when the chemical substances X and Y combined.—Suppose that the colour struck you as brighter on one day than on another; would you not sometimes say: "I must be wrong, the colour is certainly the same as yesterday"? This shews that we do not always resort to what memory tells us as the verdict of the highest court of appeal [56].

There is, indeed, such a thing as checking one memory against another, e.g., I check my recollection of the time of departure of a train by calling up a memory image of how a page of the time-table looked—but "this process has got to produce a memory which is actually *correct*. If the mental image of the time-table could not itself be *tested* for correctness, how could it confirm the correctness of the first memory?" (265).

If I have a language that is really private (i.e., it is a logical impossibility that anyone else should understand it or should have any basis for knowing whether I am using a particular name consistently), my assertion that my memory tells me so and so will be utterly empty. 'My memory' will not even mean—my memory *impression*. For by a memory impression we understand something that is either accurate or inaccurate; whereas there would not be, in the private language, any *conception* of what would establish a memory impression as correct, any conception of what 'correct' would mean here.

The same. One wants to say, 'Surely there can't be a difficulty in knowing whether a feeling of mine is or isn't the *same* as the feeling I now have. I will call this feeling "pain" and will thereafter call the *same* thing "pain" whenever it occurs. What could be easier than to follow that rule?' To understand Wittgenstein's reply to this attractive proposal we must come closer to his treatment of rules and of what it is to follow a rule. (Here he forges a remarkably illuminating connection between the philosophy of psychology and the philosophy of mathematics.) Consider his example of the pupil who has been taught to write down a cardinal number series of the form 'o, n, 2n, 3n . . .' at an order of the form '+n,' so that at the order '+1' he writes down the series of natural numbers (185). He has successfully done exercises and tests up to the number 1,000. We then ask him to continue the series '+2' beyond 1,000; and he writes 1,000, 1,004, 1,008, 1,012. We tell him that this is wrong. His instructive reply is, "But I went on in the same way" (185). There was nothing in the previous explanations, examples and exercises that made it *impossible* for him to regard that as the continuation of the series. Repeating *those* examples and explanations won't help him. One must say to him, in effect, 'That isn't what we *call* going on in the *same* way.' It is a fact, and a fact of the kind whose importance Wittgenstein constantly stresses, that it is *natural* for human beings to continue the series in the manner 1,002, 1,004, 1,006, given the previous training. But that is merely what it is—a fact of human nature.

One is inclined to retort, 'Of course he can misunderstand the instruction and misunderstand the order '+2'; but if he *understands* it he must go on in the right way.' And here one has the idea that "The understanding itself is a state which is the *source* of the correct use" (146)—that the correct continuation of the series, the right application of the rule or formula, springs from one's understanding of the rule. But the question of whether one understands the rule cannot be divorced from the question of whether one will go on in that one particular way that we call 'right.' The correct use is a criterion of understanding. If you say that knowing the formula is a state of the mind and that making this and that application of the formula is merely a *manifestation* of the knowledge, then you are in a difficulty: for you are postulating a mental apparatus that explains the manifestations, and so you ought to have (but do not have) a knowledge of the construction of the apparatus, quite apart from what it does (149). You would like to think that your understanding of the formula determines in advance the steps to be taken, that when you understood or meant the formula in a certain way "your mind as it were flew ahead and took all the steps before you physically arrived at this or that one" (188). But how you meant it is not independent of how in fact you use it. "We say, for instance, to someone who uses a sign unknown to us: 'If by '$x!2$' you mean x^2, then you get *this* value for y, if you mean $2x$, *that* one!—Now ask yourself: how does one *mean* the one thing or the other by '$x!2$'?" (190). The answer is that his putting down *this* value for y shows whether he meant the one thing and not the other: "*That* will be how meaning it can determine the steps in advance" (190). How he meant the formula determines his subsequent use of it, only in the sense that the latter is a criterion of how he meant it.

It is easy to suppose that when you have given a person the order 'Now do the *same* thing,' you have pointed out to him the way to go on. But consider the example of the man who obtains the series 1, 3, 5, 7 . . . by working out the formula $2x + 1$ and then asks himself, "Am I always doing the same thing, or something different every time?" (226). One answer is as good as the other; it doesn't matter which he says, so long as he continues in the right way. If we could not observe his work, his mere remark 'I am going on in the same way' would not tell us what he was doing. If a child writing down a row of 2's obtained '2, 2, 2' from the segment '2, 2' by adding '2' once, he might deny that he had gone on in the *same* way. He might declare that it would be doing the same thing only if he went from '2, 2' to '2, 2, 2, 2' in *one* jump, i.e., only if he *doubled* the original segment (just as it doubled the original single '2'). That could strike one as a *reasonable* use of 'same.' This connects up with Wittgenstein's remark: "If you have to have an intuition in order to develop the series 1 2 3 4 . . . you must also have one in order to develop the series 2 2 2 2 . . ." (214). One is inclined to say of the latter series, 'Why, all that is necessary is that you keep on doing the *same* thing.' But isn't this just as true of the other series? In both cases one has already *decided* what the correct continuation is, and one calls that continuation, and no other, 'doing the same thing.' As Wittgenstein says: "One might say to the person one was training: 'Look, I always do the same thing: I . . .'" (223). And then one proceeds to show him what 'the same' *is*. If the pupil does not acknowledge that what you have shown him is the *same*, and if he is not persuaded by your examples and explanations to carry on as you wish him to—then you have reached bedrock and will be inclined to say "This is simply what I do" (217). You cannot give him more reasons than you yourself have for proceeding in that way. Your reasons will soon give out. And then you will proceed, without reasons (211).

Private rules. All of this argument strikes at the idea that there can be such a thing as my following a rule in my private language —such a thing as naming something of which only I can be aware, 'pain,' and then going on to call the same thing, 'pain,' whenever it occurs. There is a charm about the expression 'same' which makes one think that there cannot be any difficulty or any chance of going wrong in deciding whether A is the *same* as B—as if one did not have to be *shown* what the 'same' is. This may be, as Wittgenstein suggests, because we are inclined to suppose that we can take the identity of a thing *with itself* as "an infallible paradigm" of the *same* (215). But he destroys this notion with one blow: "Then are two things the same when they are what *one* thing is? And how am I to apply what the *one* thing shows me to the case of two things?" (215).

The point to be made here is that when one has given oneself the private rule 'I will call this same thing "pain" whenever it occurs,' one is then free to do anything or nothing. That 'rule' does not point in any direction. On the private-language hypothesis, no one can teach me what the correct use of 'same' is. I shall be the sole arbiter of whether this is the *same* as that. What I choose to call the 'same' will *be* the same. No restriction whatever will be imposed upon my application of the word. But a sound that I can use *as I please* is not a *word*.

How would you teach someone the meaning of 'same'? By example and practice: you might show him, for instance, collections of the same colors and same shapes and make him find and produce them and perhaps get him to carry on a certain ornamental pattern uniformly (208). Training him to form collections and produce patterns is teaching him what Wittgenstein calls "techniques." Whether he has mastered various techniques determines whether he understands 'same.' The exercise of a technique is what Wittgenstein calls a "practice." Whether your pupil has understood any of the rules that you taught him (e.g., the rule; this is the 'same' color as that) will be shown in his practice. But now there cannot be a 'private' practice, i.e., a practice that cannot be exhibited. For there would then be no distinction between believing that you have that practice and having it. 'Obeying a rule' is itself a practice. "And to *think* one is obeying a rule is not to obey a rule. Hence it is not possible to obey a rule 'privately'; otherwise thinking one was obeying a rule would be the same thing as obeying it" (202. cf. 380).

If I recognize that my mental image is the 'same' as one that I had previously, how am I to know that this public word 'same' describes what I recognize? "Only if I can express my recognition in some other way, and if it is possible for someone else to teach me that 'same' is the correct word here" (378). The notion of the private language doesn't admit of there being 'some other way.' It doesn't allow that my behavior and circumstances can be so related to my utterance of the word that another person, by noting my behavior and circumstances, can discover that my use of the word is correct or incorrect. Can I discover this for myself, and how do I do it? That discovery would presuppose that I have a conception of correct use which comes from outside my private language and against which I measure the latter. If this were admitted, the private language would lose its privacy and its point. So it isn't admitted. But now the notion of 'correct' use that will exist within the private language will be such that if I *believe* that my use is correct then it is correct; the rules will be only impressions of rules; my 'language' will not be a language, but merely the impression of a language. The most that can be said for it is that I *think* I understand it (cf. 269).

Sensations of others. The argument that I have been outlining has the form of *reductio ad absurdum:* postulate a 'private' language; then deduce that it is not *language.* Wittgenstein employs another argument that is an external, not an internal, attack upon private language. What is attacked is the assumption that once I know from my *own* case what pain, tickling, or consciousness is, then I can transfer the ideas of these things to objects outside myself (283). Wittgenstein says:

> If one has to imagine someone else's pain on the model of one's own, this is none too easy a thing to do: for I have to imagine pain which I *do not feel* on the model of the pain which I *do feel.* That is, what I have to do is not simply to make a transition in imagination from one place of pain to another. As, from pain in the hand to pain in the arm. For I am not to imagine that I feel pain in some region of his body. (Which would also be possible.) [302]

The argument that is here adumbrated is, I think, the following: If I were to learn what pain is from perceiving my own pain then I should, necessarily, have learned that pain is something that exists only when *I* feel pain. For the pain that serves as my paradigm of pain (i.e., my own) has the property of existing only when *I* feel it.[2] That property is essential, not accidental; it is

---

[2] [This is an error. Apparently I fell into the trap of assuming that if two people, A and B, are in pain, the pain that A feels must be *numerically* different from the pain that B feels. Far from making this assumption, Wittgenstein attacks it when he says: "In so far as it makes *sense* to say that my pain is the same as his, it is also possible for us both to have the same pain" (*op. cit.,* 253). There is not some sense of "same pain" (*numerically* the same) in which A and B *cannot* have the same pain. "Today I have that same backache that you had last week" is something we say. "Same" means here, answering to the same description. We attach no meaning to the "question" of whether the backache you had and the one I have are or are not "numerically" the same.

A more correct account of Wittgenstein's point in sec. 302 is the following: A proponent of the privacy of sensations rejects circumstances and behavior as a criterion of the sensations of others, this being essential to his viewpoint. He does not need (and could not have) a criterion for the existence of pain that he feels. But surely he will need a criterion for the existence of pain that *he* does *not* feel. Yet he cannot have one and still hold to the privacy of sensation. If he sticks to the latter, he ought to admit that he has not the faintest idea of what would count for or against the occurrence of sensations that he does not feel. His conclusion should be, not that it is a contradiction, but that it is unintelligible to speak of the sensations of others.

nonsense to suppose that the pain I feel could exist when I did not feel it. So if I obtain my *conception* of pain from pain that I experience, then it will be part of my conception of pain that *I* am the only being that can experience it. For me it will be a *contradiction* to speak of *another's* pain. This strict solipsism is the necessary outcome of the notion of private language. I take the phrase "this is none too easy" to be a sarcasm.

One is tempted at this point to appeal to the 'same' again: "But if I suppose that someone has a pain, then I am simply supposing that he has just the same as I have so often had" (350). I will quote Wittgenstein's brilliant counterstroke in full:

That gets us no further. It is as if I were to say: "You surely know what 'It is 5 o'clock here' means; so you also know what 'It's 5 o'clock on the sun' means. It means simply that it is just the same time there as it is here when it is 5 o'clock."—The explanation by means of *identity* does not work here. For I know well enough that one can call 5 o'clock here and 5 o'clock there "the same time," but what I do not know is in what cases one is to speak of its being the same time here and there.

In exactly the same way it is no explanation to say: the supposition that he has a pain is simply the supposition that he has the same as I. For *that* part of the grammar is quite clear to me: that is, that one will say that the stove has the same experience as I, *if* one says: it is in pain and I am in pain [350].

Expressions of sensation. Wittgenstein says that he destroys "houses of cards" ("Luftgebaüde": 118) and that his aim is to show one how to pass from disguised to obvious nonsense (464). But this is not all he does or thinks he does. For he says that he changes one's *way of looking at things* (144). What is it that he wishes to substitute for that way of looking at things that is represented by the idea of private language? One would *like* to find a continuous exposition of his own thesis, instead of mere hints here and there. But this desire reflects a misunderstanding of Wittgenstein's philosophy. He rejects the assumption that he should put forward a *thesis* (128). "We may not advance any kind of theory" (109). A philosophical problem is a certain sort of

(There is a short exposition of Wittgenstein's attack on the idea that we learn what sensation is *from our own case,* in "Knowledge of Other Minds," see pp. 136-138.)]

confusion. It is like being lost; one can't see one's way (123). Familiar surroundings suddenly seem strange. We need to command a view of the country, to get our bearings. The country is well known to us, so we need only to be *reminded* of our whereabouts. "The work of the philosopher consists in assembling reminders for a particular purpose" (127). "The problems are solved, not by giving new information, but by arranging what we have always known" (109). When we describe (remind ourselves of) certain functions of our language, what we do must have a definite bearing on some particular confusion, some "deep disquietude" (111), that ensnares us. Otherwise our work is irrelevant—to *philosophy*. It is philosophically pointless to formulate a general theory of language or to pile up descriptions for their own sake. "This description gets its light, that is to say its purpose —from the philosophical problems" (109). Thus we may not complain at the absence from the *Investigations* of elaborate theories and classifications.

Wittgenstein asks the question "How do words *refer* to sensations?" transforms it into the question "How does a human being learn the meaning of the names of sensations?" and gives this answer: "Words are connected with the primitive, the natural expressions of the sensation and used in their place. A child has hurt himself and he cries; and then the adults talk to him and teach him exclamations and, later, sentences. They teach the child new pain-behaviour" (244). Wittgenstein must be talking about how it is that a human being learns to refer with words to his *own* sensations—about how he learns to use 'I am in pain'; not about how he learns to use 'He is in pain.' What Wittgenstein is saying is indeed radically different from the notion that I learn what 'I am in pain' means by fixing my attention on a 'certain' sensation and calling it 'pain.' But is he saying that what I do instead is to fix my attention on my *expressions* of pain and call them 'pain'? Is he saying that the word 'pain' means crying? "On the contrary: the verbal expression of pain replaces crying and does not describe it" (244). My words for sensations are used *in place of* the behavior that is the natural expression of the sensations; they do not *refer* to it.

Wittgenstein does not expand this terse reminder. He repeats at least once that my words for sensations are "tied up with my natural expressions of sensation" (256) and frequently alludes to the importance of the connection between the language for sensations and the behavior which is the expression of sensation (e.g., 288, 271). The following questions and objections will arise:

(1) What shows that a child has made this 'tie up'? I take Wittgenstein to mean that the child's utterances of the word for a sensation must, in the beginning, be frequently concurrent with some nonverbal, natural expression of that sensation. This concomitance serves as the criterion of his understanding the word. Later on, the word can be uttered in the absence of primitive expressions. ('It hurts' can be said without cries or winces.)

(2) In what sense does the verbal expression 'replace' the nonverbal expression? In the sense, I think, that other persons will react to the child's mere words in the same way that they previously reacted to his nonverbal sensation-behavior; they will let the mere words serve as a *new* criterion of his feelings.

(3) I feel inclined to object: 'But has the child *learned* what the words *mean*? Hasn't he merely picked up the *use* of the word from his parents?' My objection probably arises from assimilating the learning of the meaning of words to the labeling of bottles— a tendency that is easily decried but not easily resisted. 'Learning *ought* to consist in attaching the right name to the right object,' I should like to say (cf. 26). The example of 'the beetle in the box' is pertinent here (see 293). The aim of this fantasy is to prove that attending to a private object can have nothing to do with learning words for sensations. Suppose you wanted to teach a child what a tickling feeling is. You tickle him in the ribs, and he laughs and jerks away. You say to him, 'That's what the feeling of tickling is.' Now imagine he felt something that you can't know anything about. Will this be of any interest to you when you decide from his subsequent use of the word 'tickling' whether he understands it? Others understand the word too. If each one has something that only he can know about, then all the somethings may be different. The something could even be nothing! Whatever it is, it can have no part in determining whether the person who has it understands the word. "If we construe the grammar of the expression of sensation on the model of 'object and name' the object drops out of consideration as irrelevant" (293, cf. 304).

My previous objection could be put like this: the teaching and learning of names of sensations cannot stop at the mere expressions of sensation; the names must be brought *right up* to the sensations themselves, must be applied *directly* to the sensations! Here we can imagine Wittgenstein replying, "Like *what*, e.g.?" as he replies to an analogous objection in a different problem (191). In *what* sense is Wittgenstein denying that names are applied directly to sensations? Do I have a model of what it would be to apply the name 'directly'? No. I have this picture—that learning the meaning of 'pain' is applying the sign 'pain' to pain itself. I have that picture, to be sure, but what does it teach me, what is its "application"? When shall I say that what it pictures has taken place, i.e., that someone has learned the meaning of 'pain'? It doesn't tell me; it is *only* a picture. It cannot conflict with, cannot refute, Wittgenstein's reminder of what it is that determines whether a child has learned the word for a sensation. (4) Wittgenstein says that the verbal expressions of sensation can take the place of the nonverbal expressions and that in learning the former one learns "new pain-behavior." This seems to mean that the words (and sentences) for sensations are related to sensations in the same way as are the primitive expressions of sensations. I am inclined to object again. I want to say that the words are used to *report* the occurrence of a sensation and to inform others of it. The natural expressions, on the contrary, are not used to inform others; they are not 'used' at all; they have no purpose, no function; they *escape* from one. But I have oversimplified the difference, because (a) a sentence can be forced from one, can escape one's lips ('My God, it hurts!'), and (b) a natural expression of sensation can be used to inform another, e.g., you moan to let the nurse know that your pain is increasing (you would have suppressed the moan if she hadn't entered the room), yet the moan is genuine. Perhaps my objection comes to this: I don't *learn* to moan; I do learn the words. But this is the very distinction that is made by saying that moaning is a "natural," a "primitive," expression of sensation.

It is a mistake to suppose that Wittgenstein is saying that the utterance 'My leg hurts' is *normally called* an 'expression of sensation.' (Of course it isn't. For that matter, only a facial expression, not a groan, is called an '*expression* of pain.' But this is of no importance.) He is not reporting ordinary usage, but drawing our attention to an *analogy* between the groan of pain and the utterance of those words. The important similarity that he is trying to bring to light (here I may misinterpret him) is that the verbal utterance and the natural pain-behavior are each (as I shall express it) 'incorrigible.' [3] A man cannot be in *error* as to whether he is in pain; he cannot say 'My leg hurts' by mistake, any more than he can groan by mistake. It is senseless to suppose that he has wrongly identified a tickle as pain or that he falsely believes that it is in his leg when in fact it is in his shoulder. True, he may be undecided as to whether it is best described as an 'ache' or a 'pain' (one is often hard put to give satisfactory descriptions of one's feelings); but his very indecision *shows* us what his sensation is, i.e., something between an ache and a pain. His hesitant observation, 'I'm not sure whether it is a pain or an ache,' is itself an *expression* of sensation. What it expresses is an indefinite, an ambiguous sensation. The point about the incorrigibility of the utterance 'I'm in pain' lies behind Wittgenstein's reiterated remark that 'I *know* I'm in pain' and 'I don't know whether I'm in pain' are both senseless (e.g., 246, 408).[4] Wherever it is *meaningless* to speak of 'false belief,' it is also meaningless to speak of 'knowledge'; and wherever you cannot say 'I don't know . . .' you also cannot say 'I know. . . .' Of course, a philosopher can say of me that I *know* I am in pain. But "What is it supposed to mean—except perhaps that I *am* in pain?" (246).[5]

There are many 'psychological' sentences, other than sentences about sensations, that are incorrigible, e.g., the *truthful* report of a dream is a criterion for the occurrence of the dream and, unless some other criterion is introduced, "the question cannot arise" as to whether the dreamer's memory deceives him (pp. 222-223). If

[3] [I try to explain the notion of "incorrigibility," as I understand it, in "Direct Perception" (see pp. 77-86). I concentrate there on the seeing of after-images, but with appropriate changes the notion carries over to bodily sensations.]

[4] It is interesting to note that as long ago as 1930 Wittgenstein had remarked that it has no sense to speak of *verifying* "I have a toothache." (See G. E. Moore, "Wittgenstein's Lectures in 1930-33," *Mind*, LXIII, January 1954, 14.)

[5] [In "A Definition of Factual Memory," I mention a sense in which an adult person (but not an infant or a dog) can be said to know that he has a pain (see p. 239).]

one who has a mental image were asked whom the image is of, "his answer would be decisive," just as it would be if he were asked whom the drawing represents that he has just made (p. 177). When you say 'It will stop soon' and are asked whether you *meant* your pain or the sound of the piano-tuning, your truthful answer *is* the answer (666-684).

When Wittgenstein says that learning the words for sensations is learning "new pain-behavior" and that the words "replace" the natural expressions, he is bringing to light the arresting fact that my sentences about my present sensations have the same logical status as my outcries and facial expressions. And thus we are helped to "make a radical break with the idea that language always functions in one way, always serves the same purpose: to convey thoughts—which may be about houses, pains, good and evil, or anything else you please" (304).

This is not to deny that first-person sentences about sensations may, in other respects, be more or less like natural expressions of sensation. Wittgenstein's examples of the use of 'I am afraid' (pp. 187-188) show how the utterance of that sentence can be a cry of fear, a comparison, an attempt to tell someone how I feel, a confession, a reflection on my state of mind, or something in between. "A cry is not a description. But there are transitions. And the words 'I am afraid' may approximate more, or less, to being a cry. They may come quite close to this and also be *far* removed from it" (p. 189). The words 'I am in pain' "may be a cry of complaint, and may be something else" (p. 189); and 'it makes me shiver' may be a "shuddering reaction" or may be said "as a piece of information" (p. 174). If we pursue these hints, it is not hard to construct a list of examples of the use of the words 'My head hurts,' in which the variety is as great as in Wittgenstein's list for 'I am afraid.' E.g., compare 'Oh hell, how my head hurts!' with 'If you want to know whether to accept the invitation for tonight then I must tell you that my head hurts again.' In one case the sentence 'My head hurts' belongs to an exclamation of pain, not in the other. In saying that in *both* cases it is an 'expression' of pain, Wittgenstein stretches ordinary language and in so doing illuminates the hidden continuity between the utterance of that sentence and—expressions of pain.

Criterion. That the natural pain-behavior and the utterance 'It hurts' are each incorrigible is what makes it possible for each of them to be a criterion of pain. With some reluctance I will undertake to say a little bit about this notion of 'criterion,' a most difficult region in Wittgenstein's philosophy. Perhaps the best way to elucidate it is to bring out its connection with *teaching* and *learning* the use of words. "When I say the ABC to myself, what is the criterion of my doing the same as someone else who silently repeats it to himself? It might be found that the same thing took place in my larynx and in his. (And similarly when we both think of the same thing, wish the same, and so on.) But then did we learn the use of the words, 'to say such-and-such to oneself,' by someone's pointing to a process in the larynx or the brain?" (376). Of course we did not, and this means that a physiological process is not our 'criterion' that *A* said such-and-such to himself. Try to imagine, realistically and in detail, how you would teach someone the meaning of 'saying the ABC silently to oneself.' This, you may think, is merely psychology. But if you have succeeded in bringing to mind what it is that would show that he *grasped* your teaching, that he *understood* the use of the words, then you have elicited the 'criterion' for their use—and that is not psychology. Wittgenstein exhorts us, over and over, to bethink ourselves of how we learned to use this or that form of words or of how we should teach it to a child. The purpose of this is not to bring philosophy down to earth (which it does), but to bring into view those features of someone's circumstances and behavior that *settle* the question of whether the words (e.g., 'He is calculating in his head') rightly apply to him. Those features constitute the 'criterion' of calculating in one's head. It is logically possible that someone should have been born with a knowledge of the use of an expression or that it should have been produced in him by a drug; that his knowledge came about by way of the normal process of teaching is not necessary. What is necessary is that there should be something on the basis of which we *judge* whether he *has* that knowledge. To undertake to describe this may be called a 'logical' investigation, even though one should arrive at the description by reflecting on that logically inessential process of teaching and learning.

If someone says, e.g., 'I feel confident . . . ,' a question can arise as to whether he understands those words. Once you admit the untenability of 'private ostensive definition' you will see that there must be a *behavioral* manifestation of the feeling of confidence (579). There must be behavior against which his words 'I feel confident . . . ,' can be checked, if it is to be possible to judge that he does not understand them. Even if you picture a feeling of confidence as an "inner process," still it requires "outward criteria" (580).

Wittgenstein contrasts 'criterion' with 'symptom,' employing both words somewhat technically. The falling barometer is a 'symptom' that it is raining; its looking like *that* outdoors (think how you would teach the word 'rain' to a child) is the 'criterion' of rain (354). A process in a man's brain or larynx might be a symptom that he has an image of red; the criterion is "what he says and does" (377, 376). What makes something into a symptom of *y* is that experience teaches that it is always or usually associated with *y*; that so-and-so is the criterion of *y* is a matter, not of experience, but of "definition" (354). The satisfaction of the criterion of *y* establishes the existence of *y* beyond question. The occurrence of a symptom of *y* may also establish the existence of *y* 'beyond question'—but in a different sense. The observation of a brain process may make it certain that a man is in pain—but not in the same way that his pain-behavior makes it certain. Even if physiology has established that a specific event in the brain accompanies bodily pain, still it *could* happen (it makes sense to suppose) that a man was not in pain although that brain event was occurring. But it will not make sense for one to suppose that another person is not in pain if one's criterion of his being in pain is satisfied. (Sometimes, and especially in science, we *change* our criteria: "what to-day counts as an observed concomitant of a phenomenon will to-morrow be used to define it" [79].)

The preceding remarks point up the following question: Do the propositions that describe the criterion of his being in pain *logically imply* the proposition 'He is in pain'? Wittgenstein's answer is clearly in the negative. A criterion is satisfied *only in certain circumstances*. If we come upon a man exhibiting violent pain-behavior, couldn't something show that he is not in pain? Of course. For example, he is rehearsing for a play; or he has been hypnotized and told, 'You will act as if you are in pain, although you won't be in pain,' and when he is released from the hypnotic state he has no recollection of having been in pain; or his pain-behavior suddenly ceases and he reports in apparent bewilderment that it was as if his body had been possessed—for his movements had been entirely involuntary, and during the 'seizure' he had felt no pain; or he has been narrowly missed by a car and as soon as a sum for damages has been pressed into his hand, his pain-behavior ceases and he laughs at the hoax; or . . . , etc. The expressions of pain are a criterion of pain in *certain* "surroundings," not in others (cf. 584).

Now one would like to think that one can still formulate a logical implication by taking a description of his pain-behavior and conjoining it with the negation of every proposition describing one of those circumstances that would count against saying he is in pain. Surely, the conjunction will logically imply 'He is in pain'! But this assumes there is a *totality* of those circumstances such that if none of them were fulfilled, and he was also pain-behaving, then he *could not but* be in pain (cf. 183). There is no totality that can be exhaustively enumerated, as can the letters of the alphabet. It is quite impossible to list six or nine such circumstances and then to say 'That is all of them; no other circumstances can be imagined that would count against his being in pain.' The list of circumstances has no 'all,' in that sense; the list is, not infinite, but *indefinite*. Therefore, entailment-conditions cannot be formulated; there are none.

The above thought is hard to accept. It is not in line with our *ideal* of what language should be. It makes the 'rules' for the use of 'He is in pain' too vague, too loose, not really *rules*. Wittgenstein has deep things to say about the nature of this 'ideal': "We want to say that there can't be any vagueness in logic. The idea now absorbs us, that the ideal '*must*' be found in reality. Meanwhile we do not as yet see *how* it occurs there, nor do we understand the nature of this 'must.' We think it must be in reality; for we think we already see it there" (101). "The strict and clear rules of the logical structure of propositions appear to us as something in the background—hidden in the medium of the understanding" (102). "The more narrowly we examine actual language, the sharper becomes the conflict between it and our requirement. (For the crystalline purity of logic was, of course, not a *result of investigation*: it was a requirement.)" (107). What we need to do is to remove from our noses the logical glasses through which we look at reality (103). We must study our language as it is, without preconceived ideas. One thing this study will teach us is that the criteria for the use of third-person psychological statements are not related to the latter by an entailment-relation.

Wittgenstein suggests that propositions describing the fulfillment of behavioral criteria are related to third-person psychological statements in the way that propositions describing sense-impressions are related to physical-object statements (compare 486 and p. 180). It does not *follow* from the propositions describing my sense-impressions that there is a chair over there (486). The relation cannot be reduced to a *simple* formula (p. 180). *Why* doesn't it follow? Wittgenstein does not say, but the reason would appear to be of the same sort as in the example of 'He is in pain.' The propositions describing my sense-impressions would have to be conjoined with the proposition that I am not looking in a mirror, or at a painted scenery, or at a movie film, or . . . , etc. Here too there cannot be an exhaustive enumeration of the negative conditions that would have to be added to the description of sense-impressions *if* 'There's a chair over there' *were* to be logically implied.

The puzzling problem now presents itself: if it does not *follow* from his behavior and circumstances that he is in pain, then how can it ever be *certain* that he is in pain? "I can be as *certain* of someone else's sensations as of any fact," says Wittgenstein (p. 224). How can this be so, since there is not a definite set of six or eight conditions (each of which would nullify his pain-behavior) to be checked off as not fulfilled? It *looks* as if the conclusion ought to be that we cannot 'completely verify' that he is in pain. This conclusion is wrong, but it is not easy to see why. I comprehend Wittgenstein's thought here only dimly. He says:

A doctor asks: "How is he feeling?" The nurse says: "He is groaning." A report on his behaviour. But need there be any question for them whether the groaning is really genuine, is really the expression of anything? Might they not, for example, draw the conclusion "If he groans, we must give him more analgesic"—without suppressing a middle term? Isn't the point the service to which they put the description of behaviour [p. 179]?

One hint that I take from this is that there can be situations of real life in which a question as to whether someone who groans is pretending, or rehearsing, or hypnotized, or . . . , simply does not exist. "Just try—in a real case—to doubt someone else's fear or pain" (303). A doubt, a question, would be rejected as absurd by anyone who knew the actual surroundings. 'But might there not be still further surroundings, unknown to you, that would change the whole aspect of the matter?' Well, we go only *so* far—and then we are certain. "Doubting has an end" (p. 180). Perhaps we can *imagine* a doubt; but we do not take it seriously (cf. 84). Just as it becomes certain to us that there is a chair over there, although we can imagine a *possible* ground of doubt. There is a concept of certainty in these language-games only because we stop short of what is conceivable.

" 'But, if you are *certain,* isn't it that you are shutting your eyes in face of doubt?'—They are shut" (p. 224). This striking remark suggests that what we sometimes do is draw a boundary around *this* behavior in *these* circumstances and say 'Any additional circumstances that might come to light will be irrelevant to whether this man is in pain.' Just as we draw a line and say 'No further information will have any bearing on whether there is a chair in the corner—that is settled.' If your friend is struck down by a car and writhes with a broken leg, you do not think: Perhaps it was prearranged in order to alarm me; possibly his leg was anesthetized just before the 'accident' and he isn't suffering at all. Someone *could* have such doubts whenever another person was ostensibly in pain. Similarly: "I can easily imagine someone always doubting before he opened his front door whether an abyss did not yawn behind it; and making sure about it before he went through the door (and he might on some occasion prove to be right)—but that does not make me doubt in the same case" (84).

The man who doubts the other's pain may be neurotic, may 'lack a sense of reality,' but his reasoning is perfectly sound. *If* his doubts are true then the injured man is *not* in pain. His reaction is abnormal but not illogical. The certainty that the injured man is in pain (the normal reaction) ignores the endless doubts that *could* be proposed and investigated.

And it is important to see that the abnormal reaction *must* be the exception and not the rule. For if someone *always* had endless doubts about the genuineness of expressions of pain, it would mean that he was not using *any criterion* of another's being in pain. It would mean that he did not accept anything as an *expression* of pain. So what could it mean to say that he even had the *concept* of another's being in pain? It is senseless to suppose that he has this concept and yet always doubts.

Third-person sensation-sentences. Wittgenstein assimilates first-person, not third-person, sensation-sentences to *expressions* of sensation. I will say one or two things more about his conception of the use of third-person sensation-sentences.

(1) "Only of a living human being and what resembles (behaves like) a living human being can one say: it has sensations; it sees; is blind; hears; is deaf; is conscious or unconscious" (281). The *human* body and *human* behavior are the *paradigm* to which third-person attributions of consciousness, sensations, feelings are related. (The use of first-person sensation-sentences is governed by *no* paradigm.) Thus there cannot occur in ordinary life a question as to whether other human beings ever possess consciousness, and I can have this question when I philosophize only if I forget that I use that paradigm in ordinary life. It is by analogy with the human form and behavior that I attribute consciousness (or unconsciousness) to animals and fish: the more remote the analogy the less sense in the attribution. (Just as it is by analogy with our ordinary language that anything is called 'language') (494). In order to imagine that a pot or a chair has thoughts or sensations one must give it, in imagination, something like a human body, face, and speech (282, 361). A child says that its doll has stomach-ache, but this is a "secondary" use of the concept of pain. "Imagine a case in which people ascribed pain *only* to inanimate things; pitied *only* dolls!" (282; cf. 385, p. 216). Wittgenstein means, I think, that this is an impossible supposition because we should not want to say that those people *understood* ascriptions of pain. If they did not ever show pity for human beings or animals or expect it for themselves, then their treatment of dolls would not be *pity*.

(2) My criterion of another's being in pain is, first, his behavior and circumstances and, second, his words (after they have been found to be connected in the right way with his behavior and

circumstances). Does it follow that my interest is in his behavior and words, not in his pain? Does 'He is in pain' *mean* behavior? In lectures Wittgenstein imagined a tribe of people who had the idea that their slaves had no feelings, no souls—that they were automatons—despite the fact that the slaves had human bodies, behaved like their masters, and even spoke the same language. Wittgenstein undertook to try to give sense to that idea. When a slave injured himself or fell ill or complained of pains, his master would try to heal him. The master would let him rest when he was fatigued, feed him when he was hungry and thirsty, and so on. Furthermore, the masters would apply to the slaves our usual distinctions between genuine complaints and malingering. So what could it mean to say that they had the idea that the slaves were automatons? Well, they would *look* at the slaves in a peculiar way. They would observe and comment on their movements *as if* they were machines. ('Notice how smoothly his limbs move.') They would discard them when they were worn and useless, like machines. If a slave received a mortal injury and twisted and screamed in agony, no master would avert his gaze in horror or prevent his children from observing the scene, any more than he would if the ceiling fell on a printing press. Here is a difference in 'attitude' that is not a matter of believing or expecting different facts.

So in the *Investigations,* Wittgenstein says, "My attitude towards him is an attitude towards a soul. I am not of the *opinion* that he has a soul" (p. 178). I do not *believe* that the man is suffering who writhes before me—for to what facts would a 'belief' be related, such that a change in the facts would lead me to alter it? I *react* to his suffering. I look at him with compassion and try to comfort him. If I complain of headache to someone and he says 'It's not so bad,' does this prove that he believes in something *behind* my outward expression of pain? "His attitude is a proof of his attitude. Imagine not merely the words 'I am in pain' but also the answer 'It's not so bad' replaced by instinctive noises and gestures" (310). The thought that behind someone's pain-behavior is the pain itself does not enter into our use of 'He's in pain,' but what does enter into it is our sympathetic, or unsympathetic, reaction to him. The fact that the latter does enter into our use of that sentence (but might not have) gives sense to saying that the sentence 'He is in pain' does not just *mean* that his behavior, words, and circumstances are such and such—although these are the criteria for its use.

When he groans we do not *assume*, even tacitly, that the groaning expresses pain. We fetch a sedative and try to put him at ease. A totally different way of reacting to his groans would be to make exact records of their volume and frequency—and do nothing to relieve the sufferer! But our reaction of seeking to comfort him does not involve a presupposition, for, "Doesn't a presupposition imply a doubt? And doubt may be entirely lacking" (p. 180).

Form of life. The gestures, facial expressions, words, and activities that constitute pitying and comforting a person or a dog are, I think, a good example of what Wittgenstein means by a "form of life." One could hardly place too much stress on the importance of this latter notion in Wittgenstein's thought. It is intimately related to the notion "language-game." His choice of the latter term is meant to "bring into prominence the fact that the *speaking* of language is part of an activity, or of a form of life" (23; cf. 19). If we want to understand any concept we must obtain a view of the human behavior, the activities, the natural expressions, that surround the words for that concept. What, for example, is the concept of *certainty* as applied to *predictions*? The nature of my certainty that fire will burn me comes out in the fact that "Nothing could induce me to put my hand into a flame" (472). That reaction of mine to fire shows the *meaning* of certainty in this language-game (474). (Of course, it is *different* from the concept of certainty in, e.g., mathematics. "The kind of certainty is the kind of language-game" [p. 124].) But is my certainty justified? Don't I need reasons? Well, I don't normally think of reasons, I can't produce much in the way of reasons, and I don't feel a need of reasons (cf. 477). Whatever was offered in the way of reasons would not strengthen my fear of fire, and if the reasons turned out to be weak I still wouldn't be induced to put my hand on the hot stove.

As far as 'justification' is concerned, "What people accept as a justification—is shewn by how they think and live" (325). If we want to elucidate the concept of justification we must take note of what people *accept* as justified; and it is clearly shown in our lives that we accept as justified both the certainty that fire will burn and the certainty that this man is in pain—even without reasons. Forms of life, embodied in language-games, teach us what justification is. As philosophers we must not attempt to justify the forms of life, to give reasons for *them*—to argue, for example, that we pity the injured man because we believe, assume, presuppose, or know that in addition to the groans and writhing, there is pain. The fact is, we pity him! "What has to be accepted, the given, is—so one could say—*forms of life*" (p. 226). What we should say is: "*This language-game is played*" (654).

From this major theme of Wittgenstein's thought one passes easily to another major theme—that "Philosophy simply puts everything before us, and neither explains nor deduces anything" (126). "It leaves everything as it is" (124).

Strawson's criticism. Mr. Peter Strawson's critical notice[6] of the *Investigations* contains misunderstandings that might obtain currency. To Strawson it appears that, for Wittgenstein, "no word whatever stands for or names a special experience,"[7] "no words name sensations (or 'private experiences'); and in particular the word 'pain' does not."[8] Wittgenstein "has committed himself to the view that one cannot sensibly be said to recognize or identify anything, unless one uses *criteria;* and, as a consequence of this, that one cannot recognize or identify sensations."[9] His "obsession with the *expression* of pain" leads him "to deny that sensations can be recognized and bear names."[10] Wittgenstein is hostile to "the idea of what is not observed (seen, heard, smelt, touched, tasted), and in particular to the idea that what is not observed can in any sense be recognized or described or reported"[11]—although at one place in the book (p. 189) "it looks as if he were almost prepared to acknowledge" that 'I am in pain' "may be just a report of my sensations."[12] His "prejudice against 'the inner'" leads him to deny that it is possible for a person to report the words that went through his mind when he was saying something

---

[6] "Critical Notice: *Philosophical Investigations,*" *Mind*, LXIII, January 1954, 70-99. (References to Strawson will be placed in footnotes, references to Wittgenstein will remain in the text.)
[7] P. 83.   [8] P. 84.   [9] P. 86.   [10] P. 87.   [11] P. 90.   [12] P. 94.

to himself in his thoughts.[13] Strawson attributes Wittgenstein's errors not only to prejudice and, possibly, to "the old verification-ist horror of a claim that cannot be checked," [14] but also to various confusions and muddles.[15]

It is important to see how very erroneous is this account of Wittgenstein. The latter says, "Don't we talk about sensations every day, and give them names?" and then asks, "How does a human being learn the names of sensations?—of the word 'pain' for example?" (244) So Wittgenstein does not deny that we *name* sensations. It is a howler to accuse Wittgenstein of "hostility to the idea of what is not observed" ("observed" apparently means 'perceived by one of the five senses') and of "hostility to the idea that what is not observed can in any sense be recognized or described or reported." [16] Dreams and mental pictures are not observed, in Strawson's sense; yet Wittgenstein discusses *reports* of dreams (p. 222; also p. 184) and *descriptions* of mental pic-tures (e.g., 367). Consider this general remark: "Think how many different kinds of things are called 'description': description of a body's position by means of its co-ordinates; description of a fa-cial expression; *description of a sensation of touch*; of a mood" (24, my italics). And at many places in the *Investigations,* Witt-genstein *gives* descriptions of various sensations, although sensa-tions are not observed, in Strawson's sense. Strawson's belief that Wittgenstein thinks that "one cannot sensibly be said to recognize or identify anything, unless one uses criteria," [17] is proved false by the remarks about mental images: I have *no* criterion for saying that two images of mine are the same (377); yet there is such a thing as *recognition* here, and a correct use of 'same' (378). How can it be maintained that Wittgenstein has a prejudice against 'the inner' when he allows that in our ordinary language a man *can* write down or give vocal expression to his "inner experiences —his feelings, moods, and the rest—for his private use"? (243). Wittgenstein does not deny that there are *inner* experiences any more than he denies that there are *mental* occurrences. Indeed, he gives examples of things that he calls *"seelische Vorgänge,"* e.g., "a pain's growing more or less," and in contrast with which a

[13] P. 91.   [14] P. 92.   [15] See p. 86 and p. 98.   [16] P. 90.   [17] P. 86.

thing like *understanding a word* is not, he argues a *"seelischen Vorgang"* (154). Either to deny that such occurrences exist or to claim that they cannot be named, reported, or described is entirely foreign to Wittgenstein's outlook. For what would the denial amount to other than an attempt to "reform language," which is not his concern? It may *look* as if he were trying to reform language, because he is engaged in "giving prominence to distinctions which our ordinary forms of language easily make us overlook" (132). For example, Wittgenstein suggests that when we think about the philosophical problem of sensation the word 'describe' *tricks* us (290). Of course he does not mean that it is a mistake to speak of 'describing' a sensation. He means that the similarity in "surface grammar" (664) between 'I describe my sensations' and 'I describe my room' may mislead, may cause us to fail "to call to mind the differences between the language-games" (290).

Strawson rightly avers, "To deny that 'pain' is the name of a (type of) sensation is comparable to denying that 'red' is the name of a colour." [18] I suppose that, conversely, to affirm that 'pain' is the name of a sensation is like affirming that 'red' is the name of a color, and also that '0' is the name of a number. This classification tells us nothing of philosophical interest. What we need to notice is the *difference* between the way that '0' and '2,' say, function, although both are 'names of numbers' (think how easily one may be tempted to deny that 0 is a number), and the difference between the way 'red' and 'pain' function, although both are 'names.' "We call very different things 'names'; the word 'name' is used to characterize many different kinds of use of a word, related to one another in many different ways" (38). To suppose that the uses of 'pain' and 'red,' as *names*, are alike is just the sort of error that Wittgenstein wants to expose. If one thinks this, one will want to by-pass the *expression* of pain and will wonder at Wittgenstein's 'obsession' with it. Not that Strawson does by-pass it, but he seems to attach the wrong significance to it. He appears to think that the fact that there is a characteristic pain-behavior is what makes possible a *common* "language of pain," and he seems to imply that if we did not care to have a

[18] P. 87.

common language of pain each of us would still be able to name and describe his pains in "a private language-game," even if there were no characteristic pain-behavior.[19] It looks as if he thinks that with his private language he could step between pain and its expression, and apply names to the bare sensations themselves (cf. 245).

For Strawson the conception of a private language possesses no difficulty. A man "might simply be struck by the recurrence of a certain sensation and get into the habit of making a certain mark in a different place every time it occurred. The making of the marks would help to impress the occurrence on his memory." [20] Just as, I suppose, he might utter a certain sound each time a cow appeared. But we need to ask, what makes the latter sound a *word*, and what makes it the word for *cow*? Is there no difficulty here? Is it sufficient that the sound is uttered when and only when a cow is present? Of course not. The sound might refer to anything or nothing. What is necessary is that it should play a part in various activities, in calling, fetching, counting cows, distinguishing cows from other things and pictures of cows from pictures of other things. If the sound has no fixed place in activities ("language-games") of this sort, then it isn't a word for *cow*. To be sure, I can sit in my chair and talk about cows and not be engaged in any of those activities—but what makes my words *refer* to cows is the fact that I have already mastered those activities; they lie in the background. The kind of way that 'cow' refers is the kind of language-game to which it belongs. If a mark or sound is to be a word for a *sensation* it, too, must enter into language-games, although of a very different sort. What sort? Well, such things as showing the location of the sensation, exhibiting different reactions to different intensities of stimulus, seeking or avoiding causes of the sensation, choosing one sensation in preference to another, indicating the duration of the sensation, and so on. Actions and reactions of that sort constitute the sensation-behavior. They are the "outward criteria" (580) with which the sign must be connected if it is to be a sign for a sensation *at all*, not merely if it is to be a sign in a *common* language. In the mere

---

[19] See pp. 84-88.
[20] P. 85.

supposition that there is a man who is "struck by the recurrence of a certain sensation" and who gets into the habit of "making a certain mark in a different place every time it occurred," no ground *whatever* has been given for saying that the mark is a sign for a sensation. The necessary surroundings have not been supplied. Strawson sees no problem here. He is surprised that "Wittgenstein gives himself considerable trouble over the question of how a man would *introduce* a name for a sensation into this private language." [21] It is as if Strawson thought: There is no difficulty about it; the man just *makes* the mark refer to a sensation. How the man does it puzzles Strawson so little that he is not even inclined to feel that the connection between the name and the sensation is queer, occult (cf. 38)—which it would be, to say the least, if the name had no fixed place in those activities and reactions that constitute sensation-behavior, for that, and not a magical act of the mind, is what *makes* it refer to a sensation.

The conception of private language that Wittgenstein attacks is not the conception of a language that only the speaker does understand, but of a language that no other person *can* understand (243). Strawson thinks that Wittgenstein has not refuted the conception of a private language but has only shown that certain conditions must be satisfied if a common language is to exist. Strawson appears to believe (I may misunderstand him) that each of us not only can have but does have a private language of sensations, that if we are to understand one another when we speak of our sensations there must be criteria for the use of our sensation-words, and that therefore the words with which we *refer* to our sensations must, in addition, contain "allusions" either to behavior or to material substances that are "associated" with the sensations.[22] The allusions must be to things that can be perceived by us all. By virtue of this the use of sensation-words can be taught and misuses corrected, and so those words will belong to a common language. There is another feature of their use (namely, their reference) that cannot be taught. Thus sensation-words will have both a public and a private meaning. Strawson's view appears to be accurately characterized by Witt-

[21] *Ibid.*
[22] P. 86.

genstein's mock conjecture: "Or is it like this: the word 'red' means something known to everyone; and in addition, for each person, it means something known only to him? (Or perhaps rather: it *refers* to something known only to him.)" (273)

But if my words, *without* these allusions, can refer to my sensations, then what is alluded to is only *contingently* related to the sensations. Adding the "allusions to what can be seen and touched" [23] will not help one little bit in making us understand one another. For the behavior that is, for me, contingently associated with 'the sensation of pain' may be, for you, contingently associated with 'the sensation of tickling'; the piece of matter that produces in you what you call 'a metallic taste' may produce in me what, if you could experience it, you would call 'the taste of onions'; my 'sensation of red' may be your 'sensation of blue'; we do not know and cannot know whether we are talking about the same things; we cannot *learn* the essential thing about one another's use of sensation-words—namely, their reference. The language in which the private referring is done cannot be turned into a common language by having something grafted on to it. Private language cannot be the understructure of the language we all understand. It is as if, in Strawson's conception, the sensation-words were supposed to perform two functions—to refer and to communicate. But if the reference is incommunicable, then the trappings of allusion will not communicate it, and what they do communicate will be irrelevant.

Strawson's idea that expressions like 'jabbing pain,' 'metallic taste,' mean something known to everyone and, in addition, for each person, refer to something known only to him, is responsible, I believe, for his failure to understand Wittgenstein on the topic of recognizing and identifying sensations. There is *a* sense of 'recognize' and 'identify' with respect to which Wittgenstein does deny that we can recognize or identify our own sensations, feelings, images. Consider, for example, that although a man understands the word 'alcohol' he may fail to identify the alcohol in a bottle as alcohol, because the bottle is marked 'gasoline' or because the cork smells of gasoline; or, although he understands 'rabbit' and is familiar with rabbits, he may fail to recognize a

[23] *Ibid.*

rabbit as a rabbit, taking it for a stump instead; or, he may be in doubt and say, 'I don't know whether this is alcohol,' 'I'm not sure whether that is a rabbit or a stump.' But can a man who understands the word 'pain' be in doubt as to whether he has pain? Wittgenstein remarks:

If anyone said "I do not know if what I have got is a pain or something else," we should think something like, he does not know what the English word "pain" means; and we should explain it to him.— How? Perhaps by means of gestures, or by pricking him with a pin and saying: "See, that's what pain is!" This explanation, like any other, he might understand right, wrong, or not at all. And he will show which he does by his use of the word, in this as in other cases.

If he now said, for example: "Oh, I know what 'pain' means; what I don't know is whether *this*, that I have now, is pain"—we should merely shake our heads and be forced to regard his words as a queer reaction which we have no idea what to do with [288].

That a man wonders whether what he has is pain can only mean that he does not understand the word 'pain'; he cannot both understand it and have that doubt. Thus there is a sense of 'identify' that has no application to sensations. One who understands the word 'alcohol' may fail to identify *this* as alcohol or may be in doubt as to its identity or may correctly identify it. These possibilities have no meaning in the case of pain. There is not over and above (or underneath) the understanding of the word 'pain' a further process of correctly identifying or failing to identify *this* as pain. There would be if Strawson's conception was right. But there is not, and this is why "That expression of doubt ['Oh, I know what 'pain' means; what I don't know is whether *this*, that I have now, is pain'] has no place in the language-game" (288). (Strawson does not have, but in consistency should have, an inclination to dispute this last remark of Wittgenstein's.)[24] The fact that there is no *further* process of identifying a particular sensation is a reason why "the object drops out of consideration as irrelevant" when "we construe the grammar of the expression of sensation on the model of 'object and name'" (293)—a remark that Strawson misunderstands as the thesis that "no words name sensations." [25] If my use of a sensation-word

[24] See p. 85.
[25] P. 84.

satisfies the normal outward criteria and if I truthfully declare that I have that sensation, then I *have* it—there is not a further problem of my applying the word right or wrong within myself. If a man used the word 'pain' in accordance with "the usual symptoms and presuppositions of pain" then it would have no sense to suppose that perhaps his memory did not retain *what* the word 'pain' refers to, "so that he constantly called different things by that name" (271). If my use of the word fits those usual criteria there is not an added problem of whether I accurately pick out the objects to which the word applies. In this sense of 'identify,' the hypothesis that I identify my sensations is "a mere ornament, not connected with the mechanism at all" (270).

It does not follow nor, I think, does Wittgenstein mean to assert that there is *no* proper use of 'identify' or 'recognize' with sensations. He acknowledges a use of 'recognize' with mental images, as previously noted. It would be a natural use of language, I believe, if someone who upon arising complained of an unusual sensation were to say, 'Now I can identify it! It is the same sensation that I have when I go down in an elevator.' Wittgenstein, who has no interest in reforming language, would not dream of calling this an incorrect use of 'identify.' He attacks a philosophical use of the word only, the use that belongs to the notion of the private object. In this example of a non-philosophical use, if the speaker employed the rest of the sensation-language as we all do, and if his behavior in this case was approximately what it was when he was affected by the downward motion of an elevator, then his declaration that he was feeling the elevator-sensation would be decisive; and also his declaration that it was *not* the elevator-sensation would be decisive. It is *out of the question* that he should have made a mistake in identifying the sensation. His identification of his sensation is an *expression* of sensation (in Wittgenstein's extended sense of this phrase). The identification is 'incorrigible.' We have here a radically different use of 'identify' from that illustrated in the examples of alcohol and rabbit.

The philosophical use of 'identify' seems to make possible the committing of *errors* of identification of sensations and inner experiences. The idea is that my sensation or my image is an object that I cannot show to anyone and that I identify it and from it derive its description (374). But if this is so, why cannot my identification and description go wrong, and not just sometimes but always? Here we are in a position to grasp the significance of Wittgenstein's maneuver: "Always get rid of the idea of the private object in this way: assume that it constantly changes, but that you do not notice the change because your memory constantly deceives you" (p. 207). We are meant to see the *senselessness* of this supposition: for what in the world would *show* that I was deceived constantly or even once? Do I look again—and why can't I be deceived that time, too? The supposition is a knob that doesn't turn anything (cf. 270). Understanding this will perhaps remove the temptation to think that I have something that I cannot show to you and from which I derive a knowledge of its identity. This is what Wittgenstein means in saying that when I related to another what I just said to myself in my thoughts " 'what went on within me' is not the point at all" (p. 222). He is not declaring, as Strawson thinks, that I cannot report what words went through my mind.[26] He is saying that it is a report "whose truth is guaranteed by the special criteria of truthfulness" (p. 222). It is *that* kind of report. So it is not a matter of trying faithfully to observe something within myself and of trying to produce a correct account of it, of trying to do something at which I might unwittingly fail.

The influence of the idea of the private object on Strawson's thinking is subtly reflected, I believe, in his declaration that a metallic taste is "quite certainly recognizable and identifiable in itself" and in his remark that "if the question 'What is the criterion of identity here?' is pushed, one can only answer: 'Well, the taste itself' (cf. 'the sensation itself')." [27] Strawson realizes that we don't identify a sensation by means of criteria (e.g., a metallic taste by means of the metallic material that produces it). He is inclined to add that we identify it by 'the sensation itself.' This seems to me to misconstrue the 'grammar' of 'identify' here. It may be to the point to consider again the comparison of colors and sensations. Wittgenstein says, "How do I know that this colour is red?—It would be an answer to say 'I have learned English'" (381). One thing this answer does is to deny that I

[26] See pp. 90, 91.
[27] P. 86.

have *reasons* for saying that this color before me is red. We might put this by saying that I identify it as red by 'the color itself,' not by anything else. The cases of red and pain (or metallic taste) so far run parallel. Equally, I don't have reasons for saying that this color is red or that this sensation is pain. But it *can* happen that I should fail to identify this color correctly, even though I have learned English (e.g., the moonlight alters its appearance). Here the parallel ends. Nothing can alter the 'appearance' of the sensation. Nothing counts as mistaking its identity. If we assimilate identifying sensations to identifying colors, because in neither instance reasons are relevant, we conceal the philosophically more important difference. To insist that the parallel is perfect, that one identifies sensations in the same sense that one identifies colors, is like saying that "there must also be something boiling in the pictured pot" (297). Identifying one's own sensation is nothing that is either in error or *not* in error. It is not, in *that* sense, *identifying*. When I identify my sensation, I do not *find out* its identity, not even from 'the sensation itself.' My identification, one could say, *defines* its identity.

We use a man's identification of his sensation as a criterion of what his sensation is. But this is a *dependent* criterion. His verbal reports and identifications would not *be* a criterion unless they were grounded in the primitive sensation-behavior that is the primary and independent criterion of his sensations. If we cut out human behavior from the language-game of sensations (which Strawson does in defending the 'private language-game') one result will be that a man's identifying a sensation as the 'same' that he had a moment before will no longer be a criterion of its being the same. Not only the speaker but *no one* will have a criterion of identity. Consequently, for no one will it have any meaning to speak of a man's being "struck by the *recurrence* of a certain sensation." [28]

---

[28] P. 85, my italics.

Knowledge of Other Minds

I

I believe that the argument from analogy for the existence of other minds still enjoys more credit than it deserves, and my first aim will be to show that it leads nowhere. J. S. Mill is one of many who have accepted the argument and I take his statement of it as representative. He puts to himself the question, "By what evidence do I know, or by what considerations am I led to believe, that there exist other sentient creatures; that the walking and speaking figures which I see and hear, have sensations and thoughts, or in other words, possess Minds?" His answer is the following:

I conclude that other human beings have feelings like me, because, first, they have bodies like me, which I know, in my own case, to be the antecedent condition of feelings; and because, secondly, they exhibit the acts, and other outward signs, which in my own case I know by experience to be caused by feelings. I am conscious in myself of a series of facts connected by an uniform sequence, of which the beginning is modifications of my body, the middle is feelings, the end is outward demeanor. In the case of other human beings I have the evidence of my senses for the first and last links of the series, but not for the intermediate link. I find, however, that the sequence between the first and last is as regular and constant in those other cases as it is in mine. In my own case I know that the first link produces the last through the intermediate link, and could not produce it without. Experience, therefore, obliges me to conclude that there must be an intermediate link; which must either be the same in others as in myself, or a different one: I must either believe them to be alive, or to be automatons: and by believing them to be alive, that is, by supposing the link to be of the same nature as in the case of which I have experience, and which is in all other respects similar, I bring other human beings, as phenomena, under the same generalizations which I know by experience to be the true theory of my own existence.[1]

I shall pass by the possible objection that this would be very *weak* inductive reasoning, based as it is on the observation of a single instance. More interesting is the following point: Suppose this reasoning could yield a conclusion of the sort "It is probable that that human figure" (pointing at some person other than one-self) "has thoughts and feelings." Then there is a question as to whether this conclusion can *mean* anything to the philosopher who draws it, because there is a question as to whether the sentence "That human figure has thoughts and feelings" can mean anything to him. Why should this be a question? Because the assumption from which Mill starts is that he has *no criterion* for determining whether another "walking and speaking figure" does or does not have thoughts and feelings. If he had a criterion he could apply it, establishing with certainty that this or that human figure does or does not have feelings (for the only plausible criterion would lie in behavior and circumstances that are open to view), and there would be no call to resort to tenuous analogical reasoning that yields at best a probability. If Mill has no criterion for the existence of feelings other than his own then in that sense he does not understand the sentence "That human figure has feelings" and therefore does not understand the sentence "It is *probable* that that human figure has feelings."

There is a familiar inclination to make the following reply: "Although I have no criterion of verification still I *understand*, for example, the sentence 'He has a pain.' For I understand the meaning of 'I have a pain,' and 'He has a pain' means that he has the *same* thing I have when I have a pain." But this is a fruitless maneuver. If I do not know how to establish that someone has a

---

[1] J. S. Mill, *An Examination of Sir William Hamilton's Philosophy*, 6th ed. (New York: Longmans, Green & Co., Inc., 1889), pp. 243-244.

pain then I do not know how to establish that he has the *same* as I have when I have a pain.[2] You cannot improve my understanding of "He has a pain" by this recourse to the notion of "the same," unless you give me a criterion for saying that someone *has* the same as I have. If you can do this you will have no use for the argument from analogy: and if you cannot then you do not understand the supposed conclusion of that argument. A philosopher who purports to rely on the analogical argument cannot, I think, escape this dilemma.

There have been various attempts to repair the argument from analogy. Mr. Stuart Hampshire has argued [3] that its validity as a method of inference can be established in the following way: Others sometimes infer that I am feeling giddy from my behavior. Now I have direct, non-inferential knowledge, says Hampshire, of my own feelings. So I can check inferences made about me against the facts, checking thereby the accuracy of the "methods" of inference.

All that is required for testing the validity of any method of factual inference is that each one of us should sometimes be in a position to confront the conclusions of the doubtful method of inference with what is known by him to be true independently of the method of inference in question. Each one of us is certainly in this position in respect of our common methods of inference about the feelings of persons other than ourselves, in virtue of the fact that each one of us is constantly able to compare the results of this type of inference with what he knows to be true directly and non-inferentially; each one of us is in the position to make this testing comparison, whenever he is the designated subject of a statement about feelings and sensations. I, Hampshire, know by what sort of signs I may be misled in inferring Jones's and Smith's feelings, because I have implicitly noticed (though probably not formulated) where Jones, Smith and others generally go wrong in inferring my feelings (*op. cit.*, pp. 4-5).

Presumably I can also note when the inferences of others about my feelings do not go wrong. Having ascertained the reliability

---

[2] "It is no explanation to say: the supposition that he has a pain is simply the supposition that he has the same as I. For *that* part of the grammar is quite clear to me: that is, that one will say that the stove has the same experience as I, *if* one says: it is in pain and I am in pain" (Ludwig Wittgenstein, *Philosophical Investigations* (New York: The Macmillan Company, 1953), sec. 350).

[3] "The Analogy of Feeling," *Mind*, January 1952, pp. 1-12.

of some inference-procedures I can use them myself, in a guarded way, to draw conclusions about the feelings of others, with a modest but justified confidence in the truth of those conclusions.

My first comment is that Hampshire has apparently forgotten the purpose of the argument from analogy, which is to provide some probability that "the walking and speaking figures which I see and hear, have sensations and thoughts" (Mill). For the reasoning that he describes involves the assumption that other human figures *do* have thoughts and sensations: for they are assumed to *make inferences* about me from *observations* of my behavior. But the philosophical problem of the existence of other minds *is* the problem of whether human figures other than one-self do, among other things, make observations, inferences, and assertions. Hampshire's supposed defense of the argument from analogy is an *ignoratio elenchi*.

If we struck from the reasoning described by Hampshire all assumption of thoughts and sensations in others we should be left with something roughly like this: "When my behavior is such and such there come from nearby human figures the sounds 'He feels giddy.' And generally I do feel giddy at the time. Therefore when another human figure exhibits the same behavior and I say 'He feels giddy,' it is probable that he does feel giddy." But the reference here to the sentence-like sounds coming from other human bodies is irrelevant, since I must not assume that those sounds express inferences. Thus the reasoning becomes simply the classical argument from analogy: "When my behavior is such and such I feel giddy; so probably when another human figure behaves the same way he feels the same way." This argument, again, is caught in the dilemma about the criterion of the *same*.

The version of analogical reasoning offered by Professor H. H. Price[4] is more interesting. He suggests that "one's evidence for the existence of other minds is derived primarily from the under-standing of language" (p. 429). His idea is that if another body gives forth noises one understands, like "There's the bus," and if these noises give one new information, this "provides some evidence that the foreign body which uttered the noises is animated

---

[4] "Our Evidence for the Existence of Other Minds," *Philosophy*, XIII (1938), 425-456.

by a mind like one's own. . . . Suppose I am often in its neighborhood, and it repeatedly produces utterances which I can understand, and which I then proceed to verify for myself. And
suppose that this happens in many different kinds of situations.
I think that my evidence for believing that this body is animated
by a mind like my own would then become very strong" (p. 430).
The body from which these informative sounds proceed need not
be a human body. "If the rustling of the leaves of an oak formed
intelligible words conveying new information to me, and if gorse-
bushes made intelligible gestures, I should have evidence that the
oak or the gorse-bush was animated by an intelligence like my
own" (p. 436). Even if the intelligible and informative sounds
did not proceed from a body they would provide evidence for the
existence of a (disembodied) mind (p. 435).

Although differing sharply from the classical analogical argument, the reasoning presented by Price is still analogical in form:
I know by introspection that when certain combinations of sounds
come from me they are "symbols in acts of spontaneous thinking";
therefore similar combinations of sounds, not produced by me,
"probably function as instruments to an act of spontaneous thinking, which in this case is not my own" (p. 446). Price says that
the reasoning also provides an *explanation* of the otherwise mysterious occurrence of sounds which I understand but did not produce. He anticipates the objection that the hypothesis is nonsensical because unverifiable. "The hypothesis is a perfectly
conceivable one," he says, "in the sense that I know very well
what the world would have to be like if the hypothesis were
true—what sorts of entities there must be in it, and what sorts of
events must occur in them. I know from introspection what acts
of thinking and perceiving are, and I know what it is for such
acts to be combined into the unity of a single mind . . ." (pp.
446-447).

I wish to argue against Price that no amount of intelligible
sounds coming from an oak tree or a kitchen table could create
any probability that it has sensations and thoughts. The question
to be asked is: What would show that a tree or table *understands*
the sounds that come from it? We can imagine that useful warn-
ings, true descriptions and predictions, even "replies" to questions, should emanate from a tree, so that it came to be of

enormous value to its owner. How should we establish that it understood those sentences? Should we "question" it? Suppose that the tree "said" that there was a vixen in the neighborhood, and we "asked" it "What is a vixen?," and it "replied," "A vixen is a female fox." It might go on to do as well for "female" and "fox." This performance might incline us to say that the tree understood the words, in contrast to the possible case in which it answered "I don't know" or did not answer at all. But would it show that the tree understood the words in the same sense that a person could understand them? With a person such a performance would create a presumption that he could make correct *applications* of the word in question; but not so with a tree. To see this point think of the normal teaching of words (e.g., "spoon," "dog," "red") to a child and how one decides whether he understands them. At a primitive stage of teaching one does not require or expect definitions, but rather that the child should *pick out* reds from blues, dogs from cats, spoons from forks. This involves his looking, pointing, reaching for and going to the right things and not the wrong ones. That a child says "red" when a red thing and "blue" when a blue thing is put before him is indicative of a mastery of those words *only* in conjunction with the other activities of looking, pointing, trying to get, fetching, and carrying. Try to suppose that he says the right words but looks at and reaches for the wrong things. Should we be tempted to say that he has mastered the use of those words? No, indeed. The disparity between words and behavior would make us say that he does not understand the words. In the case of a tree there could be no disparity between its words and its "behavior" because it is logically incapable of behavior of the relevant kind.

Since it has nothing like the human face and body it makes no sense to say of a tree, or an electronic computer, that it is looking or pointing at or fetching something. (Of course one can always *invent* a sense for these expressions.) Therefore it would make no sense to say that it did or did not understand the above words. Trees and computers cannot either pass or fail the tests that a child is put through. They cannot take them. That an object was a source of intelligible sounds or other signs (no matter how sequential) would not be enough by itself to establish that it had thoughts or sensations. How informative sentences and valuable predictions could emanate from a gorse-bush might be a grave scientific problem, but the explanation could never be that the gorse-bush has a mind. Better no explanation than nonsense!

It might be thought that the above difficulty holds only for words whose meaning has a "perceptual content" and that if we imagined, for example, that our gorse-bush produced nothing but pure mathematical propositions we should be justified in attributing thought to it, although not sensation. But suppose there was a remarkable "calculating boy" who could give right answers to arithmetical problems but could not apply numerals to reality in empirical propositions, e.g., he could not *count* any objects. I believe that everyone would be reluctant to say that he *understood* the mathematical signs and truths that he produced. If he could count in the normal way there would not be this reluctance. And "counting in the normal way" involves looking, pointing, reaching, fetching, and so on. That is, it requires the human face and body, and human behavior—or something similar. Things which do not have the human form, or anything like it, not merely do not but *cannot* satisfy the criteria for thinking. I am trying to bring out part of what Wittgenstein meant when he said, "We only say of a human being and what is like one that it thinks" (*Investigations*, sec. 360), and "The human body is the best picture of the human soul" (*ibid.*, p. 178).

I have not yet gone into the most fundamental error of the argument from analogy. It is present whether the argument is the classical one (the analogy between my body and other bodies) or Price's version (the analogy between my language and the noises and signs produced by other things). It is the mistaken assumption that *one learns from one's own case* what thinking, feeling, sensation are. Price gives expression to this assumption when he says: "I know from introspection what acts of thinking and perceiving are . . ." (*op. cit.*, p. 447). It is the most natural assumption for a philosopher to make and indeed seems at first to be the only possibility. Yet Wittgenstein has made us see that it leads first to solipsism and then to nonsense. I shall try to state as briefly as possible how it produces those results.

A philosopher who believes that one must learn what thinking, fear, or pain is "from one's own case," does not believe that the thing to be observed is one's behavior, but rather something "inward." He considers behavior to be related to the inward states and occurrences merely as an accompaniment or possibly an effect. He cannot regard behavior as a *criterion* of psychological phenomena: for if he did he would have no use for the analogical argument (as was said before) and also the priority given to "one's own case" would be pointless. He believes that he notes something in himself that he calls "thinking" or "fear" or "pain," and then he tries to infer the presence of the *same* in others. He should then deal with the question of what his criterion of the *same* in others is. This he cannot do because it is of the essence of his viewpoint to reject circumstances and behavior as a criterion of mental phenomena in others. And what else could serve as a criterion? He ought, therefore, to draw the conclusion that the notion of thinking, fear, or pain in others is in an important sense meaningless. He has no idea of what would count for or against it.[5] "That there should be thinking or pain other than my own is unintelligible," he ought to hold. This would be a rigorous solipsism, and a correct outcome of the assumption that one can know only from one's own case what the mental phenomena are. An equivalent way of putting it would be: "When I say 'I am in pain,' by 'pain' I mean a certain inward state. When I say '*He* is in pain,' by 'pain' I mean *behavior*. I cannot attribute pain to others *in the same sense* that I attribute it to myself."

Some philosophers before Wittgenstein may have seen the solipsistic result of starting from "one's own case." But I believe he is the first to have shown how that starting point destroys itself. This may be presented as follows: One supposes that one inwardly picks out something as thinking or pain and thereafter identifies it whenever it presents itself in the soul. But the question to be pressed is, Does one make *correct* identifications? The proponent of these "private" identifications has nothing to say here. He feels sure that he identifies correctly the occurrences in his soul; but feeling sure is no guarantee of being right. Indeed he has no idea of what being *right* could mean. He does not know

---

[5] One reason why philosophers have not commonly drawn this conclusion may be, as Wittgenstein acutely suggests, that they assume that they have "an infallible paradigm of identity in the identity of a thing with itself" (*Investigations*, sec. 215).

how to distinguish between actually making correct identifications and being under the impression that he does. (See *Investigations*, secs. 258-9.) Suppose that he identified the emotion of anxiety as the sensation of pain? Neither he nor anyone else could know about this "mistake." Perhaps he makes a mistake *every* time! Perhaps all of us do! We ought to see now that we are talking nonsense. We do not know what a *mistake* would be. We have no standard, no examples, no customary practice, with which to compare our inner recognitions. The inward identification cannot hit the bull's-eye, or miss it either, because there is no bull's-eye. When we see that the ideas of correct and incorrect have no application to the supposed inner identification, the latter notion loses its appearance of sense. Its collapse brings down both solipsism and the argument from analogy.

II

The destruction of the argument from analogy also destroys the *problem* for which it was supposed to provide a solution. A philosopher feels himself in a difficulty about other minds because he assumes that first of all he is acquainted with mental phenomena "from his own case." What troubles him is how to make the transition from his own case to the case of others. When his thinking is freed of the illusion of the priority of his own case, then he is able to look at the familiar facts and to acknowledge that the circumstances, behavior, and utterances of others actually are his *criteria* (not merely his evidence) for the existence of their mental states. Previously this had seemed impossible.

But now he is in danger of flying to the opposite extreme of behaviorism, which errs by believing that through observation of one's own circumstances, behavior, and utterances one can find out that one is thinking or angry. The philosophy of "from one's own case" and behaviorism, though in a sense opposites, make the common assumption that the first-person, present-tense psychological statements are verified by self-observation. According to the "one's own case" philosophy the self-observation cannot be checked by others; according to behaviorism the self-observation would be by means of outward criteria that are available to all. The first position becomes unintelligible; the second is false for at least many kinds of psychological statements. We are forced to conclude that the first-person psychological statements are not (or hardly ever) verified by self-observation. It follows that they have no verification at all; for if they had a verification it would have to be by self-observation.

But if sentences like "My head aches" or "I wonder where she is" do not express observations then what do they do? What is the relation between my declaration that my head aches and the fact that my head aches, if the former is not the report of an observation? The perplexity about the existence of *other* minds has, as the result of criticism, turned into a perplexity about the meaning of one's own psychological sentences about oneself. At our starting point it was the sentence "*His* head aches" that posed a problem; but now it is the sentence "*My* head aches" that puzzles us.

One way in which this problem can be put is by the question, "How does *one know when to say* the words 'My head aches'?" The inclination to ask this question can be made acute by imagining a fantastic but not impossible case of a person who has survived to adult years without ever experiencing pain. He is given various sorts of injections to correct this condition, and on receiving one of these one day, he jumps and exclaims, "Now I feel pain!" One wants to ask, "How did he *recognize* the new sensation as a *pain?*"

Let us note that if the man gives an answer (e.g., "I knew it must be pain because of the way I jumped") then he proves by that very fact that he has not mastered the correct use of the words "I feel pain." They cannot be used to state a *conclusion*. In telling us *how* he did it he will convict himself of a misuse. Therefore the question "How did he recognize his sensation?" requests the impossible. The inclination to ask it is evidence of our inability to grasp the fact that the use of this psychological sentence has nothing to do with recognizing or identifying or observing a state of oneself.

The fact that this imagined case produces an especially strong temptation to ask the "How?" question shows that we have the idea that it must be more difficult to give the right name of one's sensation *the first time.* The implication would be that it is not so difficult *after* the first time. Why should this be? Are we thinking that then the man would have a paradigm of pain with which he could compare his sensations and so be in a position to know right off whether a certain sensation was or was not a pain? But the paradigm would be either something "outer" (behavior) or something "inner" (perhaps a memory impression of the sensation). If the former then he is misusing the first-person sentence. If the latter then the question of whether he compared *correctly* the present sensation with the inner paradigm of pain would be without sense. Thus the idea that the use of the first-person sentences can be governed by paradigms must be abandoned. It is another form of our insistent misconception of the first-person sentence as resting somehow on the identification of a psychological state.

These absurdities prove that we must conceive of the first-person psychological sentences in some entirely different light. Wittgenstein presents us with the suggestion that the first-person sentences are to be thought of as similar to the natural nonverbal, behavioral expressions of psychological states. "My leg hurts," for example, is to be assimilated to crying, limping, holding one's leg. This is a bewildering comparison and one's first thought is that two sorts of things could not be more unlike. By saying the sentence one can make a *statement*; it has a *contradictory*; it is *true* or *false*; in saying it one *lies* or *tells the truth*; and so on. None of these things, exactly, can be said of crying, limping, holding one's leg. So how can there be any resemblance? But Wittgenstein knew this when he deliberately likened such a sentence to "the primitive, the natural, expressions" of pain, and said that it is "new pain-behavior" (*ibid.*, sec. 244). This analogy has at least two important merits: first, it breaks the hold on us of the question "How does one *know when to say* 'My leg hurts'?", for in the light of the analogy this will be as nonsensical as the question "How does one know when to cry, limp, or hold one's leg?"; second, it explains how the utterance of a first-person psychological sentence by another person can have *importance* for us, although not as an identification—for in the light of the analogy it will have the same importance as the natural behavior which serves as our preverbal criterion of the psychological states of others.

Anselm's Ontological Arguments

I believe that in Anselm's *Proslogion* and *Responsio editoris* there are two different pieces of reasoning which he did not distinguish from one another, and that a good deal of light may be shed on the philosophical problem of "the ontological argument" if we do distinguish them. In Chapter 2 of the *Proslogion*[1] Anselm says that we believe that God is *something a greater than which cannot be conceived.* (The Latin is *aliquid quo nihil maius cogitari possit.* Anselm sometimes uses the alternative expressions *aliquid quo maius nihil cogitari potest, id quo maius cogitari nequit, aliquid quo maius cogitari non valet.*) Even the fool of the Psalm who says in his heart there is no God, when he hears this very thing that Anselm says, namely, "something a greater than which cannot be conceived," understands what he hears, and what he understands is in his understanding though he does not understand that it exists.

Apparently Anselm regards it as tautological to say that whatever is understood is in the understanding (*quidquid intelligitur in intellectu est*): he uses *intelligitur* and *in intellectu est* as interchangeable locutions. The same holds for another formula

---

[1] I have consulted the Latin text of the *Proslogion,* of *Gaunilonis Pro Insipiente,* and of the *Responsio editoris,* in S. Anselmi, *Opera Omnia,* edited by F. C. Schmitt (Secovii, 1938), Vol. I. With numerous modifications, I have used the English translation by S. N. Deane: *St. Anselm* (La Salle, Ill.: Open Court Publishing Co., 1948).

of his: whatever is thought is in thought (*quidquid cogitatur in cogitatione est*).[2]

Of course many things may exist in the understanding that do not exist in reality; for example, elves. Now, says Anselm, something a greater than which cannot be conceived exists in the understanding. But it cannot exist *only* in the understanding, for to exist in reality is greater. Therefore that thing a greater than which cannot be conceived cannot exist only in the understanding, for then a greater thing could be conceived: namely, one that exists both in the understanding and in reality.[3]

Here I have a question. It is not clear to me whether Anselm means that (a) existence in reality by itself is greater than existence in the understanding, or that (b) existence in reality and existence in the understanding together are greater than existence in the understanding alone. Certainly he accepts (b). But he might also accept (a), as Descartes apparently does in *Meditation III* when he suggests that the mode of being by which a thing is "objectively in the understanding" is *imperfect*.[4] Of course Anselm might accept both (a) and (b). He might hold that in general something is greater if it has both of these "modes of existence" than if it has either one alone, but also that existence in reality is a more perfect mode of existence than existence in the understanding.

In any case, Anselm holds that something is greater if it exists both in the understanding and in reality than if it exists merely in the understanding. An equivalent way of putting this interesting proposition, in a more current terminology, is: something is greater if it is both conceived of and exists than if it is merely conceived of. Anselm's reasoning can be expressed as follows: *id quo maius cogitari nequit* cannot be merely conceived of and not exist, for then it would not be *id quo maius cogitari nequit*. The doctrine that something is greater if it exists in addition to

---

[2] See *Proslogion* 1 and *Responsio* 2.

[3] Anselm's actual words are: "Et certe id quo maius cogitari nequit, non potest esse in solo intellectu. Si enim vel in solo intellectu est, potest cogitari esse et in re, quod maius est. Si ergo id quo maius cogitari non potest, est in solo intellectu: id ipsum quo maius cogitari non potest, est quo maius cogitari potest. Sed certe hoc esse non potest." *Proslogion* 2.

[4] Haldane and Ross, *The Philosophical Works of Descartes*, Vol. I (New York: The Macmillan Company, 1931), 163.

being conceived of, than if it is only conceived of, could be called the doctrine that *existence is a perfection*. Descartes maintained, in so many words, that existence is a perfection,[5] and presumably he was holding Anselm's doctrine, although he does not, in *Meditation V* or elsewhere, argue in the way that Anselm does in *Proslogion* 2.

When Anselm says "And certainly, that than which nothing greater can be conceived cannot exist merely in the understanding. For suppose it exists merely in the understanding, then it can be conceived to exist in reality, which is greater," [6] he is claiming that if I conceived of a being of great excellence, that being would be *greater* (more excellent, more perfect) if it existed than if it did not exist. His supposition that "it exists merely in the understanding" is the supposition that it is conceived of but does not exist. Anselm repeated this claim in his reply to the criticism of the monk Gaunilo. Speaking of the being a greater than which cannot be conceived, he says:

I have said that if it exists merely in the understanding it can be conceived to exist in reality, which is greater. Therefore, if it exists merely in the understanding obviously the very being a greater than which cannot be conceived, is one a greater than which can be conceived. What, I ask, can follow better than that? For if it exists merely in the understanding, can it not be conceived to exist in reality? And if it can be so conceived does not he who conceives of this conceive of a thing greater than it, if it does exist merely in the understanding? Can anything follow better than this: that if a being a greater than which cannot be conceived exists merely in the understanding, it is something a greater than which can be conceived? What could be plainer? [7]

He is implying, in the first sentence, that if I conceive of something which does not exist then it is possible for it to exist, and *it will be greater if it exists than if it does not exist.*

The doctrine that existence is a perfection is remarkably queer. It makes sense and is true to say that my future house will be a better one if it is insulated than if it is not insulated; but what could it mean to say that it will be a better house if it exists than if it does not? My future child will be a better man if he is honest

---

[5] *Op. cit.*, p. 182.
[6] *Proslogion* 2, Deane, *St. Anselm*, p. 8.
[7] *Responsio* 2; Deane, *St. Anselm*, pp. 157-158.

than if he is not; but who would understand the saying that he will be a better man if he exists than if he does not? Or who understands the saying that if God exists He is more perfect than if He does not exist? One might say, with some intelligibility, that it would be better (for oneself or for mankind) if God exists than if He does not—but that is a different matter.

A king might desire that his next chancellor should have knowledge, wit, and resolution; but it is ludicrous to add that the king's desire is to have a chancellor who exists. Suppose that two royal councilors, A and B, were asked to draw up separately descriptions of the most perfect chancellor they could conceive, and that the descriptions they produced were identical except that A included existence in his list of attributes of a perfect chancellor and B did not. (I do not mean that B put nonexistence in his list.) One and the same person could satisfy both descriptions. More to the point, any person who satisfied A's description would *necessarily* satisfy B's description and *vice versa*! This is to say that A and B did not produce descriptions that differed in any way but rather one and the same description of necessary and desirable qualities in a chancellor. A only made a show of putting down a desirable quality that B had failed to include.

I believe I am merely restating an observation that Kant made in attacking the notion that "existence" or "being" is a "real predicate." He says:

By whatever and by however many predicates we may think a thing —even if we completely determine it—we do not make the least addition to the thing when we further declare that this thing *is*. Otherwise, it would not be exactly the same thing that exists, but something more than we had thought in the concept; and we could not, therefore, say that the exact object of my concept exists.[8]

Anselm's ontological proof of *Proslogion* 2 is fallacious because it rests on the false doctrine that existence is a perfection (and therefore that "existence" is a "real predicate"). It would be desirable to have a rigorous refutation of the doctrine but I have not been able to provide one. I am compelled to leave the matter at the more or less intuitive level of Kant's observation. In any

[8] *The Critique of Pure Reason,* tr. by Norman Kemp Smith (New York: The Macmillan Company, 1929), p. 505.

case, I believe that the doctrine does not belong to Anselm's other formulation of the ontological argument. It is worth noting that Gassendi anticipated Kant's criticism when he said, against Descartes:

Existence is a perfection neither in God nor in anything else; it is rather that in the absence of which there is no perfection. . . . Hence neither is existence held to exist in a thing in the way that perfections do, nor if the thing lacks existence is it said to be imperfect (or deprived of a perfection), so much as to be nothing.[9]

II

I take up now the consideration of the second ontological proof, which Anselm presents in the very next chapter of the *Proslogion.* (There is no evidence that he thought of himself as offering two different proofs.) Speaking of the being a greater than which cannot be conceived, he says:

And it so truly exists that it cannot be conceived not to exist. For it is possible to conceive of a being which cannot be conceived not to exist; and this is greater than one which can be conceived not to exist. Hence, if that, than which nothing greater can be conceived, can be conceived not to exist, it is not that than which nothing greater can be conceived. But this is a contradiction. So truly, therefore, is there something than which nothing greater can be conceived, that it cannot even be conceived not to exist.
And this being thou art, O Lord, our God.[10]

Anselm is saying two things: first, that a being whose nonexistence is logically impossible is "greater" than a being whose nonexistence is logically possible (and therefore that a being a greater than which cannot be conceived must be one whose nonexistence is logically impossible); second, that *God* is a being than which a greater cannot be conceived.

In regard to the second of these assertions, there certainly is *a* use of the word "God," and I think far the more common use, in accordance with which the statements "God is the greatest of all beings," "God is the most perfect being," "God is the supreme being," are *logically* necessary truths, in the same sense that the statement "A square has four sides" is a logically necessary truth.

[9] Haldane and Ross, *The Philosophical Works of Descartes,* II, 186.
[10] *Proslogion* 3; Deane, *St. Anselm,* pp. 8-9.

If there is a man named "Jones" who is the tallest man in the world, the statement "Jones is the tallest man in the world" is merely true and is not a logically necessary truth. It is a virtue of Anselm's unusual phrase, "a being a greater than which cannot be conceived," [11] to make it explicit that the sentence "God is the greatest of all beings" expresses a logically necessary truth and not a mere matter of fact such as the one we imagined about Jones.

With regard to Anselm's first assertion (namely, that a being whose nonexistence is logically impossible is greater than a being whose nonexistence is logically possible) perhaps the most puzzling thing about it is the use of the word "greater." It appears to mean exactly the same as "superior," "more excellent," "more perfect." This equivalence by itself is of no help to us, however, since the latter expressions would be equally puzzling here. What is required is some explanation of their use.

We do think of *knowledge,* say, as an excellence, a good thing. If A has more knowledge of algebra than B we express this in common language by saying that A has a *better* knowledge of algebra than B, or that A's knowledge of algebra is *superior* to B's, whereas we should not say that B has a better or superior *ignorance* of algebra than A. We do say "greater ignorance," but here the word "greater" is used purely quantitatively.

Previously I rejected *existence* as a perfection. Anselm is maintaining in the remarks last quoted, not that existence is a perfection, but that *the logical impossibility of nonexistence is a perfection.* In other words, *necessary existence is a perfection.* His first ontological proof uses the principle that a thing is greater if it exists than if it does not exist. His second proof employs the different principle that a thing is greater if it necessarily exists than if it does not necessarily exist.

Some remarks about the notion of *dependence* may help to make this latter principle intelligible. Many things depend for their existence on other things and events. My house was built

[11] Professor Robert Calhoun has pointed out to me that a similar locution had been used by Augustine. In *De moribus Manichaeorum* (Bk. II, ch. 11, sec. 24), he says that God is a being *quo esse aut cogitari melius nihil possit* (*Patrologiae Patrum Latinorum,* J. P. Migne, ed. [Paris, 1841-1845], Vol. 32; *Augustinus,* Vol. 1).

by a carpenter: its coming into existence was dependent on a certain creative activity. Its continued existence is dependent on many things: that a tree does not crush it, that it is not consumed by fire, and so on. If we reflect on the common meaning of the word "God" (no matter how vague and confused this is), we realize that it is incompatible with this meaning that God's existence should *depend* on anything. Whether we believe in Him or not we must admit that the "almighty and everlasting God" (as several ancient prayers begin), the "Maker of heaven and earth, and of all things visible and invisible" (as is said in the Nicene Creed), cannot be thought of as being brought into existence by anything or as depending for His continued existence on anything. To conceive of anything as dependent upon something else for its existence is to conceive of it as a lesser being than God.

If a housewife has a set of extremely fragile dishes, then as dishes they are *inferior* to those of another set like them in all respects except that they are *not* fragile. Those of the first set are *dependent* for their continued existence on gentle handling; those of the second set are not. There is a definite connection in common language between the notions of dependency and inferiority, and independence and superiority. To say that something which was dependent on nothing whatever was superior to ("greater than") anything that was dependent in any way upon anything is quite in keeping with the everyday use of the terms "superior" and "greater." Correlative with the notions of dependence and independence are the notions of *limited* and *unlimited*. An engine requires fuel and this is a limitation. It is the same thing to say that an engine's operation is *dependent* on as that it is *limited* by its fuel supply. An engine that could accomplish the same work in the same time and was in other respects satisfactory, but did not require fuel, would be a *superior* engine.

God is usually conceived of as an *unlimited* being. He is conceived of as a being who *could not* be limited, that is, as an absolutely unlimited being. This is no less than to conceive of Him as *something a greater than which cannot be conceived*. If God is conceived to be an absolutely unlimited being He must be conceived to be unlimited in regard to His existence as well as His operation. In this conception it will not make sense to say that He depends on anything for coming into or continuing in existence. Nor, as Spinoza observed, will it make sense to say that something could *prevent* Him from existing.[12] Lack of moisture can prevent trees from existing in a certain region of the earth. But it would be contrary to the concept of God as an unlimited being to suppose that anything other than God Himself could prevent Him from existing, and it would be self-contradictory to suppose that He Himself could do it.

Some may be inclined to object that although nothing could prevent God's existence, still it might just *happen* that He did not exist. And if He did exist that too would be by chance. I think, however, that from the supposition that it could happen that God did not exist it would follow that, if He existed, He would have mere duration and not eternity. It would make sense to ask, "How long has He existed?," "Will He still exist next week?," "He was in existence yesterday but how about today?," and so on. It seems absurd to make God the subject of such questions. According to our ordinary conception of Him, He is an eternal being. And eternity does not mean endless duration, as Spinoza noted. To ascribe eternity to something is to exclude as senseless all sentences that imply that it has duration. If a thing has duration then it would be merely a *contingent* fact, if it was a fact, that its duration was endless. The moon could have endless duration but not eternity. If something has endless duration it will *make sense* (although it will be false) to say that it will cease to exist, and it will make sense (although it will be false) to say that something will *cause* it to cease to exist. A being with endless duration is not, therefore, an absolutely unlimited being. That God is conceived to be eternal follows from the fact that He is conceived to be an absolutely unlimited being.

I have been trying to expand the argument of *Proslogion* 3. In *Responsio* 1 Anselm adds the following acute point: if you can conceive of a certain thing and this thing does not exist then if it *were* to exist its nonexistence would be *possible*. It follows, I believe, that if the thing were to exist it would depend on other things both for coming into and continuing in existence, and also that it would have duration and not eternity. Therefore it would

[12] *Ethics*, Part I, prop. 11.

not be, either in reality or in conception, an unlimited being, *aliquid quo nihil maius cogitari possit.*

Anselm states his argument as follows:

If it [the thing a greater than which cannot be conceived] can be conceived at all it must exist. For no one who denies or doubts the existence of a being a greater than which is inconceivable, denies or doubts that if it did exist its non-existence, either in reality or in the understanding, would be impossible. For otherwise it would not be a being a greater than which cannot be conceived. But as to whatever can be conceived but does not exist: if it were to exist its non-existence either in reality or in the understanding would be possible. Therefore, if a being a greater than which cannot be conceived, can even be conceived, it must exist.[13]

What Anselm has proved is that the notion of contingent existence or of contingent nonexistence cannot have any application to God. His existence must either be logically necessary or logically impossible. The only intelligible way of rejecting Anselm's claim that God's existence is necessary is to maintain that the concept of God, as a being a greater than which cannot be conceived, is self-contradictory or nonsensical.[14] Supposing that this is false, Anselm is right to deduce God's necessary existence from his characterization of Him as a being a greater than which cannot be conceived.

Let me summarize the proof. If God, a being a greater than which cannot be conceived, does not exist then He cannot *come* into existence. For if He did He would either have been *caused* to come into existence or have *happened* to come into existence, and in either case He would be a limited being, which by our conception of Him He is not. Since He cannot come into exist-

---

[13] *Responsio* 1; Deane, *St. Anselm,* pp. 154-155.

[14] Gaunilo attacked Anselm's argument on this very point. He would not concede that a being a greater than which cannot be conceived existed in his understanding (*Gaunilonis Pro Insipiente,* secs. 4 and 5; Deane, *St. Anselm,* pp. 148-150). Anselm's reply is: "I call on your faith and conscience to attest that this is most false" (*Responsio* 1; Deane, *St. Anselm,* p. 154). Gaunilo's faith and conscience will attest that it is false that "God is not a being a greater than which is inconceivable," and false that "He is not understood (*intelligitur*) or conceived (*cogitatur*)" (*ibid.*). Descartes remarks that one would go to "strange extremes" who denied that we understand the words *"that thing which is the most perfect that we can conceive;* for that is what all men call God" (Haldane and Ross, *The Philosophical Works of Descartes,* II, 129).

ence, if He does not exist His existence is impossible. If He does exist He cannot have come into existence (for the reasons given), nor can He cease to exist, for nothing could cause Him to cease to exist nor could it just happen that He ceased to exist. So if God exists His existence is necessary. Thus God's existence is either impossible or necessary. It can be the former only if the concept of such a being is self-contradictory or in some way logically absurd. Assuming that this is not so, it follows that He necessarily exists.[15]

It may be helpful to express ourselves in the following way: to say, not that *omnipotence* is a property of God, but rather that *necessary omnipotence* is; and to say, not that omniscience is a property of God, but rather that *necessary omniscience* is. We have criteria for determining that a man knows this and that and can do this and that, and for determining that one man has greater knowledge and abilities in a certain subject than another. We could think of various tests to give them. But there is nothing we should wish to describe, seriously and literally, as "testing" God's knowledge and powers. That God is omniscient and omnipotent has not been determined by the application of criteria: rather these are requirements of our conception of Him. They are internal properties of the concept, although they are also rightly said to be properties of God. *Necessary existence* is a property of God in the *same sense* that *necessary omnipotence* and *necessary omniscience* are His properties. And we are not to think that "God necessarily exists" means that it follows necessarily from something that God exists *contingently*. The a priori proposition "God necessarily exists" entails the proposition "God exists," if and only if the latter also is understood as an a priori proposition: in which case the two propositions are equivalent. In this sense Anselm's proof is a proof of God's existence.

[15] [The following elegant argument occurs in *Responsio* 1: "That than which a greater cannot be conceived cannot be conceived to begin to exist. Whatever can be conceived to exist and does not exist, can be conceived to begin to exist. Therefore, that than which a greater cannot be conceived, cannot be conceived to exist and yet not exist. So if it can be conceived to exist it exists from necessity." (*Nam quo maius cogitari nequit non potest cogitari esse nisi sine initio. Quidquid autem potest cogitari esse et non est, per initium potest cogitari esse. Non ergo quo maius cogitari nequit cogitari potest esse et non est. Si ergo cogitari potest esse, ex necessitate est.*) (Schmitt, *Opera Omnia*, p. 131; Deane, *St. Anselm*, p. 154.)]

Descartes was somewhat hazy on the question of whether existence is a property of things that exist, but at the same time he saw clearly enough that *necessary existence* is a property of God. Both points are illustrated in his reply to Gassendi's remark, which I quoted above:

I do not see to what class of reality you wish to assign existence, nor do I see why it may not be said to be a property as well as omnipotence, taking the word property as equivalent to any attribute or anything which can be predicated of a thing, as in the present case it should be by all means regarded. Nay, necessary existence in the case of God is also a true property in the strictest sense of the word, because it belongs to Him and forms part of His essence alone.[16]

Elsewhere he speaks of "the necessity of existence" as being "that crown of perfections without which we cannot comprehend God." [17] He is emphatic on the point that necessary existence applies solely to "an absolutely perfect Being." [18]

III

I wish to consider now a part of Kant's criticism of the ontological argument which I believe to be wrong. He says:

If, in an identical proposition, I reject the predicate while retaining the subject, contradiction results; and I therefore say that the former belongs necessarily to the latter. But if we reject subject and predicate alike, there is no contradiction; for nothing is then left that can be contradicted. To posit a triangle, and yet to reject its three angles, is self-contradictory; but there is no contradiction in rejecting the triangle together with its three angles. The same holds true of the concept of an absolutely necessary being. If its existence is rejected, we reject the thing itself with all its predicates; and no question of contradiction can then arise. There is nothing outside it that would then be contradicted, since the necessity of the thing is not supposed to be derived from anything external; nor is there anything internal that would be contradicted, since in rejecting the thing itself we have at the same time rejected all its internal properties. "God is omnipotent" is a necessary judgment. The omnipotence cannot be rejected if we posit a Deity, that is, an infinite being; for the two concepts are identical. But if we say "There is no God" neither the omnipotence nor any other of its predicates is given; they are one and all rejected

---

[16] Haldane and Ross, *The Philosophical Works of Descartes*, II, 228.
[17] *Ibid.*, I, 445.
[18] E.g., *ibid.*, Principle 15, p. 225.

together with the subject, and there is therefore not the least contradiction in such a judgment.[19]

To these remarks the reply is that when the concept of God is correctly understood one sees that one cannot "reject the subject." "There is no God" is seen to be a necessarily false statement. Anselm's demonstration proves that the proposition "God exists" has the same a priori footing as the proposition "God is omnipotent."

Many present-day philosophers, in agreement with Kant, declare that existence is not a property and think that this overthrows the ontological argument. Although it is an error to regard existence as a property of things that have contingent existence, it does not follow that it is an error to regard necessary existence as a property of God. A recent writer says, against Anselm, that a proof of God's existence "based on the necessities of thought" is "universally regarded as fallacious: it is not thought possible to build bridges between mere abstractions and concrete existence." [20] But this way of putting the matter obscures the distinction we need to make. Does "concrete existence" mean contingent existence? Then to build bridges between concrete existence and mere abstractions would be like inferring the existence of an island from the concept of a perfect island, which both Anselm and Descartes regarded as absurd. What Anselm did was to give a demonstration that the proposition "God necessarily exists" is entailed by the proposition "God is a being a greater than which cannot be conceived" (which is equivalent to "God is an absolutely unlimited being"). Kant declares that when "I think a being as the supreme reality, without any defect, the question still remains whether it exists or not." [21] But once one has grasped Anselm's proof of the necessary existence of a being a greater than which cannot be conceived, no question remains as to whether it exists or not, just as Euclid's demonstration of the existence of an infinity of prime numbers leaves no question on that issue.

[19] *Op. cit.,* p. 502.

[20] J. N. Findlay, "Can God's Existence Be Disproved?" *New Essays in Philosophical Theology,"* A. N. Flew and A. MacIntyre, eds. (New York: The Macmillan Company, 1955), p. 47.

[21] *Op. cit.,* pp. 505-506.

Kant says that "every reasonable person" must admit that "all existential propositions are synthetic." [22] Part of the perplexity one has about the ontological argument is in deciding whether or not the proposition "God necessarily exists" is or is not an "existential proposition." But let us look around. Is the Euclidean theorem in number theory, "There exists an infinite number of prime numbers," an "existential proposition"? Do we not want to say that *in some sense* it asserts the existence of something? Cannot we say, with equal justification, that the proposition "God necessarily exists" asserts the existence of something, *in some sense*? What we need to understand, in each case, is the particular sense of the assertion. Neither proposition has the same sort of sense as do the propositions "A low pressure area exists over the Great Lakes," "There still exists some possibility that he will survive," "The pain continues to exist in his abdomen." One good way of seeing the difference in sense of these various propositions is to see the variously different ways in which they are proved or supported. It is wrong to think that all assertions of existence have the same kind of meaning. There are as many kinds of existential propositions as there are kinds of subjects of discourse.

Closely related to Kant's view that all existential propositions are "synthetic" is the contemporary dogma that all existential propositions are contingent. Professor Gilbert Ryle tells us that "Any assertion of the existence of something, like any assertion of the occurrence of something, can be denied without logical absurdity." [23] "All existential statements are contingent," says Mr. I. M. Crombie.[24] Professor J. J. C. Smart remarks that "Existence is not a property" and then goes on to assert that "There can never be any *logical contradiction* in denying that God exists." [25] He declares that "The concept of a logically necessary being is a self-contradictory concept, like the concept of a round square. . . . No existential proposition can be logically necessary," he maintains, for "the truth of a logically necessary proposi-

[22] *Ibid.*, p. 504.
[23] *The Nature of Metaphysics*, D. F. Pears, ed. (New York: St. Martin's Press, Inc., 1957), p. 150.
[24] *New Essays in Philosophical Theology*, p. 114.
[25] *Ibid.*, p. 34.

tion depends only on our symbolism, or to put the same thing in
another way, on the relationship of concepts" (p. 38). Professor
K. E. M. Baier says, "It is no longer seriously in dispute that the
notion of a logically necessary being is self-contradictory. Whatever can be conceived of as existing can equally be conceived of
as not existing." [26] This is a repetition of Hume's assertion,
"Whatever we conceive as existent, we can also conceive as non-
existent. There is no being, therefore, whose non-existence implies
a contradiction." [27]

Professor J. N. Findlay ingeniously constructs an ontological
*dis*proof of God's existence, based on a "modern" view of the
nature of "necessity in propositions": the view, namely, that
necessity in propositions "merely reflects our use of words, the
arbitrary conventions of our language." [28] Findlay undertakes to
characterize what he calls "religious attitude," and here there
is a striking agreement between his observations and some of the
things I have said in expounding Anselm's proof. Religious
attitude, he says, presumes *superiority* in its object and superiority
so great that the worshiper is in comparison as nothing. Religious
attitude finds it "anomalous to worship anything *limited* in any
thinkable manner. . . . And hence we are led on irresistibly to
demand that our religious object should have an *unsurpassable*
supremacy along all avenues, that it should tower *infinitely* above
all other objects" (p. 51). We cannot help feeling that "the
worthy object of our worship can never be a thing that merely
happens to exist, nor one on which all other objects merely *happen* to depend. The true object of religious reverence must not
be one, merely, to which no *actual* independent realities stand
opposed: it must be one to which such opposition is totally *inconceivable*. . . . And not only must the existence of *other* things
be unthinkable without him, but his own non-existence must be
wholly unthinkable in any circumstances" (p. 52). And now,
says Findlay, when we add up these various requirements, what
they entail is "not only that there isn't a God, but that the
Divine Existence is either senseless or impossible" (p. 54). For

[26] *The Meaning of Life,* Inaugural Lecture, Canberra University College
(Canberra, 1957), p. 8.
[27] *Dialogues Concerning Natural Religion,* Part IX.
[28] Findlay, *op. cit.,* p. 154.

on the one hand, "if God is to satisfy religious claims and needs, He must be a being in every way inescapable, One whose existence and whose possession of certain excellences we cannot possibly conceive away." On the other hand, "modern views make it self-evidently absurd (if they don't make it ungrammatical) to speak of such a Being and attribute existence to Him. It was indeed an ill day for Anselm when he hit upon his famous proof. For on that day he not only laid bare something that is of the essence of an adequate religious object, but also something that entails its necessary non-existence" (p. 55).

Now I am inclined to hold the "modern" view that logically necessary truth "merely reflects our use of words" (although I do not believe that the conventions of language are always *arbitrary*). But I confess that I am unable to see how that view is supposed to lead to the conclusion that "the Divine existence is either senseless or impossible." Findlay does not explain how this result comes about. Surely he cannot mean that this view entails that nothing can have necessary properties: for this would imply that mathematics is "senseless or impossible," which no one wants to hold. Trying to fill in the argument that is missing from his article, the most plausible conjecture I can make is the following: Findlay thinks that the view that logical necessity "reflects the use of words" implies, not that nothing has necessary properties, but that *existence* cannot be a necessary property of anything. That is to say, every proposition of the form "*x exists*," including the proposition "God exists," must be *contingent*.[29] At the same time, our concept of God requires that His existence be *necessary*, that is, that "God exists" be a necessary truth. Therefore, the modern view of necessity proves that what the concept of God requires *cannot* be fulfilled. It proves that God *cannot* exist.

The correct reply is that the view that logical necessity merely reflects the use of words cannot possibly have the implication that every existential proposition must be contingent. That view

---

[29] The other philosophers I have just cited may be led to this opinion by the same thinking. Smart, for example, says that "the truth of a logically necessary proposition depends only on our symbolism, or to put the same thing in another way, on the relationship of concepts" (*supra*). This is very similar to saying that it "reflects our use of words."

requires us to *look at* the use of words and not manufacture a priori theses about it. In the Ninetieth Psalm it is said: "Before the mountains were brought forth, or ever thou hadst formed the earth and the world, even from everlasting to everlasting, thou art God." Here is expressed the idea of the necessary existence and eternity of God, an idea that is essential to the Jewish and Christian religions. In those complex systems of thought, those "languages-games," God has the status of a necessary being. Who can doubt that? Here we must say with Wittgenstein, "This language-game is played!" [30] I believe we may rightly take the existence of those religious systems of thought in which God figures as a necessary being to be a disproof of the dogma, affirmed by Hume and others, that no existential proposition can be necessary.

Another way of criticizing the ontological argument is the following: "Granted that the concept of necessary existence follows from the concept of a being a greater than which cannot be conceived, this amounts to no more than granting the *a priori* truth of the *conditional* proposition, 'If such a being exists then it necessarily exists.' This proposition, however, does not entail the *existence of anything*, and one can deny its antecedent without contradiction." Kant, for example, compares the proposition (or "judgment," as he calls it) "A triangle has three angles" with the proposition "God is a necessary being." He allows that the former is "absolutely necessary" and goes on to say:

The absolute necessity of the judgment is only a conditional necessity of the thing, or of the predicate in the judgment. The above proposition does not declare that three angles are absolutely necessary, but that, under the condition that there is a triangle (that is, that a triangle is given), three angles will necessarily be found in it.[31]

He is saying, quite correctly, that the proposition about triangles is equivalent to the conditional proposition "If a triangle exists, it has three angles." He then makes the comment that there is no contradiction "in rejecting the triangle together with its three angles." He proceeds to draw the alleged parallel: "The same holds true of the concept of an absolutely necessary being. If its

[30] *Philosophical Investigations* (New York: The Macmillan Company, 1953), sec. 654.
[31] *Op. cit.*, pp. 501-502.

existence is rejected, we reject the thing itself with all its predicates; and no question of contradiction can then arise." [32] The priest, Caterus, made the same objection to Descartes when he said:

Though it be conceded that an entity of the highest perfection implies its existence by its very name, yet it does not follow that that very existence is anything actual in the real world, but merely that the concept of existence is inseparably united with the concept of highest being. Hence you cannot infer that the existence of God is anything actual, unless you assume that that highest being actually exists; for then it will actually contain all its perfections, together with this perfection of real existence. [33]

I think that Caterus, Kant, and numerous other philosophers have been mistaken in supposing that the proposition "God is a necessary being" (or "God necessarily exists") is equivalent to the conditional proposition "If God exists then He necessarily exists." [34] For how do they want the antecedent clause "*If* God exists" to be understood? Clearly they want it to imply that it is *possible* that God does *not* exist. [35] The whole point of Kant's

[32] *Ibid.*, p. 502.

[33] Haldane and Ross, *The Philosophical Works of Descartes*, II, 7.

[34] I have heard it said by more than one person in discussion that Kant's view was that it is really a misuse of language to speak of a "necessary being," on the grounds that necessity is properly predicated only of propositions (judgments) not of *things.* This is not a correct account of Kant. (See his discussion of "The Postulates of Empirical Thought in General," *op. cit.*, pp. 239-256, esp. p. 239 and pp. 247-248.) But if he had held this, as perhaps the above philosophers think he should have, then presumably his view would not have been that the pseudo-proposition "God is a necessary being" is equivalent to the conditional "If God exists then He necessarily exists." Rather his view would have been that the genuine proposition " 'God exists' is necessarily true" is equivalent to the conditional "If God exists then He exists" (*not* "If God exists then He necessarily exists," which would be an illegitimate formulation, on the view imaginatively attributed to Kant). "If God exists then He exists" is a foolish tautology which says nothing different from the tautology "If a new earth satellite exists then it exists." If "If God exists then He exists" were a correct analysis of " 'God exists' is necessarily true," then "If a new earth satellite exists then it exists" would be a correct analysis of " 'A new earth satellite exists' is necessarily true." If the *analysans* is necessarily true then the *analysandum* must be necessarily true, provided the analysis is correct. If this proposed Kantian analysis of " 'God exists' is necessarily true" were correct, we should be presented with the consequence that not only is it necessarily true that God exists, but also it is necessarily true that a new earth satellite exists, which is absurd.

[35] When summarizing Anselm's proof (in Part II, *supra*) I said: "If God exists He necessarily exists." But there I was merely stating an entailment.

analysis is to try to show that it is possible to "reject the subject." Let us make this implication explicit in the conditional proposition, so that it reads: "If God exists (and it is possible that He does not) then He necessarily exists." But now it is apparent, I think, that these philosophers have arrived at a self-contradictory position. I do not mean that this conditional proposition, taken alone, is self-contradictory. Their position is self-contradictory in the following way. On the one hand, they agree that the proposition "God necessarily exists" is an a priori truth; Kant implies that it is "absolutely necessary," and Caterus says that God's existence is implied by His very name. On the other hand, they think that it is correct to analyze this proposition in such a way that it will entail the proposition "It is possible that God does not exist." But so far from its being the case that the proposition "God necessarily exists" entails the proposition "It is possible that God does not exist," it is rather the case that they are *incompatible* with one another! Can anything be clearer than the conjunction "God necessarily exists but it is possible that He does not exist" is self-contradictory? Is it not just as plainly self-contradictory as the conjunction "A square necessarily has four sides but it is possible for a square not to have four sides"? In short, this familiar criticism of the ontological argument is self-contradictory, because it accepts *both* of two incompatible propositions.[36]

One conclusion we may draw from our examination of this criticism is that (contrary to Kant) there is a lack of symmetry, in an important respect, between the propositions "A triangle has three angles" and "God has necessary existence," although both are a priori. The former can be expressed in the conditional assertion "If a triangle exists (and it is possible that none does) it has three angles." The latter cannot be expressed in the corresponding conditional assertion without contradiction.

"If God exists" did not have the implication that it is possible He does not exist. And of course I was not regarding the conditional as *equivalent* to "God necessarily exists."

[36] This fallacious criticism of Anselm is implied in the following remarks by Gilson: "To show that the affirmation of necessary existence is analytically implied in the idea of God, would be . . . to show that God is necessary if He exists, but would not prove that He does exist" (E. Gilson, *The Spirit of Medieval Philosophy* [New York: Charles Scribner's Sons, 1940], p. 62).

IV

I turn to the question of whether the idea of a being a greater than which cannot be conceived is self-contradictory. Here Leibniz made a contribution to the discussion of the ontological argument. He remarked that the argument of Anselm and Descartes

is not a paralogism, but it is an imperfect demonstration, which assumes something that must still be proved in order to render it mathematically evident; that is, it is tacitly assumed that this idea of the all-great or all-perfect being is possible, and implies no contradiction. And it is already something that by this remark it is proved that, assuming that God is possible, he exists, which is the privilege of divinity alone.[37]

Leibniz undertook to give a proof that God is possible. He defined a *perfection* as a simple, positive quality in the highest degree.[38] He argued that since perfections are *simple* qualities they must be compatible with one another. Therefore the concept of a being possessing all perfections is consistent.

I will not review his argument because I do not find his definition of a perfection intelligible. For one thing, it assumes that certain qualities or attributes are "positive" in their intrinsic nature, and others "negative" or "privative," and I have not been able to clearly understand that. For another thing, it assumes that some qualities are intrinsically simple. I believe that Wittgenstein has shown in the *Investigations* that nothing is *intrinsically* simple, but that whatever has the status of a simple, an indefinable, in one system of concepts, may have the status, of a complex thing, a definable thing, in another system of concepts.

I do not know how to demonstrate that the concept of God— that is, of a being a greater than which cannot be conceived— is not self-contradictory. But I do not think that it is legitimate to demand such a demonstration. I also do not know how to demonstrate that either the concept of a material thing or the

---

[37] *New Essays Concerning the Human Understanding*, Bk. IV, ch. 10; A. G. Langley, ed. (La Salle, Ill.: Open Court Publishing Company, 1949), p. 504.
[38] See *Ibid.*, Appendix X, p. 714.

concept of *seeing* a material thing is not self-contradictory, and philosophers have argued that both of them are. With respect to any particular reasoning that is offered for holding that the concept of seeing a material thing, for example, is self-contradictory, one may try to show the invalidity of the reasoning and thus free the concept from the charge of being self-contradictory *on that ground*. But I do not understand what it would mean to demonstrate *in general*, and not in respect to any particular reasoning, that the concept is not self-contradictory. So it is with the concept of God. I should think there is no more of a presumption that it is self-contradictory than is the concept of seeing a material thing. Both concepts have a place in the thinking and the lives of human beings.

But even if one allows that Anselm's phrase may be free of self-contradiction, one wants to know how it can have any *meaning* for anyone. Why is it that human beings have even *formed* the concept of an infinite being, a being a greater than which cannot be conceived? This is a legitimate and important question. I am sure there cannot be a deep understanding of that concept without an understanding of the phenomena of human life that give rise to it. To give an account of the latter is beyond my ability. I wish, however, to make one suggestion (which should not be understood as autobiographical).

There is the phenomenon of feeling guilt for something that one has done or thought or felt or for a disposition that one has. One wants to be free of this guilt. But sometimes the guilt is felt to be so great that one is sure that nothing one could do oneself, nor any forgiveness by another human being, would remove it. One feels a guilt that is beyond all measure, a guilt "a greater than which cannot be conceived." Paradoxically, it would seem, one nevertheless has an intense desire to have this incomparable guilt removed. One requires a forgiveness that is beyond all measure, a forgiveness "a greater than which cannot be conceived." Out of such a storm in the soul, I am suggesting, there arises the conception of a forgiving mercy that is limitless, beyond all measure.[39] This is one important feature of the Jewish and Christian conception of God.

[39] [*Psalm* 116: "The sorrows of death compassed me, and the pains of hell gat hold upon me: I found trouble and sorrow. Then called I upon the name

I wish to relate this thought to a remark made by Kierkegaard, who was speaking about belief in Christianity but whose remark may have a wider application. He says:

> There is only one proof of the truth of Christianity and that, quite rightly, is from the emotions, when the dread of sin and a heavy conscience torture a man into crossing the narrow line between despair bordering upon madness—and Christendom.[40]

One may think it absurd for a human being to feel a guilt of such magnitude, and even more absurd that, if he feels it, he should *desire* its removal. I have nothing to say about that. It may also be absurd for people to fall in love, but they do it. I wish only to say that there *is* that human phenomenon of an unbearably heavy conscience and that it is importantly connected with the genesis of the concept of God, that is, with the formation of the "grammar" of the word "God." I am sure that this concept is related to human experience in other ways. If one had the acuteness and depth to perceive these connections one could grasp the *sense* of the concept. When we encounter this concept as a problem in philosophy, we do not consider the human phenomena that lie behind it. It is not surprising that many philosophers believe that the idea of a necessary being is an arbitrary and absurd construction.

What is the relation of Anselm's ontological argument to religious belief? This is a difficult question. I can imagine an atheist going through the argument, becoming convinced of its validity, acutely defending it against objections, yet remaining an atheist. The only effect it could have on the fool of the Psalm would be that he stopped saying in his heart "There is no God," because he would now realize that this is something he cannot meaningfully say or think. It is hardly to be expected that a demonstrative argument should, in addition, produce in him a living faith. Surely there is a level at which one can view the argument as a piece of logic, following the deductive moves but not being touched religiously? I think so. But even at this level the argument may not be without religious value, for it may help to

---

of the Lord; O Lord, I beseech thee, deliver my soul."
Psalm 130: "'Out of the depths have I cried unto thee, O Lord.'"]
    [40] *The Journals,* tr. by A. Dru (New York: Oxford University Press, 1938), sec. 926.

remove some philosophical scruples that stand in the way of faith. At a deeper level, I suspect that the argument can be thoroughly understood only by one who has a view of that human "form of life" that gives rise to the idea of an infinitely great being, who views it from the *inside* not just from the outside and who has, therefore, at least some inclination to *partake* in that religious form of life. This inclination, in Kierkegaard's words, is "from the emotions." This inclination can hardly be an *effect* of Anselm's argument, but is rather presupposed in the fullest understanding of it. It would be unreasonable to require that the recognition of Anselm's demonstration as valid must produce a conversion.[41]

[41] [Since the appearance of this essay many acute criticisms of it have been published or communicated to me in private correspondence. In *The Philosophical Review*, LXX, No. 1, January 1961, there are the following articles: Raziel Abelson, "Not Necessarily"; R. E. Allen, "The Ontological Argument"; Paul Henle, "Uses of the Ontological Argument"; Gareth B. Matthews, "On Conceivability in Anselm and Malcolm"; Alvin Plantinga, "A Valid Ontological Argument?"; Terence Penelhum, "On the Second Ontological Argument." Some other published articles are: Jan Berg, "An Examination of the Ontological Proof," *Theoria*, XXVII, No. 3 (1961); T. P. Brown, "Professor Malcolm on 'Anselm's Ontological Arguments,'" *Analysis*, October 1961; W. J. Huggett, "The Nonexistence of Ontological Arguments," *The Philosophical Review*, LXXI, No. 3, July 1962; Jerome Shaffer, "Existence, Prediction, and the Ontological Argument," *Mind*, LXXI, No. 283, July 1962. It would be a major undertaking to attempt to reply to all of the criticisms, and I hope that my not doing so will not be construed as a failure to appreciate them. I do not know that it is possible to meet all of the objections; on the other hand, I do not know that it is impossible.]

George Edward Moore

I

I should like to say something about the character
of G. E. Moore, the man and philosopher, whom I knew for the
last twenty years of his life. He was a very gentle and sweet-
natured human being, as anyone acquainted with him would
testify. For one thing, he had a wonderful way with children.
When he read or told a story or explained something to a child,
the scene was so delightful that the adults within hearing were
enthralled, as well as the child. He liked to spend time with
children. To one son, Moore gave a music lesson every day from
his third year until he went away to prep school; and that son
is now a music teacher and composer. Moore loved to sing and
play the piano. He also took great joy in flowers and plants, and
was anxious to learn their names.

Moore was himself a childlike person. One thing
that contributed to this quality in him was an extreme modesty.
It was as if the thought had never occurred to Moore that he
was an eminent philosopher. I recall that once when lecturing
before a small class he had occasion to refer to an article that he
had published some years before, and he went on to remark,
without embarrassment, that it was a *good* article. I was much
struck by this. Most men would be prevented by false modesty

163

from saying a thing of this sort in public. Moore's modesty was so genuine that he could say it without any implication of self-satisfaction. How many times, both in public and private, did he declare that some previous work of his was a "dreadful muddle" or "utterly mistaken"!

Another aspect of the childlike in him was the constant freshness of his interest, his eager curiosity. This was manifest in all things, but was particularly surprising and impressive in his philosophical work. During the approximately two and a half years I spent in Cambridge at two different periods, I had regular weekly discussions with him; also I went to his weekly "at-homes," which were given over to discussion with whomever showed up. I was amazed at the way he reacted whenever anyone proposed a problem for discussion. He was all eagerness: never casual, never bored, never suggesting in his manner, "Oh, yes, I have heard of that problem before." His reaction was rather as if he had not known of it before and was anxious to look into it at once! This was so even if the topic was one that the others and himself had been thinking about together for many months. In the course of a discussion he would listen to everyone's remarks with breathless attention, as if what they were saying was entirely new and extraordinarily exciting. His younger son, who was then about seventeen years of age and a freshman at Cambridge, began to attend Moore's lectures, and I recall how in the course of a discussion that occurred after the lecture, Moore listened with this same intensity to a comment made by the young man, a beginner in philosophy and his own offspring! This continuously fresh interest and eager desire to learn was certainly one of Moore's most remarkable qualities as a philosopher.

Another aspect of the childlike in Moore was his simplicity. This was exhibited in both his speech and his writing. Although he had a mastery of the classical languages, as well as of French and German, he did not ever adorn his prose with phrases from those languages. And his writing is largely free of the jargon that philosophers typically fall into. He wrote in the plainest possible English, employing no elegant variation but rather continuous repetition. Rarely did he ever use any of the technical phrases or terms of art of philosophy; and when he did, he went to great pains to explain their meaning in the common language of everyday life.

Moore wrote an "Autobiography," which is printed in the volume entitled *The Philosophy of G. E. Moore*.[1] In it he describes a striking episode of his youth. When he was eleven or twelve years old, he was converted by a group of young men whose evangelical views were similar to those of the Salvation Army. Moore says he felt it to be his duty to try to convert others as he had been converted, but that he "had to fight against a very strong feeling of reluctance." He did, however, drive himself to do various things which he "positively hated"—for example, to distribute religious tracts. "But I constantly felt," he says, "that I was not doing nearly as much as I ought to do. I discovered that I was very deficient in moral courage." [2] The three features of Moore's childlike quality that I have mentioned, his modesty, freshness, and simplicity, present themselves very clearly in his account of this incident, which I will not quote in full.

As a philosopher he was not very imaginative. He was not fertile in ideas, as was Russell. He was not a profound thinker, as was Wittgenstein. I believe that what gave Moore stature as a philosopher was his *integrity*, an attribute of character rather than of intellect. He had the depth of seriousness. When he addressed himself to a philosophical difficulty what he said about it had to be *exactly* right. Philosophical problems vexed him: but it was impossible for him to get one out of the way by ignoring some aspect of it with which he did not know how to deal. His lectures at Cambridge were always freshly written, and during a course of lectures he would continuously revise or take back what he had previously said. His lecturing was always new research, which is perhaps one reason why he never availed himself of sabbatical leave. His labor on any piece of philosophical writing was intensive and prolonged. To one paper, "Four Forms of Scepticism," [3] he applied himself for some fifteen years. He gave the Tarner Lectures in Cambridge, but could not bring

[1] P. A. Schilpp, ed. (Evanston: Northwestern, 1942).
[2] *Op. cit.*, pp. 10-11.
[3] Published posthumously in G. E. Moore, *Philosophical Papers* (New York: The Macmillan Company, 1959).

himself to publish them and therefore received no fee for the lectures.

The address that Moore delivered to the British Academy, entitled "Proof of an External World," caused him a great deal of torment in its preparation. He worked hard at it, but the concluding portion displeased him, and he could not get it right as the time approached for his appearance before the Academy. On the day of the lecture he was still distressed about the ending of the paper. As he was about to leave the house to take the train to London, Mrs. Moore said, in order to comfort him, "Cheer up! I'm sure they will like it." To which Moore made this emphatic reply: "If they *do*, they'll be *wrong!*"

The anecdote is entirely typical of Moore. It is not what people *believe* that matters, but the truth and only the truth. When I dwell in my mind on this true love of the truth, it disturbs me. A thinker with that kind of devotion to truth must go it alone, and this is awesome and frightening.

Moore's steady, immovable integrity was exhibited in every lecture, every discussion, everything he wrote. He had a stubbornness, not of pride, but of honesty.

Along with his perfect honesty there was another thing that contributed to Moore's stature, namely, his utter absorption in philosophy. He worked at it the better part of each day. He worked very slowly with intense concentration, and he came back to the same topics again and again. The philosophical problems stayed with him; they were part of his nature; for Moore to have given up philosophy would have been inconceivable.

Let me relate another anecdote which helps to point up this side of Moore. He was awarded the Order of Merit, the highest honor that a man of letters can receive in the British Empire. The presentation was to be made by King George VI, in a private audience. Moore and his wife went to London on the day appointed and took a cab to Buckingham Palace. Mrs. Moore waited in the cab while Moore went into the palace. There he was met by the King's secretary and taken to the King's library. The secretary was a man of culture and also a Cambridge man, and while they waited for the King, he and Moore chatted about Cambridge. The King entered. He invited Moore to sit down and they talked for a while. Then the King presented the medal to

Moore. After some further conversation the King arose, indicating that the audience was at an end. They shook hands and Moore was taken back to the gates of the palace. He reentered the cab and, leaning over excitedly, said to Mrs. Moore: "Do you know that the King had never heard of *Wittgenstein!*"

This exclamation of Moore's illustrates not only his naïveté, but also his complete preoccupation with philosophy. Here is philosophy, the most exciting thing in the world; here is Wittgenstein, the most exciting figure in philosophy; and here is the King, who had not even heard of Wittgenstein!

Finally, Moore had an acute and energetic mind. He could hold together all of the strands of a long, complex, and subtle discussion. As he pushed deeper and deeper into a topic he would always know what the road behind had been, how he had got to the place he was in the argument.

Thus the qualities that contributed to Moore's philosophical eminence (and by eminence I do not mean fame, but rather the quality of being first-rate) were, I think, these: complete modesty and simplicity, saving him from the dangers of jargon and pomposity; thorough absorption in philosophy, which he found endlessly exciting; strong mental powers; and a pure integrity that accounted for his solidity and his passion for clarity. These were the primary ingredients in the nature of this remarkable philosopher.

II

Let us turn now to Moore's philosophical work. He made interesting contributions on many topics: perception, knowledge, facts and propositions, the reality of time, hedonism, idealism, universals and particulars; whether goodness is a quality, whether existence is a predicate; the proof of an external world, the nature of philosophical analysis: these are some of the topics on which Moore wrote. But as I reflect on his writings, his lectures, and his oral discussions, the thing that stands out most prominently for me is his so-called "Defence of Common Sense." I suspect that if Moore is remembered in the history of philosophy it will be because of this theme embedded in his philosophical thought. It was not there merely as an implicit assumption. He made it an explicit principle of his philosophy, so much so that in 1925 when he published an essay intended to describe his philosophical position he actually entitled it "A Defence of Common Sense."

Now what did Moore mean by "Common Sense" and what is its importance in relation to philosophy? Writing in 1910, Moore said the following: "There are, it seems to me, certain views about the nature of the Universe, which are held, now-a-days, by almost everybody. They are so universally held that they may, I think, fairly be called the views of Common Sense." [4] He goes on to say: "It seems to me that what is most amazing and most interesting about the views of many philosophers is the way in which they go beyond or positively contradict the views of Common Sense."

He proceeds to mention some of these "views of Common Sense." For example: "We certainly believe that there are in the Universe enormous numbers of material objects, of one kind or another. We know, for instance, that there are upon the surface of the earth, besides our own bodies, the bodies of millions of other men; we know that there are the bodies of millions of other animals; millions of plants too; and, besides all these, an even greater number of inanimate objects—mountains, and all the stones upon them, grains of sand, different sorts of minerals and soils, all the drops of water in rivers and in the sea, and moreover ever so many different objects manufactured by men; houses and chairs and tables and railway engines, etc., etc." [5] "All this we now believe about the material Universe," he says; "It is surely Common Sense to believe it all." Another "Common Sense belief" is this: "We believe that we men, besides having bodies, also have minds." [6] And another belief of Common Sense is that we *know* all of the things that have just been mentioned. [7]

In his essay "A Defence of Common Sense," published fifteen years later, [8] Moore put down another list of "Common Sense beliefs." Among the sentences on this list are the following: "I am a human being"; "There exists at present a living human

---

[4] G. E. Moore, *Some Main Problems of Philosophy* (New York: The Macmillan Company, 1953), p. 2.

[5] *Ibid.*, pp. 2-3.   [6] *Ibid.*, p. 4.   [7] *Ibid.*, p. 12.

[8] Republished in *Philosophical Papers*.

body, which is my body"; "This body was born at a certain time in the past, and has existed continuously ever since." He declares that each of us *knows* these things to be true of himself, and that it would be "the height of absurdity" for any philosopher "to speak with contempt" of these Common Sense beliefs.

It might be useful to stop for a moment to examine this phrase "common sense." To me it sounds odd to speak of "a common sense belief," whereas the phrases "common belief" and "common knowledge" are quite familiar. It is, for example, a common belief that colds can be transmitted from one person to another. I doubt that we should call it a "common sense belief" or a "common sense view." How do we actually use this expression "common sense"? I can imagine one person saying to another: "If you want so very much to enter the Civil Service, then it is common sense that you have to start preparing yourself for the examination." "It is common sense" means here "It is the obvious conclusion." I am inclined to think that this is how we commonly use the phrase "common sense." Something falls under that heading if it is an obvious conclusion from information at hand. In this common use of "common sense," common sense has nothing to do with views about the universe, nor with the so-called "belief" that there are enormous numbers of material objects in the world. We say of one person that he is lacking in common sense, and of another that he has lots of common sense. What this means is that the former has a tendency to arrive at conclusions which ignore obvious facts, and that the latter does not have this tendency. In general, the expression "lacking in common sense" means "lacking in good judgment." Thomas Reid, the eighteenth-century Scotsman, who, like Moore, made "an appeal to common sense" a foundation of his philosophical work, connected "common sense" quite explicitly with good judgment:

A man of sense is a man of judgment. Good sense is good judgment. Nonsense is what is evidently contrary to right judgment. Common sense is that degree of judgment which is common to men with whom we can converse and transact business.[9]

---

[9] *Reid's Essays on the Intellectual Powers of Man*, A. D. Woozley, ed. (New York: The Macmillan Company, 1941), pp. 330-331.

A man of common sense is a *sensible* man—one who makes sensible judgments. He is not to be identified as a man who holds a certain set of *views*—about the world or anything else.

Suppose that a mother has a daughter, sixteen years of age, who takes singing lessons and is said by her teacher and others to have a pretty voice. Suppose this lady tries to persuade her husband to sell his prosperous business in the small town where they live and move to New York City, so that their daughter can study in a famous school of music. Her idea is that after six months of training, during which time they will live on savings, their daughter will become an opera and concert singer, and support them for the rest of their lives. This mother's proposal could be said to be extravagant and unrealistic on a number of counts. It could also be said to show a complete lack of common sense. Her husband, in arguing against this proposal and pointing out various objections, is showing common sense. He takes a common sense view of the matter. This is a faithful example of the actual use of the expression "a common sense view" whereas to say that it is "a common sense view" that there are an enormous number of material objects in the universe is to violate the ordinary use of the expression "common sense." It is not a matter of common sense at all. Common sense has nothing to do with it.

III

Since, as I hold, the examples that Moore gives of alleged "common sense views of the world" actually are not examples of common sense, let us ask whether they are "common beliefs," or "widespread beliefs," or "universal beliefs," or "things which we all commonly assume to be true," as Moore says they are. There is one item on Moore's list of which some, at least, of the above things are true: namely, the belief that "the sun and moon and the visible stars are great masses of matter, most of them many times larger than the earth." [10] This might even be said to be common knowledge, whereas at one time it was not. But consider the following examples: "There are enormous numbers of material objects"; "Acts of consciousness are quite definitely

[10] *Some Main Problems,* p. 3.

attached in a particular way to some material objects";[11] "Our acts of consciousness . . . occur *in the same places* in which our bodies are";[12] "There exists at present a living human body, which is my body"; "I am a human being." Is it right to say that nearly everyone assumes these things to be true, and even knows them to be true?

If you stop to think about the things on this list you will begin to see that all of them are queer sentences. Their queerness is brought out if we ask of each of them a question that Wittgenstein taught us to ask, namely, "What is supposed to be the *use* of the sentence?" When would you seriously say it to someone? What would the circumstances be? What would be the purpose of saying it? Would it be to give someone information, or to admonish or warn him, or to remind him of something, or to teach him the meaning of a word, or what?

Let us try out this kind of inquiry with the sentence "I am a human being." When would you say this to someone or to yourself? If you think about it a bit, certain ways in which this sentence might be used will occur to you: *a*. The first example that I think of is this: Suppose we lived in a region where there were beings who looked like bears but who talked our language, so that if you heard someone talking in the next room, you often could not tell whether it was a human being or a bear. If I were to knock on someone's door he might ask me through the door, "Are you a bear?" and I could reply, "I am a human being." *b*. Second example: A child might ask me, "What is a human being?" and I could reply, "I am a human being; you are a human being; the cat there is not a human being; the baby is a human being, but the dog is not." Here I should be trying to teach him, by examples, to master the range of application of the expression "human being." *c*. Third example: Suppose that someone had been falsely informed of my death. When I appear before him he exclaims in terror, "Are you a ghost?" I reply: "I am a human being."

Those are three sorts of cases in which you could seriously say the sentence "I am a human being" and if we tried we could

[11] *Ibid.*, p. 6.
[12] *Ibid.*

think of still others. Now when Moore wrote and spoke the sentence "I am a human being," in which of these circumstances was he using it? In none of them, of course. Did he believe that someone somewhere supposed he might be a bear? No. Was he trying to teach someone the application of the expression "human being"? No.

There is an inclination to think that if anyone were to utter the sentence "I am a human being," he would be stating an *obvious fact*. But there is something wrong with this. I should not know whether he was stating an obvious fact until I knew how he was using the sentence: to what question he was addressing himself or what doubt he was trying to remove. I do not think this is overly sophisticated. If some stranger should come up to me and say, "I am a human being," I should probably be at a loss as to what he meant. (Is he complaining of unfair treatment?) I should not know whether or not he was stating an obvious fact.

I am not holding, of course, that the sentence "I am a human being" is meaningless. On the contrary, it is a sentence for which we can, without much effort, imagine various contexts of use. But if I hear or see that sentence and it is not clear to me what the context of its use is, then it is not clear to me what the person meant by that sentence on that occasion. It would be useless for him to reply, "I meant that I am a human being!" That would be repeating the sentence without explaining what he meant by it.

One is strongly tempted to make something like the following reply: "There is a certain assertion that a person normally makes when he speaks or writes the sentence 'I am a human being.' The sentence is ordinarily used to make that assertion. You may not know what the speaker's *purpose* is (Moore's, for example) in making the assertion in question. But you know that Moore used the sentence in its *ordinary sense* to make the assertion that it is normally used to make."

Let us leave aside the cases in which one would not have made *any* assertion at all by saying that sentence. (For example, alone in my study, thinking about the "Defence of Common Sense," I say aloud, "I am a human being." Have I made an assertion?)

Why should we suppose that when the sentence is used to make an assertion, there is some *one and the same* assertion that is "normally" made? How does one tell whether it is the same assertion that is made in different cases? Does not the particular doubt, the particular question at issue, have some bearing on this? In one of our examples the speaker *informed* someone that he was *not a bear;* in another, that he was *not a ghost;* in another, that he is *called* "a human being" (in contrast to a dog or a cat). If these differences in what is in doubt, in what comparisons are made, in what information is given, do not make for differences in *what is asserted,* then it will have no definite meaning to speak of one assertion as being "different" or the "same" as another one.

When Moore says "I am a human being," I do not wish to agree or to disagree. It is not clear to me what he is saying. Of course he is addressing himself to philosophers, and it would be reasonable to assume that his utterance is relevant to some philosophical view. But what view? Could it be some thesis of Cartesian philosophy? But which one? What philosophical thesis has the implication that Moore is not a human being? When Moore's sentence is, instead, "I *know* I am a human being," it is much easier to supply philosophical surroundings for it.

My general point is that not only does the famous "Defence of Common Sense" have no clear relationship to *common sense* but, furthermore, if we go through Moore's list of so-called "Common Sense views" it is far from clear, with regard to some at least, either what assertions he was making or that he was making any at all.

IV

So far I have not succeeded in explaining why the "Defence of Common Sense" was an important development in philosophy. I do not doubt that it was. I was strongly influenced by it, and so were many others. *Prima facie* it is not easy to understand what philosophical interest it has. Of what possible interest could it be to remind us that it is a universal or widespread belief that the sun is many times larger than the earth? Moore's list of "common sense views" is an odd assortment. Some of the items in it, like the one just mentioned, are genuine common beliefs—but they have no apparent philosophical relevance. Some, like "I am a human being," cannot be said to express common beliefs, nor am I certain that they have any philosophical relevance.

But there are some that are of real philosophical interest, although they are neither "common sense views" nor "common beliefs." An example in this category is the following statement from "A Defence of Common Sense":

> I have often perceived both my own body and other things which formed part of its environment, including other human bodies; I have not only perceived things of this kind, but have also observed facts about them, such as, for instance, the fact which I am now observing, that that mantel-piece is at present nearer to my body than that book-case.[13]

Considering that some philosophers have said that it is impossible for a person to perceive a material thing, this statement of Moore's has philosophical interest. In another work Moore discusses what he calls "judgments of perception," and his examples are seeing an inkstand, or a door, or a finger. He makes this remark:

> Some people may no doubt think that it is very unphilosophical in me to say that we ever can perceive such things as these. But it seems to me that we do, in ordinary life, constantly talk of seeing such things, and that, when we do so, we are neither using language incorrectly, nor making any mistake about the facts—supposing something to occur which never does in fact occur. The truth seems to me to be that we are using the term "perceive" in a way which is both perfectly correct and expresses a kind of thing which constantly does occur. . . . I am not, therefore, afraid to say that I do now perceive that that is a door, and that that is a finger.[14]

In still another work Moore was commenting on a feature of Hume's philosophy, which has the consequence that no person can ever know of the existence of any material thing. He says:

> If Hume's principles are true, then, I have admitted, I do *not* know *now* that this pencil—the material object—exists. If, therefore, I am to prove that I *do* know that this pencil exists, I must prove, somehow, that Hume's principles, one or both of them, are *not* true. In what sort of way, by what sort of argument, can I prove this?

[13] *Philosophical Papers,* p. 33.
[14] *Philosophical Studies* (New York: Harcourt, Brace & World, Inc., 1922), pp. 226-227.

It seems to me that, in fact, there really is no stronger and better argument than the following. I *do* know that this pencil exists; I could not know this, if Hume's principles were true; *therefore,* Hume's principles, one or both of them, are false. I think this argument really is as strong and good a one as any that could be used; and I think it really is conclusive.[15]

Here there appears to be some sort of issue joined between Moore and some other philosophers. But I expect that some will be puzzled as to how anyone in his right mind can *deny* that we see doors and know that pencils exist. Others, who feel no difficulty about this, will be perplexed as to how Moore could think of himself as *disproving* these views; for all he does is to declare that he *does* see a door and does know that there is a pencil in front of him; so he appears to be begging the question. I should like to say something on both of these points.

With regard to the first point, anyone who begins to study problems in the philosophy of perception will soon come upon a number of arguments which appear to prove that it is impossible to see a material thing. For example, H. A. Prichard, who held a chair at Oxford and wrote and lectured from about 1910 to 1940, produced various arguments to prove that it is impossible to see bodies. Prichard accepted these arguments, and I expect he had many followers. Speaking of the "view" that we do see such things as chairs, tables, and boats going downstream, he remarked: "It need hardly be said that this view, much as we should all like to be able to vindicate it, will not stand examination." [16] He said that the "consideration of any so-called illusion of sight . . . is enough to destroy this view." [17]

I will not try to give a detailed account of how he thought that the occurrence of "illusions of sight" proves that we do not see bodies, but the gist of the argument is something like this: If you are to really see a body then "the whole fact of seeing must include the thing seen," [18] and furthermore the body cannot "look other than what it is." [19] "A body, if it be really seen and seen along with other bodies, can only present to us just

---

[15] *Some Main Problems,* pp. 119-120.
[16] *Knowledge and Perception* (New York: Oxford University Press, 1950), p. 53.
[17] *Ibid.*   [18] *Ibid.,* p. 53.   [19] *Ibid.,* p. 54.

that appearance which its relations to the other bodies really require."[20] For example, if a body were really seen it could not "present the appearance which a body similar but reversed as regards right and left can present," as happens when we "see" something in a mirror.[21] When it seems to us that we see a man moving in front of us (we are looking in a mirror), if "that state, activity, or process which really only seems to us to be seeing a man move across in front of us had an intrinsic character of its own, in virtue of which it was only *like*, without *being*, seeing a man move thus, then that character ought to be recognizable at the time, in an act of self-consciousness, and if so it need not be true, as in fact it always is, that we can still have the illusion even though we are not taken in by it."[22] "If the state had a character other than being just like seeing a man move across, we ought to be able while in this state to recognize that it has this character, and if we did we should no longer have the illusion."[23] There is no difference in "intrinsic character," Prichard is saying, between what is ordinarily *called* seeing a body and the cases in which we are under an illusion of seeing a body. If there is no difference in "intrinsic character" between two "states," then if one of them is not seeing a body neither is the other. "No one doubts that in certain cases we have or are under an illusion, and all I have been doing is to contend that all so-called seeing involves an illusion just as much as that so-called seeing which everyone admits to involve an illusion."[24]

The argument may be briefly recapitulated as follows: Suppose there are two "states," or "states of mind,"[25] A and B. They are states of either seeing or seeming to see a man in front of us. When state A occurs there actually is a man in front of us; state B is an illusion produced by a mirror. States A and B have the *same intrinsic character*—that is, if we considered state B "in itself we could not say that it was not a state of seeing" a man in front of us.[26] State A, therefore, which is ordinarily *called* "seeing a man in front of us" is not actually seeing a man in front of us, any more than is the admittedly illusory state B.

The reasoning is undoubtedly obscure; but at the same time it

---

[20] *Ibid.*, p. 53.   [21] *Ibid.*   [22] *Ibid.*, p. 50.   [23] *Ibid.*   [24] *Ibid.*
[25] *Ibid.*, p. 49.   [26] *Ibid.*

is extremely persuasive, and it is extremely difficult to put one's finger on any serious error in it. It is one of a number of attractive arguments that Prichard and others have used to prove, to the satisfaction of many philosophers, that we do not see bodies, and that what we really see are "sense-data" or "sensations." Those arguments and that conclusion, in one form or another, dominated the philosophy of perception for centuries. If you consider Moore's remark, "I am not . . . afraid to say that I do now perceive that that is a door and that that is a finger," and view it against this background of the history of philosophy, you will appreciate it as being a bold line to take.

This brings us to the second point, namely, what does Moore *achieve* by insisting that he does see material things? Is not this merely a stubborn refusal to accept the various arguments against it? Distinguished philosophers have given ingenious and persuasive proofs that we do not see material things. Moore says that we do, and that the proofs are wrong. But he does not say *how* they are wrong; so is he not begging the question?

It must be admitted that Moore never gave a satisfactory account of what he was doing; and so we ourselves must supply some explanation of this particular feature of the so-called "defence of common sense," if we are to attribute any cogency to it. In the following I will attempt an explanation.

Prichard and the others must admit that we use such sentences as "See my finger," "Now you see the dog," "Now you don't see him," every day of our lives; and furthermore that we are taught to use such sentences and teach their use to others. We are taught and do teach that the correct way to speak, in certain circumstances, is to say "I see the dog," and in other circumstances to say "I don't see him now," and in still other circumstances to say "I think I see him," and so on. Undoubtedly Prichard used such forms of speech every day (and taught them to his children, if he had any) and would have acknowledged in various ways in practical life that they are correct forms of speech.

His philosophical position, however, stands in opposition to this obvious fact. I believe that Prichard was contending that we *cannot* see bodies, not merely that we do not. He says: "I, of course, take it for granted that if it can be shown in certain cases that what we see cannot be a body, the same thing must be true of all cases." [27] He implies, I believe, that if there is just *one* case in which someone is under the illusion of seeing a certain body in front of him then no one ever sees a body. As we noted, he offers the example of seeing something in a mirror as an instance of illusion.[28] I do not believe, however, that Prichard's real point could have been that visual illusions do occur *in point of fact*. Suppose that they should cease to occur (e.g., there are no more mirrors or reflecting surfaces): would Prichard be willing to admit then that we see bodies? Obviously not. The "state" that we call "seeing a body" would not have changed its "intrinsic character" and could not do so. Visual illusions would be logically possible, and this would be enough to prove that we do not see bodies. Prichard says: "A body, if it be really seen and seen along with other bodies, can only present to us just that appearance which its relations to the other bodies really require." [29] It cannot cease to be a logical possibility that a body should present an appearance "different from what its relations to the other bodies really require." Prichard is holding that if we could see bodies then visual illusions could not occur. The actual occurrence of illusions is not necessary for his position. The logical possibility of illusions suffices. The logical possibility of visual illusions is an a priori truth. When Prichard's view is drawn out in the only direction it can go, it turns out to be the claim that it is an a priori truth that we cannot see bodies. He is holding that the very notion of *seeing a body* is absurd. It contains a requirement that *could not* be satisfied, namely, that visual illusion should be logically impossible. In order for this requirement to be satisfied the concept of seeing a body would have to be identical with the concept of seeing an after-image —which is an impossibility of an a priori sort.[30] Prichard is holding that there is a conceptual absurdity in saying such a thing

---

[27] *Ibid.*, p. 54.

[28] J. L. Austin justly remarks that, normally, seeing something in a mirror is *not* an illusion (*Sense and Sensibilia* [New York: Oxford University Press, 1962], p. 26).

[29] Prichard, *Knowledge and Perception*, p. 53.

[30] The two concepts are compared in "Direct Perception," pp. 85-87.

as "I see a raccoon in your corn patch," or in making *any* affirmative statement expressed by a sentence whose main verb is some form of the verb "see," used in a visual sense and taking for its object the name of a body.

If those sentences embodied some conceptual absurdity then they would not have a correct use. They could never express true statements. But those sentences do have a correct use. A child is taught that he is wrong when he says "I see pussy cat" while he is looking the wrong way, but that he is right when his eyes are following the cat's movements. If the sentence involved a conceptual absurdity he would never be right and he would not be told that he was. The language has the use that we give it.

To come back to Moore: When he said, against the skeptics, such a thing as "I now see that door," it did not matter whether he was actually looking at a *door*. He did not have to produce an example of a *true* perceptual statement. In order to refute the claim that there is an absurdity in the concept of seeing a body, Moore did not have to present a *paradigm* of seeing a body, as I once thought.[31] He only had to remind his listeners and readers that the sentence "I see a door over there" has a correct use and, therefore, *can* express a true statement. On one famous occasion Moore was actually in error in his example. This delighted his skeptical opponents in the audience. On my view he was right even when he was wrong.

I believe that Moore himself was confused about what he was doing, as is often so when one makes a philosophical advance. He always *tried* to present his audiences with examples of *true* perceptual statements. And he made a point of remarking that sentences such as "I have often seen pennies" or "I have often seen the moon" "are correct ways of expressing propositions which are true. I, personally, have in fact often seen pennies and often seen the moon, and so have many other people." [32] Why

---

[31] I misunderstood this point when I first wrote on Moore. In "Moore and Ordinary Language," I said that Moore's replies to various skeptical assertions consist in presenting *paradigms* of knowing something for certain, seeing bodies, and so on. *The Philosophy of G. E. Moore*, p. 354.

[32] "Visual Sense-Data," *British Philosophy in the Mid-Century*, C. A. Mace, ed. (New York: The Macmillan Company, 1957), p. 205.

does he have this interest in giving examples of perceptual statements which are *true,* if it is irrelevant whether they are true? Part of the explanation (perhaps all of it) is Moore's mistaken idea that when he is dealing with a proposition put forward by a philosophical skeptic he is dealing with an *empirical* proposition. That Moore has this idea is shown, for one thing, by his famous "proof" of the existence of external things.[33] In "A Reply to My Critics," he states explicitly that a philosopher who holds that there are no external objects is "making a false empirical statement." [34] Undoubtedly he would be inclined to say the same thing about Prichard's proposition that we do not see bodies, or about the common philosophical view that no one has absolutely certain knowledge of any empirical fact. But the examination of a typical argument for the latter view makes it plain that what is being held is that it is *logically* impossible for anyone to know with certainty the truth of any empirical statement.[35] Our brief study of Prichard's claim shows that, on his view, we could not see bodies unless something which is a logical possibility (visual illusion) were to become a logical impossibility—which is itself a logical impossibility. In replying to Prichard, therefore, it is both unnecessary and misleading for Moore to assert that he has often seen the moon. It does not matter whether he has. What is necessary and sufficient, and also puts the view he is attacking in its true light, is to point out that the sentence "I see the moon" has a correct use. It is surprising that anyone should think it has not: but philosophical reasoning has a peculiar power to blind one to the obvious.

It has been claimed that in previous writings I identified Moore's "appeal to common sense" with his "appeal to ordinary language," and that this is a mistake because they are different.[36]

---

[33] "Proof of an External World," *Philosophical Papers,* pp. 145-146.

[34] *The Philosophy of G. E. Moore,* p. 672.

[35] See "The Verification Argument," especially p. 56.

[36] Alan R. White, *G. E. Moore* (Oxford: Basil Blackwell & Mott, 1958): see Chapters 1-3. V. C. Chappell has an interesting discussion of various interpretations of Moore's "defence of common sense" in his article "Malcolm on Moore" (*Mind,* LXX, No. 279, July 1961, 417-425). Chappell mentions two interpretations that differ from the one put forward here. One is ascribed to Moore himself. Its principal feature is the assertion that Moore's

I want to insist, however, that if Moore's so-called "defence of common sense" has any cogency, then it is not really about *common sense* or *common beliefs*, for neither of these things is relevant to the philosophical issues in which Moore is involved. I take the philosophers with whom he is engaged to be asserting that the notion of seeing a body (or of having absolutely certain knowledge of an empirical truth, and so on) contains a logical absurdity. The actual efficacy of Moore's reply, his misnamed "defence of common sense," consists in reminding us that there is a proper use for sentences like "I see the broom under the bed" or "It is known for certain that he drowned in the lake." As Moore remarks, when we say such things we are not "using language incorrectly." [37] We should be *if* those sentences did embody some logical absurdity. The philosophical positions that Moore opposes can, therefore, be seen to be false *in advance* of an examination of the arguments adduced in support of them. We can know that something is wrong with Prichard's reasoning before we study it.

We are able to see now why Moore was not begging the question against Prichard: for when we understand the latter's position we realize that he was contending for something that is, beyond question, false. That is just the point that Moore made. He was not begging the question because the point he made (without fully realizing it) was that it is *not even a question* whether those sentences of ordinary language have a correct use.

Here there comes to light a genuine connection with common sense. Prichard showed a lack of common sense, in the ordinary meaning of the words. He was led by persuasive reasoning into losing sight of the obvious fact that it is correct to speak of seeing bodies. He was blind to something that was right before his

opponents are maintaining empirical theses. But in order to find out what kind of thesis a philosopher is maintaining, we have to consider the kind of support he offers for it. Prichard's reasoning, for example, clearly implies that his thesis is nonempirical. The other interpretation, put forward by A. Ambrose and M. Lazerowitz in their essays in *The Philosophy of G. E. Moore*, contains the claim that Moore's opponents are essentially making "verbal recommendations." But there is no natural sense of "recommend" in which Prichard, for example, can be said to have *recommended* that we should no longer *speak* of seeing bodies.

[37] *Philosophical Studies*, p. 226.

eyes. In contrast, Moore resisted that temptation. In tenaciously keeping sight of the obvious he showed common sense.[38] And also he "appealed to common sense," in the common meaning of the words, when he reminded other philosophers of the plain facts of language.

Why should we not say that what Prichard was blind to was the fact that we do see bodies? Because, as I tried to show, his denial that we see bodies is really the claim that it is logically impossible to see bodies. Moore's assertion that we do see the moon and pennies and doors can be taken as a *reply* to Prichard only if it is understood as the assertion that there is no logical absurdity in the notion of seeing a body. But is it a "common sense view" or a "common belief" that it is logically possible to see bodies? No. It is the kind of observation that only a philosopher makes or understands.

V

I believe that Moore's misnamed "defence of common sense" was a philosophical step of first importance. Its effect is to alter one's conception of the nature of philosophy and thereby to change one's philosophical practice. Clearly Prichard would have looked at what he was doing in an entirely different way had he seen the soundness of Moore's position. He would have realized that he could not possibly prove that it is impossible to see bodies! He might have been unable to detect anything wrong in his reasoning. But he would have known that *something* was wrong in it. His attitude toward his own philosophical work would have been different.

Wittgenstein says: "A philosophical problem has the form: 'I don't know my way about.'"[39] That is: "I am confused"; "I

---

[38] I owe this observation to Professor G. H. von Wright. (I would not be thought to be extolling common sense as the supreme virtue of a philosopher. Many first-rate contributions to philosophy have been made by thinkers who developed their ideas in disregard of absurd consequences. They would rather be rigorous than right. As Austin remarks: "In philosophy, there are many mistakes that it is no disgrace to have made: to make a first-water, ground-floor mistake, so far from being easy, takes one [*one*] form of philosophical genius." J. L. Austin, *Philosophical Papers*, J. O. Urmson and G. J. Warnock, eds. [New York: Oxford University Press, 1961], p. 153.)

[39] Ludwig Wittgenstein, *Philosophical Investigations*, tr. G. E. M. Anscombe (New York: The Macmillan Company, 1953), sec. 123.

am in a muddle." But I think a philosophical problem can take this form only if one sees the soundness of Moore's defence of ordinary language. One is tempted to hold that certain ordinary expressions *cannot* have a correct use: at the same time one realizes that of course they *do*. Then one knows that one is in a muddle.

Prichard did not have that attitude toward this view of his about seeing. If that had been his attitude he would have thought: "Here I am inclined to hold something absurdly false, namely, that we cannot see bodies. Where in my thinking do I go *wrong*?" Instead, he said that the "common view" that we see bodies "will not stand examination." He really thought that our ordinary language of perception needs to be corrected.

Wittgenstein says: "Philosophy may in no way interfere with the actual use of language; it can in the end only describe it." [40] This conception of philosophy is entirely different from Prichard's. He thought that philosophy *could* "interfere with the actual use of language." To think of philosophy as Prichard did is enormously different from thinking of a philosophical problem as a confusion. Philosophy has a different *feel* in the two conceptions, and the actual steps one will take in conducting one's philosophical inquiry will be different.

I believe that in order to grasp Wittgenstein's idea that a philosophical problem is essentially a confusion in our thinking, and that philosophical work cannot interfere with the actual use of language but must "leave everything as it is" (that is, leave our actual use of language as it is, not leave everything in philosophy as it is)—in order to grasp this idea, one must understand what is right in Moore's defence of ordinary language. The latter was an advance in philosophy because it brought us nearer to a true understanding of philosophy itself.

[40] *Ibid.*, sec. 124.

Three Lectures on Memory

Memory and the Past

I begin by quoting some well-known remarks by Russell in *The Analysis of Mind:*

In investigating memory-beliefs, there are certain points which must be borne in mind. In the first place, everything constituting a memory-belief is happening now, not in that past time to which the belief is said to refer. It is not logically necessary to the existence of a memory-belief that the event remembered should have occurred, or even that the past should have existed at all. There is no logical impossibility in the hypothesis that the world sprang into being five minutes ago, exactly as it then was, with a population that "remembered" a wholly unreal past. There is no logically necessary connection between events at different times; therefore nothing that is happening now or will happen in the future can disprove the hypothesis that the world began five minutes ago. Hence the occurrences which are *called* knowledge of the past are logically independent of the past; they are wholly analyzable into present contents, which might, theoretically, be just what they are even if no past had existed.

I am not suggesting that the non-existence of the past should be entertained as a serious hypothesis. Like all sceptical hypotheses, it is logically tenable, but uninteresting. All that I am doing is to use its logical tenability as a help in the analysis of what occurs when we remember.[1]

---

[1] Bertrand Russell, *The Analysis of Mind* (New York: The Macmillan Company, 1921), pp. 159-160.

187

We must not be misled by Russell's remark that his "hypothesis" is not to be taken seriously. He was perfectly serious when he said that there is no logical impossibility in it, that it is "logically tenable." In later books he expresses the same thought. In *An Outline of Philosophy* he says that "there is no logical impossibility in the view that the world was created five minutes ago, complete with memories and records." [2] In *Human Knowledge* he says: "I might have come into existence a few moments ago, complete with just those recollections which I then had." [3]

Russell's belief in the logical tenability of his "hypothesis" greatly influenced his treatment of the topic of memory. A good part of the chapter on memory in *The Analysis of Mind* is presumably devoted to finding out "what occurs when we remember." If his "skeptical hypothesis" were tenable it would follow that remembering is logically independent of the past; and it would be a further consequence that there is little left for the philosophy of memory to do except to investigate what goes on in our minds when we remember. If the hypothesis were to appear untenable it would no longer seem obvious, as it did to Russell, that philosophy should be concerned with this. One would be free to think that what happens in our minds when we remember something has little if any philosophical interest.

The idea that it is logically possible that the world began five minutes ago, "complete with memories and records," is an astonishing thought partly because, as we first mull the idea over, we cannot get hold of anything which would prove that it is *not* a logical possibility. It is worth inquiring whether this can be done. What I wish to examine at first is not the question of whether it is logically possible that the world began five minutes ago, but the question of whether it is logically possible that the world began five minutes ago "complete with memories of an unreal past."

To begin with one might think it is self-contradictory to speak of *remembering incorrectly,* and if this were so the hypothesis would be self-contradictory. A. J. Ayer says that "the verb 'to remember,' like the verb 'to know,' is used in such a way that if

[2] *An Outline of Philosophy* (New York: W. W. Norton & Company, Inc., 1927), p. 7.

[3] *Human Knowledge* (New York: Simon and Schuster, Inc., 1948), p. 228.

something is remembered it follows that it was so. To speak of remembering what never happened would be self-contradictory." [4] Is this so? Let us look into the matter of usage.

The verb "remember" occurs in various locutions. One of these is the phrase "to remember that so-and-so." This is normally so used that it is improper to say such a thing as "He remembers that so-and-so happened although it didn't happen." We have the authority of G. E. Moore for this.[5] But I want to prove the point by means of an example for which I am indebted to Jaakko Hintikka. Suppose someone was taught that Columbus discovered America in 1392. Later he is asked "When did Columbus discover America?" and he answers "1392." Can we say he *remembers* that America was discovered in 1392? Of course not, no more than we can say that he *knows* it was. If he had been taught that the date was 1492, and if when asked for the date he had answered "1492," it would have been right to say, "He remembers that 1492 is the date that Columbus discovered America." In both cases he was taught something and in both cases he remembers what he was taught. The sole difference between the two cases is that the date is wrong in one and right in the other. The example provides a proof that one cannot remember that *p* when *p* is false. Sometimes we do say such a thing as "He *remembers* that there were four men in the room but actually there were only three." But this is carelessness or possibly sarcasm. It is exactly as wrong to speak this way as to say "He *knows* that there were four men but actually there were only three."

The verb "remember" is used in other locutions. We say "As he remembers the dinner there was a lady seated on his left," or "That is how he remembers it," or "The way he remembers it is so-and-so." These locutions make it possible to speak of incorrect memory. Even if I know that at the dinner there was a gentleman, not a lady, on his left, I can still say, "That is how he remembers it—that there was a lady on his left." If someone claims to remember that *p*, and I wish to refer to his claim with-

[4] *The Problem of Knowledge* (London: Macmillan & Co., Inc., 1956), p. 168.
[5] See his *Philosophical Papers* (New York: The Macmillan Company, 1959), p. 217.

out committing myself to accepting p as true, I can say, "As he remembers it, p," "According to his memory of the occasion, p," and so on. But if I say "He remembers that p," then I have committed myself: I have myself implied that I believe it is true that p, just as I have when I say "He knows that p."

Thus it is not true without qualification, that "If something is remembered it follows that it was so." This holds for remembering *that* so-and-so, but not for those other locutions. If as Jones remembers it, p, and p is false, then Jones' memory is incorrect.

Let us look more closely at this notion of incorrect memory. If a man told us that once he lunched with Winston Churchill, and then it turned out that it was breakfast, not lunch, his memory was incorrect. He remembered the meal as lunch—here his memory was wrong. If the occasion had been a cocktail party then his memory of it as a meal was wrong. If he had never met Churchill at all, and had indeed never encountered any of the great ones of this world, and always took meals with his wife only, then there seems to be *no respect* in which his alleged memory of having lunched with the Prime Minister is *incorrect*. And also there is no respect in which it is correct.

One is reluctant to speak in this case of his "memory" of having lunched with the Prime Minister, and would prefer to speak of his "alleged" or "so-called" memory, or of his "claim" to remember so-and-so. Why is this? I believe it is because incorrect or erroneous memory is possible only in a context of correct memory. If I remember a dinner party which occurred in such and such a place, at such and such a time, attended by these persons and those persons, then there is room for some of my recollections of the occasion to be incorrect—for example, that there was a lady seated on my left. But if my belief about the supposed past incident was completely false—no social occasion of even approximately that description had occurred—one could not say that my memory was incorrect or erroneous. Or rather: you could say it, but you would not mean that I remembered the occasion, although incorrectly. You would mean that it was not memory at all. One could call it a "delusion of memory" or, a "delusive memory." But a memory which is totally delusive, as in the example, is not a memory. It stands to an erroneous memory as a counterfeit diamond stands to an imperfect diamond.

The latter is a diamond, the other not. A totally delusive memory is no more a memory than a fictitious occurrence is something that happened, or no more than a painted fire is a fire. This is not quibbling. A painted fire does not have the important properties of fire and a totally delusive memory does not have the important properties of memory. Nothing could be more unsound, therefore, than to base one's philosophical treatment of memory on the notion of a total delusion of memory, as Russell does.

Two of the chief properties of memory are *present knowledge* and *previous knowledge* of what is remembered. In the third lecture I present an analysis of one form of memory in terms of knowledge. Here I will offer the following brief considerations. Memory can be divided into correct and incorrect memory. It is pretty evident that correct memory of something involves both present and previous knowledge of it. It would be self-contradictory to say of someone that he *correctly remembers* the date of the battle of Austerlitz, but to add either that he *does not know* its date, or that *he did not know its date at any time prior* to his remembering it.

I think that incorrect memory of something involves correct memory of something and, therefore, both present and previous knowledge of the latter. Let us suppose that a man remembers the date of the battle of Austerlitz incorrectly. This can be so only if, in giving some date, he is referring to that battle. He must provide some correct information about the latter in order for it to be identified as the event whose date he purports to be giving. He must have some knowledge of it in order to be talking about *it*. And at least some part of his present knowledge of the battle of Austerlitz must be knowledge that he *previously* possessed. Otherwise it would not be a case of *remembering* its date, even incorrectly.

Thus incorrect memory of an occurrence presupposes some correct memory of it. But one may also have incorrect memory relating to an event which did not occur and which, therefore, one does not refer to by means of some correct memory of *it*. How is this to be dealt with? Different kinds of cases are possible here. Someone could point at a man in plain sight and say "I met him last week." The event he refers to is meeting-*that-*

man-last-week. His memory is wrong, let us suppose, because he and the man pointed at were in different parts of the world last week. His erroneous memory does not presuppose some correct memory of the event referred to, for it did not take place. Still, his memory might be partly correct, for it might be that he remembered meeting this man but is wrong about when it happened. Or it could be that he had never met this particular man, but had met one who could easily be mistaken for him. Correct memory would here be mixed in with incorrect memory. Another possibility would be that previously he had dreamt of meeting this man, or had hallucinated it, or had formed in some other way an erroneous impression of having met him. But if his present belief was based on a previous false impression, then the present belief would not involve an error of *memory*: the error would be in the original impression. Finally, if he had never met this man nor anyone who could be mistaken for him, and had not been under any previous erroneous impression of having met him, then if it seems to him that he remembers having met him, this would be a *delusion* of memory and not memory, not even incorrect or erroneous memory. What keeps it from being memory is that there is no element of knowledge in it.

It is interesting to observe a curious vacillation in *The Analysis of Mind* on the question of whether memory is knowledge. There is, on one hand, the thesis that memory is logically independent of the past, which entails that memory is not knowledge, since knowledge is certainly not logically independent of what is known, it being plainly self-contradictory to say, for example, "He knows that Napoleon won the Battle of Austerlitz although Napoleon actually lost it." When Russell says that occurrences of memory are "*called* knowledge of the past" he is insinuating that this is a common *error*. But elsewhere in his discussion he assumes that memory *is* knowledge, as when he says that "there can be no doubt that memory forms an indispensable part of our knowledge of the past." [6]

Let us return now to Russell's hypothesis in which the people are supposed to remember, at the first moment of their creation,

---

[6] *The Analysis of Mind*, p. 165.

"a wholly unreal past." Since what is supposed to be remembered is *wholly* unreal, the so-called memories of the past involve no knowledge of the past, which implies that they are not memories. The hypothesis, as formulated by Russell, is self-contradictory. Can we turn it into a description of what is logically possible by formulating it in another way?

II

It may be thought that it is easy to achieve a revision of the hypothesis that avoids self-contradiction. Instead of saying that the newly created people remember things that did not happen, let us say that they *think* they remember those things, or that it *seems* to them that they remember them, or that they have *delusions* of memory. Is this a logical possibility?

I believe it is not. It involves a kind of logical incoherence different from the self-contradiction previously noted, but one that goes deeper. It may help to bring this to light to consider the example of a child who is learning to speak. Let us suppose he has begun to master the use of a few verbs in the present tense indicative. By saying that he has begun to master their use, I imply that when he uses them in sentences what he says is *true*, for the most part. He says "Mama is there" when it is true, mostly, that his mother is where he points. If he is asked whether she is there when she isn't, he will usually say she isn't. If what he says is not true, it will generally be evident that he is pretending, or perhaps that he is deceived by appearances.

Let us suppose that he has not yet used the past tense forms of any verbs. But now they begin to crop up in his speech. Let us imagine that when he speaks in the past tense what he says is always or nearly always false. He says his dog "was" barking when this was not so. If he says it only when the dog is just beginning to bark, it would be plausible to think that he has not yet differentiated past and present tense: there would be some justification for thinking he *means* that the dog *is* barking. If there was not that particular regularity one could not suppose he means *that*. If there was no other regularity it would be wrong to suppose he means anything. Certainly we should have no right to say, "As he remembers it the dog was barking."

Why would it be wrong to say this? I think the answer is

that although a person can say what he remembers and what he thinks he remembers, this presupposes that he has some understanding of past tense speech. This in turn presupposes that the statements he makes with past tense sentences are mainly true. If this were not so then his sentences, even though they had past tense grammatical form, would not express statements *about the past.* It would not be *that* "language-game," but some other one, or none at all. Here we can make a comparison with chess, Wittgenstein's favorite analogy. It cannot be right to say that the members of a club who have the pastime of moving chess pieces on chess boards are playing chess unless the moves they make are mostly legal chess moves. If in their play illegal moves were the rule and not the exception, then they would not be playing chess, but some other game, or none at all. In this analogy, legal moves correspond to true statements and illegal moves to false statements about the past.

I am holding that Russell's "population" could not make false statements about past happenings unless their statements about the past were largely true. I rely, first of all, on Wittgenstein's familiar thesis that our concepts, our language-games, presuppose *agreement in judgments.* Wittgenstein asks: "Does it make sense to say that people generally agree in their judgment of colour? What would it be like for them not to? One man would say a flower was red which another called blue, and so on. But what right should we have to call these people's words 'red' and 'blue' *our* 'colour-words?' " [7] We can see that unless those people agreed almost completely with us in applying those words to things—agreed in saying that *this* is red and *that* is blue—their words would *not* be *our* color words. They would not be making color judgments.

This notion of agreement in judgments is of central importance in Wittgenstein's thought. As he says, "This consideration must . . . apply to mathematics too. If there were not complete agreement, then neither would human beings be learning the technique which we learn. It would be more or less different from ours up to the point of unrecognizability." [8] Here we are made to take

[7] Ludwig Wittgenstein, *Philosophical Investigations,* tr. G. E. M. Anscombe (New York: The Macmillan Company 1953), p. 226.
[8] *Ibid.*

note of the striking fact that there is a *normal* reaction to the explanations and examples that make up the instruction in elementary mathematics. Given a certain teaching everyone goes on in the same way. We agree that in taking such and such further steps we are doing the *same* as we were taught to do. We agree that doing *this* (not *that*) is what the rule, which we were taught, requires.

It is conceivable that someone should not have this normal reaction; conceivable that he should, as a matter of course, go on in a different way. It is even conceivable that he should be able to give a plausible explanation for saying that his way of going on is the *same* as the way he was taught, and that *our* way is *not* the same.

This is conceivable; but it does not happen, or only rarely. If this were not so, mathematics would not be possible, and the same holds for other areas of language. Agreement in judgments is "part of the framework on which the working of our language is based." [9]

The second point in support of my contention about Russell's "population" is that the concept of *truth* is bound up with the agreement in judgments that underlies our language-games. Wittgenstein puts to himself the question: "So you are saying that human agreement decides what is true and what is false?" He answers: "It is what human beings *say* that is true and false: and they agree in language." [10] In a sense, the question is answered in the affirmative. The existence of color judgments requires that there be a great many cases in which people agree that this is red and that is blue. The disagreement that there is in color judgments presupposes a background of overwhelming agreement. Furthermore, this agreement in language makes it *true* that this is red and that is blue.

The same holds for judgments about the past. People must agree, overwhelmingly, about what they have just noticed or observed, e.g., that the telephone *rang* or the lights *went out*. Otherwise they do not speak the same language. The agreement in language, which is necessary for agreement in judgments, is

[9] *Ibid.*, sec. 240.
[10] *Ibid.*, sec. 241.

an agreement about *what to say*. And this brings in *truth*.[11] In order for there to be a past tense in our language there must be a multitude of cases in which we agree that so-and-so happened; and in which it is true that so-and-so happened, because that is how we speak. We "agree in language."

We have an inclination to imagine the past as *behind* us, *out of sight,* and to think that every proposition we make about it might be false. But in imagining this we assume all along that our propositions do *refer* to the past, are genuinely propositions *about* the past. When we think out what is involved in that *reference to the past,* which we took for granted, we see that it requires that many of those propositions about the past should be true.

In opposition to this, Russell's "hypothesis" requires that the newly created people should make judgments about the past, all of which are false. What criterion would there be, then, for saying that they have a past tense in their language? An omniscient observer ought to conclude that they do not have one. The case would be similar to that of a people who apparently speak English but whose "color judgments" are always or usually false. An observer ought to conclude that, contrary to what had first been supposed, they are not making color judgments. What originally looked like that has to be interpreted in some other way. The same holds for those sentences that at first appeared to express statements about the past.

Knowing how to use the past tense cannot be completely separated from actually using it correctly, and using it correctly cannot be completely separated from making many true statements with it. From Russell's hypothesis it really follows that the people do not make statements about the past. If one of them uttered the sentence "I did so-and-so" an observer would not be

---

[11] Notice the following remark by D. M. Armstrong: "We may concede Wittgenstein the point that: 'If language is to be a means of communication there must be agreement not only in definitions but also . . . in judgments' (*Investigations,* sec. 242). But notice that Wittgenstein only speaks of *agreements* in judgments, and not that the judgments that are agreed upon must be *true*" (*Perception and the Physical World* [New York: Humanities Press and London: Routledge & Kegan Paul, Ltd., 1961], p. 168, footnote). But what would be the standard of comparison in relation to which it would have *meaning* to say that those judgments were false?

entitled to attribute to him the thought or seeming memory of having done so-and-so. If he said "I *seem to remember* doing so-and-so," that would not change matters. He cannot be saying what we should be saying if we uttered the same words. We cannot use their remarks as our criterion of their having thoughts about past events. They cannot give expression in language to seeming memories.

Nor can they express them in behavior. There is, of course, nonlinguistic behavior that expresses memory, e.g., a child buries a toy in the sand and then a little later digs it out again. Indeed, nonlinguistic memory behavior is, in a sense, more fundamental than memory language. In the beginning the latter can be taught and the understanding of it can be verified only by connecting it with the behavior of taking interest in objects, of being surprised by their disappearance, of pursuing them, searching for them, and so on. Against a background of behavior that exhibited correct memory, there could be some behavior that expressed mere seeming memory, as when the child digs in the wrong place. But as in the case of language, the exception cannot be the rule. Russell's hypothesis requires that *all* the memory behavior of the newly created people should be erroneous, as well as all of their memory statements. In that case there would be nothing in their behavior that *looked* like memory— not even like delusive memory.

Russell's people could not give expression to seeming memories either in behavior or in language. But could they not *have* seeming memories? This question may feel as if it were significant. But how could it seem to someone that he remembers something, if there was no *expression* of memory? What would be supposed to happen? Saying the words "I remember so-and-so" would be irrelevant, since Russell's hypothesis, we have argued, is incompatible with there being any language of memory. What about imagery? But imagery may also figure in daydreams and expectations. Memory-images are images that go with remembering and seeming to remember. These latter concepts require something more than imagery; and what could this "more" be, if there was neither the behavior nor the language of memory? One is tempted to supplement the imagery with feelings of "familiarity," "pastness," or "fittingness," as philosophers have done. But these inventions could not turn images into memories or make them refer to the past.

Russell's people may be compared to the dog, in Wittgenstein's example, who can believe that his master is at the door but cannot be said to believe that his master will come the day after tomorrow.[12] He can express the first belief in behavior but not the second one. The dog's inability to have beliefs about the day after tomorrow is matched by the inability of Russell's people to have beliefs about the past. They will not have the necessary language or behavior.

I conclude that it is not intelligible that they should have *thoughts* about past happenings, or the *experience* of *seeming to remember* something. They cannot, therefore, have delusive memories.

III

I wish to consider one more possible revision of the hypothesis. Instead of trying to suppose that in the first moments after their creation the people seem to remember an unreal past, let us suppose that over a considerable period of time they exhibit normal memory-reactions in daily behavior and also gradually demonstrate a mystery of language, including the past tense. In all respects they appear like ourselves. But then they begin to express, in the language which they understand, apparent memories of "a wholly unreal past." The objections I previously made will not apply here, since these people have normal memories and a language they understand. Is this new supposition "logically tenable"?

We are entitled to suppose that their apparent memories are in *agreement*: for this is what Russell envisaged when he spoke of "a population that 'remembered' a wholly unreal past." Their apparent memories will largely agree with each other and *also* with the "records." For this is how things actually are with us, and it was Russell's intention to urge that it is logically possible that *this* world, *our* world, sprang into existence five minutes ago, "complete with memories and records."

But if there was this kind of agreement then the apparent

---

[12] *Philosophical Investigations*, p. 174.

memories would be verified as true. This is what the *verification* of apparent memories *means*. There is nothing else for it to mean since, as Russell remarks, "we cannot evoke the past bodily." [13] This comment about verification does not deny that "memory is true (or false) in virtue of a past event";[14] it merely says how it is determined what the past event was. And if the apparent memories were verified it would not be intelligible to hold that, nevertheless, the past they describe may not have existed.

Thus the twice revised hypothesis destroys itself again. The supposed unreal past has turned out to be real. Russell said that his skeptical hypothesis was logically tenable but uninteresting. I believe the exact opposite has proved to be the case.

IV

I have completed what I wish to say directly about memory in relation to Russell's hypothesis. The question inevitably arises whether or not it is a logical possibility that the world sprang into being five minutes ago; so I will make a few remarks about this. I am reluctant, however, to discuss exactly this question. If the world came into existence five minutes ago then the world came into existence. But the sentence "The *world* came into existence" is one that is notoriously difficult to understand. If the world came into existence, it would seem to follow that at one time there was no world. But what could this mean? If, like Wittgenstein in the *Tractatus*, we define "the world" as "everything that is the case," then if at one time there was no world would this mean that at one time there was *nothing* that was the case? One may reasonably doubt that this makes any sense. Yet we have difficulty in giving a meaning, other than the *Tractatus* does, to the phrase "the world." So I would rather not talk about the world.

I prefer to consider a sentence that is, in a sense, easier to understand—namely, the sentence "The *earth* sprang into being five minutes ago." There seems to be no conceptual difficulty in supposing that *the earth* came into existence and that, therefore,

[13] *The Analysis of Mind*, p. 161.
[14] *Ibid.*, p. 165.

there was a time at which it did not exist. It is obvious, I think, that Russell would have held that it is logically possible that the earth came into existence five minutes ago. This would even seem to be a less radical assertion than the one about the world and one that is easier to defend.

To me it seems surprising that there is a strong tendency to assume that *of course* it is a *logical* possibility that the earth came into existence five minutes ago. Once we ask ourselves what conceivable fact could *support* the hypothesis about the earth, it will not appear obvious that it is a logical possibility. Russell remarked about his hypothesis that "nothing that is happening now or will happen in the future can disprove" it, and probably he would have agreed that nothing can *prove* it. It is worth dwelling on this. If the hypothesis were that the earth came into existence one million years ago, this could be a subject of inquiry, and it is conceivable there should be evidence, for or against it, from geology, chemistry, or radar astronomy. But nothing would count as evidence that the earth came into existence five minutes ago. Could a *document* (as Wittgenstein once asked ironically) be evidence for it; or a carbon-14 test, or someone's testimony? No one could seriously think so. The five-minute hypothesis is incompatible with the very concept of *evidence*. If a geologist thought it is a conceivable hypothesis that the earth came into existence one million years ago, he would surely imply that some discovery could be evidence for that hypothesis. A philosopher who puts forward the five-minute hypothesis does not imply this. There is "merely a difference in the quantity of time"; yet this has the consequence that one hypothesis is an empirical proposition, the other not.

Let us dwell on the point that the five-minute hypothesis is incompatible with our concept of evidence. Consider what would be implied by our "believing" that the earth and mankind have just come into existence. If one of us were to "believe" this he would have to renounce not only his previous conception of his own identity, but his entire store of common knowledge—his knowledge of natural processes; his knowledge of the normal properties of anything, so that he would no longer know what wood, water, and fire are; his knowledge of how the words of his language are used or even that he has a language; of how people live, act, and react; of what interests them and what kinds of inquiries they make; of how measurements, experiments, and arguments are conducted, and when something is held to be proved. If he thought out the consequences of this hypothesis he would realize that it is not anything he could rationally believe, because "believing" it would mean that he no longer understood anything at all. If a man were to refuse to pay his income tax on the "ground" that the earth had come into existence only five minutes before, this would literally be (and not just be called) *madness*.

To accept this "hypothesis" as true would mean the destruction of *all* our thinking. This is why we could not rationally regard *any* future disclosure as evidence for it.

Perhaps we can conceive that Martian scientists (whose technology is wonderfully advanced in the imagination of philosophers) should demonstrate their ability to produce, instantaneously, planets with complete populations. But if those scientists were to maintain that they had done this very thing with the earth five minutes ago, the least we could think would be that it was a case of mistaken identity. England is part of the earth, and by "England" we *mean* a geographical and national entity with a long history. By "Bertrand Russell" I mean a man who has written many books, lived many years, and greatly contributed to the development of logic and philosophy. No one could understand what England is and who Bertrand Russell is and also believe that they are only five minutes old. The Martians must have got their planets mixed up.

If someone admitted that nothing could serve as evidence for the five-minute hypothesis but still maintained that it is a "logical possibility," what would he mean? He might be influenced by the consideration that the sentence "The earth came into existence five minutes ago" is not self-contradictory. It is true that one cannot deduce a contradiction by means of definitions and formal manipulations. But neither can one do this with the sentence "All of our color judgments have been wrong," which nevertheless does not express a logical possibility. Nor can one do it with the sentence "I am unconscious." There is not just *one* brand of logical impossibility.

It may be that more influential than anything else is the

thought that some being could have *observed* the earth's coming into existence five minutes ago "exactly as it then was," and now *knows* this to be a fact, whereas we earth-dwellers do not know it. This thought might be accompanied by quite definite imagery. The difficulty, however, has merely been transferred to another place. What could count as evidence that some being made that observation five minutes ago? If a voice were to announce this from the heavens, in impressive circumstances, the best we could do would be to treat it as a dark saying.

Russell, following Hume, claims that "There is no logically necessary connection between events at different times." This is obviously false; keeping a promise logically implies a prior event, and so does changing one's mind or winning a bet. From this doctrine Russell draws the conclusion that nothing can disprove the five-minute hypothesis, and he may think that this proves it to be a logical possibility. It is true that no one would think that something had *disproved* it. But this is for the same reason that no one would take anything as evidence for it, namely, that we cannot rationally think of it as "possibly true."

There is a temptation to think that *for human understanding* it is inconceivable that the earth and mankind came into existence five minutes ago, but that *in itself* it is a logical possibility. If it is admitted that the truth of this proposition would be incompatible with our concepts of evidence, of proof, and of possibility, then the notion must be that there is a framework of logical possibilities which is independent of our concepts and our application of language. I believe that this attractive notion is a mere piece of imagery.

Three Forms of Memory

I wish to distinguish and compare three different *forms* of memory. These three do not exhaust the forms of memory. The verb "remember" enters into a variety of grammatical constructions and the things that are remembered are of many different kinds, e.g., faces, names, sensations, errands, the meanings of words, and so on. When the verb "remember" is used with different kinds of objects the statements we make will usually carry different implications. A familiar sense of remembering someone's *words* is to be able to repeat them: but obviously this is never a part of the meaning of remembering someone's *face*. Because of these different implications of remembering someone's words and of remembering someone's face, I call them different "forms" of memory. More than one way of classifying the forms of memory would be possible, depending on what differences of implication one wished to emphasize. It will not be possible for me to discuss all the uses of the verb "remember" that could legitimately be regarded as expressing different forms of memory. I have picked out three of them for study, partly because of their intrinsic interest, partly because of the attention they have received in the history of the philosophy of memory.

I wish to consider, first of all, that use of "remember" in which this verb is followed by a clause of the form "that *p*," where for "*p*" there may be substituted any sentence expressing a proposition. I will give this form the name of "factual memory," for the reason that if the subordinate sentence in the that-clause expresses a true proposition then the that-clause expresses a *fact*.

The verb of the subordinate sentence may be in any tense. One can remember that there *was* snow last October, that the car *is* in second gear, or that the game *will* start at 2 P.M.[1] Factual memory, therefore, is not limited in its objects to *past* things and occurrences. Also, the subordinate sentence might have no genuine tense, as when we say of a boy that he remembers that $11 \times 11 = 121$. The subordinate sentence can express a general proposition as well as a singular one, e.g., "He remembers that pigs drink milk."

In the first lecture I called attention to the fact that the natural use of the locution "He remembers that *p*" is such that it does not express a *true* proposition unless the sentence substituted for "*p*" expresses a *true* proposition: one cannot remember that *p* unless *p* is true. Let me produce another example of this. Suppose someone had visited your house previously and was invited to come again. On the second occasion he had difficulty in finding your house. He was under the impression that it was three-storied when in fact it was only two-storied. Could you say he remembered that your house was three-storied? Certainly not. If someone wondered why he had so much difficulty you could not reply: "He remembered that it was three-storied, so he looked for a three-storied house." You *could* say: "As he remembered my house it had three stories": or, "According to his memory it had three stories." These latter locutions allow for incorrect memory. In contrast, our use of the "remembering that" locution is, I believe, quite strict in not permitting incorrect memory.

Let us consider a second form of memory. The most appropriate name for it is "perceptual memory." This phrase was

[1] Many people are shocked by the suggestion that one can *remember* that a certain thing *will* happen. Aristotle said that it is impossible to "remember the future" (*De Memoria et Reminiscentia*, 449b). But it is obvious that we commonly *speak* of remembering that something will be so. ("I remember that there will be an eclipse next month.") This way of speaking is not incorrect nor is it elliptical.

coined by C. D. Broad. It will be seen, however, that I define it somewhat differently. Broad says that "perceptual memory" is "the memory of particular events, places, persons, or things." [2] He says it is the only kind of memory that "can plausibly be regarded as closely analogous to perception." [3] Some of his examples of sentences which express perceptual memory are "I remember having my hair cut last week," "I remember the tie which my friend wore yesterday," "I remember the feeling which I had when I last went to the dentist," and "I remember hearing Mr. Russell lecture."

We are likely to feel that there is an important difference in meaning between the sentences "I remember hearing Russell lecture in London" and "I remember that I heard Russell lecture in London." Apparently there is a real distinction to be got at here. Often we wish to contrast remembering something with remembering that the something occurred or existed: "I remember that there was a huge parade when war was declared, and I must have seen it, but I don't remember the parade itself," or "I remember that there was a chap named Robin in my class but I don't remember *him*." These are things we say. On the other hand, we sometimes say "Not only do I remember that there was a lad named Robin in my class but I remember *him*." When we say these things, what point are we making, what information are we giving?

The point is not always the same. But sometimes it is to announce that we cannot *see in our minds* the scenes of the parade or the face of the classmate. This meaning comes out very strongly when we say "I remember a great deal *about* him but I don't remember *him*." Remembering about him would be factual memory, e.g., remembering that he was captain of the team, that the girls liked him and that he dressed neatly. Remembering all of this and more we might still not remember him in the sense of seeing him, picturing him, "in our minds."

Similarly, one can remember a good deal about a melody (e.g., that it is in the key of G, that it is very brisk) without being

[2] *The Mind and Its Place in Nature* (New York: Harcourt, Brace & World, Inc., 1925), p. 222.
[3] *Ibid.*

able to remember the melody itself. Of course, to say that a person cannot remember a melody frequently means that he cannot play, hum or whistle it from memory. Or it may mean that he cannot recognize it when he hears it. Sometimes, however, we mean, not this, but that he cannot "hear it in his head," as we say. When a person wants to hear a melody in his head but it won't come to him, he will often express this by saying "I can't remember it": yet in the sense of recalling many facts about the melody he remembers it quite well, and he may also remember it in the sense that he would recognize it if he heard it.

A prisoner who had not seen his wife for many years might regret that he could no longer remember her face. He might remember much about her face: that her complexion was fair, her eyes blue, and so on. But he cannot *see* her face. He might give natural expression to this by saying "I don't remember her face any more." It would be a joyous experience for him to see her face in his mind. If at last this happened he could exclaim "Now I remember her face!"

Philosophers who have a reluctance to believe in mental imagery are inclined to suppose that such an exclamation could only be a sign that the prisoner suddenly *knows* something *about* his wife's face that he did not previously recall, i.e., that there has been a sudden addition to his factual memory. That this is wrong comes out when one considers that *duration* applies to memory imagery in a sense in which it does not apply to knowledge. A man trying to picture in his mind the house in which he grew up, might tell you "I saw it just for a moment, as we were talking." It need not be the case, however, that just for a moment he knew something about the house and then forgot it. An image might come and go quite often in the course of a conversation. "There! I saw him again, just for a moment," one could exclaim. Whereas it does not appear to make much sense to speak of a piece of knowledge or information as coming or going in this way. It would be senseless to say "Now I know he has a beard; now I don't"; but not to say "Now I see his beard; now I don't."

We must be warned, however, that such a sentence as "I can just see him now in the pink trousers and orange straw hat he used to wear," often does *not* mean that the speaker is, or just has been, seeing those things in his mind's eye. Often it is merely a dramatic way of expressing factual memory.

But there *is* the phenomenon of seeing someone or something in one's mind's eye, and we often express this with the verb "remember." When a person says that he remembers something in this sense, he is attributing "perceptual memory" to himself. Seeing or hearing (or smelling, if that is possible) something in one's mind or head is identical with having a "mental image" of the thing. Therefore, perceptual memory involves mental imagery. I make this part of the meaning of saying that one remembers something in this sense.[4] The imagery which is required for perceptual memory cannot be regarded, I have said, as merely a form of knowledge. Nor is it identical with a "utilization" of the knowledge of how a thing should look or sound, nor with *thinking* how it should look or sound, as Gilbert Ryle supposed.[5] Seeing something in one's mind or hearing something in one's head genuinely involves an element of what can properly be called visual or auditory experience, which I believe Ryle wished to deny.

In sentences expressing perceptual memory, the verb "remember" can be followed by a noun or pronoun, a definite or indefinite description, a participial phrase like "hearing the explosion," or a phrase starting with a possessive pronoun, e.g., "your house." It is wrong, however, to suppose that sentences of those grammatical forms always express perceptual memory. A person could say that he remembers *the* Second Law of Thermodynamics (definite description) and another person could say he too remembers *it* (pronoun); but they could hardly mean that they have a perceptual memory of it, although they might have one of a sentence that expressed that Law. Anything that is a possible object of perceptual memory must have, I think, a *definite perceptible physiognomy*. I wish to so restrict the application of "perceptual memory" that it would be incorrect to

[4] This brings out the difference between Broad's use of the phrase "perceptual memory" and my own. Broad says: "I think that the function of imitative images in perceptual memory has been greatly exaggerated" (*The Mind and Its Place in Nature*, p. 249). Certainly he intends to imply that images are not *essential* to "perceptual memory," and therefore his use of the expression is not the same as mine.

[5] *The Concept of Mind* (New York: Barnes & Noble, Inc., 1949), p. 270.

say a person had a perceptual memory of something, X, unless X was a kind of thing that could be perceived by sense.

But even when this condition is satisfied, as when one says "Yes, I remember Jones," one is commonly expressing factual rather than perceptual memory. One is not saying that one does, or even that one could, see Jones in one's mind, but instead that one remembers some facts about him, e.g., that he was formerly Dean of the Faculty and a good poker player.

Also we speak of remembering future events ("the wedding next Saturday"). And one could even see in one's mind, in anticipation, or imagination, next Saturday's wedding. Yet I am sure we shall not wish to say that one could have a perceptual memory of something before it occurred. We shall wish to say that one can have a perceptual memory of something only if one *previously* perceived it. (What we want to hold, I believe, is that perceptual memory requires "personal" memory, the third form of memory which I shall discuss.)

In short, it is only sometimes that sentences of the forms previously mentioned are used to express perceptual memory.

It belongs to the concept of perceptual memory, that it requires mental imagery. Factual memory, on the other hand, does not require imagery. A person might remember *that* the house he lived in as a boy had two floors, although he is unable to picture the house in his mind. It is tempting to apply here Russell's famous distinction between knowledge by acquaintance and knowledge by description. One might wish to call perceptual memory "memory by acquaintance," and factual memory "memory by description." Remembering the fire that burned down the city hall might be an illustration of the former: remembering that there was a fire of the description, the fire that burned down the city hall, would be an illustration of the latter. In one case one remembers the fire itself: one sees in one's mind some scene or scenes of the fire. In the other case one remembers some fact or facts (some truth or truths) about the fire.

Russell claimed that knowledge by acquaintance is "logically independent of knowledge of truths," [6] and also that "All our

---

[6] *The Problems of Philosophy* (New York: Holt, Rinehart & Winston, Inc., 1912), p. 72.

knowledge, both knowledge of things and knowledge of truths, rests upon acquaintance as its foundation."[7] A parallel claim about memory would be that perceptual memory is logically independent of factual memory and that factual memory is based on perceptual memory.

Apparently Russell actually took this view about memory. He offers as one kind of knowledge by acquaintance, "acquaintance by *memory*." He says of it:

It is obvious that we often remember what we have seen or heard or had otherwise present to our senses, and that in such cases we are still immediately aware of what we remember, in spite of the fact that it appears as past and not as present.[8]

It seems likely, although I cannot prove the point, that this form of memory, in which one is supposed to be "immediately aware" of something previously perceived by sense, is intended to be the same thing that I have called "perceptual" memory. Russell goes on to claim that "This immediate knowledge by memory is the source of all our knowledge concerning the past."[9] He seems to be holding that perceptual memory is the most fundamental form of memory.

In *The Analysis of Mind* Russell, following Bergson, distinguishes between "true" and "habit" memory. "True" memory, he says, occurs whenever I remember something I have never remembered before, and it "constitutes the essence of memory."[10] Remembering "what I had to eat for breakfast," he says, is an example of "true" memory. This example does not make it clear whether "true" memory is the same as perceptual memory. Remembering what I ate for breakfast could be factual memory: remembering *that* I ate x and y and z for breakfast. Or it could be perceptual memory: remembering *the* x and y and z that I ate for breakfast, i.e., seeing them in my mind. The example is ambiguous as between factual and perceptual memory.

Russell goes on to say something, however, which makes it quite probable that his example should be taken as perceptual

[7] *Ibid.*, p. 75.
[8] *Ibid.*, p. 76.
[9] *Ibid.*
[10] Bertrand Russell, *The Analysis of Mind* (New York: The Macmillan Company, 1921), p. 167.

memory. He says that when he remembers what he had for breakfast, "the process of remembering will *consist* of calling up images of my breakfast." [11] He must be thinking of remembering in the sense that *requires* one to picture the remembered thing in one's mind. Some memories, he says, use words and others use images, but the ones in which words replace images are really "habit" memories, and the ones that use images are the only "true" memories.[12]

It is probable that by "true" memory as well as "acquaintance by memory," Russell means perceptual memory. If so, he is holding that the form of memory in which one pictures the remembered thing in one's mind is the *essence* of memory (and also the *source* of *all* our knowledge concerning the past).

Bergson had, before Russell, distinguished two forms of memory. He notes the contrast between remembering a passage in a book, in the sense of knowing it by heart, with remembering a particular occasion of reading the passage. The latter kind of remembering is a "representation." It consists of the "spontaneous evoking of an image of the past." It appears therefore, that Bergson's "spontaneous" memory is perceptual memory. He also says that it is "memory *par excellence*," which would seem to imply that it is the most fundamental form of memory.[13]

This emphasis on the importance of perceptual memory is a noteworthy feature of previous philosophy of memory. I wish to argue against the central importance of perceptual memory. Contrary to Russell's apparent view, in both *The Problems of Philosophy* and *The Analysis of Mind*, I shall maintain that factual memory is logically independent of perceptual memory, and that perceptual memory is logically dependent on factual memory.

Taking the first point first, how can I prove that factual memory is logically independent of perceptual memory? For one thing, it seems to be a fact of experience that factual memory often occurs without perceptual memory. A person may remem-

[11] *Ibid.*, p. 175; my italics.
[12] *Ibid.*, pp. 175-176.
[13] Henri Bergson, *Matiere et Memoire,* forty-sixth ed. (Paris: Presses Universitaires, 1956), pp. 83-96.

ber that he put the hammer on the garage shelf without seeing the hammer or the garage shelf in his mind. But in philosophical proof one does not want to rest on alleged facts of experience, and so I will argue that it is logically possible that there should be a man who had a good factual memory, but *no* perceptual memory. What would show that someone had no perceptual memory at all? One thing would be his lacking any inclination to say such a thing as "I can see him now smoking his pipe!" or "I *saw* him now, just for a moment," when reminiscing about a long absent friend. Another thing would be his finding this use of language unintelligible when others employ it. "What do you mean 'you *saw* him?' How could you have *seen* him when he wasn't here and you knew he wasn't?"

The person I am imagining would not respond in the desired way to the following instruction: "Look at the fireplace. Now close your eyes and try to see it." Let us suppose this order merely bewilders or irritates him. "How can I see it when my eyes are closed!" he exclaims. He does not ever come forth with the right reaction: "Now I see it!"

Although this man would not visualize a printed page or picture his room in his mind, it would be possible for him to repeat from memory something he had read, or describe from memory the furniture in his room. Although he would not hear words or musical phrases in his head, he would be able to repeat some words he had heard or sing something from memory.

Our imaginary person's incapacity for mental imagery might not have been discovered until after he had learned a vast amount of language, including the correct use of the past tense of many verbs. We may suppose that he has learned the multiplication tables and elementary mathematics, that he remembers the names of many persons and things, and that he has a normal ability to remember where he was and what he did. We may suppose that he gives testimony with normal confidence and is counted a fairly reliable witness. In relating an incident he observed he may sometimes be in doubt about some detail. After some reflection his doubt often comes to an end: he is now certain as to what happened. But when he reflects he does not visualize the events which he proceeds to report. He puts questions to himself, he tries to recall the exact order of events, and then the answer comes to him. Picturing the past episode in his mind does not play any part.

Suppose it came to be known that this man had no mental imagery. Would this be taken as a proof that he had not really remembered the names, places, and facts that we had previously credited him with remembering? Of course not. It would be impossible to draw this conclusion. We should have discovered that he is incapable of a *certain kind* of memory, not that he has no memory at all. There is no doubt about his remembering that $8 \times 7 = 56$, or that he went on a boat trip last week. The discovery could not put this in question.

It is undeniable, I believe, that it is logically possible for there to be a man who had factual but not perceptual memory. It is even a logical possibility that *all* of mankind should have been without perceptual memory—that the phenomenon of seeing and hearing things in our minds or heads should never have existed.[14]

Is it logically possible that all mankind should have been without factual memory? Certainly not. A being without factual memory would not have the ability to remember that he was about to do so-and-so or that he had been doing such-and-such. He would not remember where he had put anything, where he was, or when he was to do a certain thing.[15] A being without factual memory would have no mental powers to speak of, and he would not really be a man even if he had the human form. That *all* of mankind should have been without normal human powers is not a logical possibility, although it is logically possible that mankind should never have existed.

Factual memory is logically independent of perceptual memory. Is the latter independent of the former? I believe not. Perceptual memory presupposes a background of remembered

[14] There is a very strong but, I believe, mistaken temptation to hold that all remembering *must* involve imagery, or something like imagery, because it is *by means of it* that we remember. I will not stop to examine that view.

[15] It is worth noting here that many locutions into which the verb "remember" enters, such as "remembering where," "remembering when," "remembering what," in many of their uses, can actually be *defined* in terms of factual memory and existential quantification. For example, the statement "He remembers where he put his hat" is logically equivalent to the statement "There is a place, p, such that he remembers that he put his hat in p."

facts. This is plainly the case if a man *claims* to have perceptual memory, for example, of the house in which he lived as a boy: for at least he would be claiming to remember that he did live in a house then, and not a hotel, flat, or tent, and also that he had perceived that house. But more than these two trivial items of factual memory would be required. For if he went on to describe the former dwelling place quite wrongly, saying that it was a two-storied, Cape Cod, frame house, when in fact it had a single story and was of yellow brick, we should not wish to allow that he really does *see* the former dwelling place in his mind. Those errors of factual memory would rule out this possibility. What is brought out here is that we should credit a man with perceptual memory of a certain thing only if we knew, or assumed, that he remembered correctly some facts about it, i.e., had some factual memory of it.

More difficult would be a case in which a person had imagery of something he had previously experienced but did not know he had experienced it. Suppose he had recurring imagery of an episode which he thought to be merely imaginary, but the imagery strikingly fitted a real episode. Suppose he says, for example, that sometimes he sees very clearly in his mind three men in black masks who seize him and carry him to a green automobile. Let us suppose that he was kidnapped when a small boy, by three men in black masks who had a green automobile. Perhaps because of the terror of the experience he no longer remembers having been kidnapped. Here we might be inclined to say, on the one hand, he does not remember that he was kidnapped, on the other, he has perceptual memory of a scene of the kidnapping.

Would this example show that perceptual memory is independent of factual memory? I think not. The main difficulty here is whether it is right to say that he *remembers* the kidnapping. There are opposing inclinations here and I believe it is neither clearly right to say he remembers it nor clearly right to say he does not. On the one hand there is the recurring imagery which corresponds strikingly with the real happening. On the other hand, he does not remember *that* he was kidnapped: he does not even believe it. These facts pull in opposite directions and I believe there is no right answer. But in so far as the character of his imagery inclines us to say that he remembers the three men in black masks, the green car, and so forth, it inclines us also to say that he remembers *that* there were three men in black masks who put him in a green car, and so forth. To the same degree that we are pulled toward saying that he has perceptual memory of the incident we are drawn also toward saying that he has factual memory of it.

When a person has imagery he must be able to give an account of what it is *of*, if it is *of* anything. If his account does not correspond to anything that he previously witnessed or experienced, then his imagery is not an instance of *remembering* what he pictures in his mind, but perhaps of imagining or anticipating it. If his account does correspond sufficiently to something he did previously observe or experience to make us say he *remembers* it, then in the respects in which his account corresponds to it he does have factual memory of it. It appears, therefore, that perceptual memory does logically require factual memory.

Since perceptual memory cannot exist without factual memory, yet the latter can exist without the former, we are justified in holding that factual memory is logically more primitive and that perceptual memory is a secondary form of memory. "Memory by description," we could say, is more fundamental than "memory by acquaintance."

Let us turn to a third form of memory. Moore once observed that, although many people remember that the Battle of Hastings occurred in 1066, "this is not a 'personal' memory of any living person." [16] The expression "personally remember" is sometimes used in ordinary language: e.g., a man might say "I personally remember the burning of the city hall." When a person says that he personally remembers so-and-so, he implies that the so-and-so occurred or existed in his lifetime. Another implication would be that he had perceived or, in some sense, "experienced" the so-and-so. Thus, if someone was contemporaneous with a certain incident but was too young to have had any knowledge of it at the time, he could not be said to personally remember it. Or if a man was unconscious when he was carried down a mountain side,

---

[16] G. E. Moore, *Philosophical Papers* (New York: The Macmillan Company, 1959), p. 215.

he could not later say, correctly, that he personally remembers the trip, although he might remember that he had been carried down a mountain side, having learned of it later. A third implication of saying that someone personally remembers a certain thing is that his memory of the thing is *based on* his perception or experience of it. Thus if a ten year old boy had witnessed the burning of the city hall, but when he was twenty years old no longer remembered it and was told about it by his parents, it might be that at age twenty-five he remembered that the city hall burned down, on the basis of what his parents had told him: but it would not be true that he personally remembered it.

The foregoing three conditions can be compressed into two conditions which will constitute, I believe, a correct definition of "personal" memory. The definition is this: "A person, B, personally remembers something, *x*, if and only if B previously perceived or experienced *x and* B's memory of *x* is based wholly or partly on his previous perception or experience of *x*." [17] This is not a definition of *memory* but only of the adverb "personally" as it modifies the verb "remembers." We should note the necessity for making a distinction between what is perceived and what is "experienced." Someone could personally remember "hearing the Leningrad Orchestra" or "his hike through the Berkshires." But he would not have *perceived* a hike, or himself hiking, or himself hearing a concert. We can say, however, that hiking through the Berkshires and hearing the concert were "experiences" he had, or things that he "experienced." Another kind of case may be noted in which someone can personally remember something he did not perceive. A speaker might say to an audience, "How many people here personally remember the Spanish-American War?" Those people could answer in the affirmative who remembered that war on the basis of having known about it at the time it was going on, even if they did not participate in it or witness any of its scenes. Their experience of the war may have been limited to hearing or reading remarks or reports about it while it was going on. In this thin sense they "experienced" it.

The foregoing definition of personal memory leaves many

---

[17] I give "personal memory" the following technical definition: "B has a personal memory of *x* if and only if B personally remembers *x*." In ordinary usage, a "personal" memory is a memory of something intimate or private.

things unsettled. For example, what *kinds* of things can be personally remembered? Events and people, surely. But could one personally remember *that* the city hall burned down? Strictly speaking, no, since it would be senseless to speak of having been contemporaneous with the *fact that* the city hall burned down. Yet in a derivative sense one could speak of personal memory in this case. A person who personally remembers the burning of the city hall could be said, in this derivative sense, to personally remember *that* it burned. The objects of personal factual memory, as we might call it, would be restricted to a narrower range than are the objects of nonpersonal factual memory. For example, no one can now personally remember an event that has not occurred but will occur, since one can personally remember only what one has been contemporaneous with. Therefore, someone cannot personally remember, even in the derivative sense, *that* a certain event *will* occur. Thus personal factual memory cannot have future facts for its objects, whereas nonpersonal factual memory is not limited in this way. Nor could one personally remember that $11 \times 11 = 121$ (although one might remember it) since there would be nothing here that one could be contemporaneous with, even in a derivative sense.

In many cases one hardly knows whether the concept of personal memory has application or not, and in this sense it is a vague concept. I can say without hesitation that I personally remember my maternal grandfather. But do I personally remember Franklin D. Roosevelt? I was contemporaneous with him; I did not ever see him in the flesh, but I saw him many times in photographs and movies; I heard him speak over the radio; I remember both what he looked like and how his voice sounded. Do I personally remember him? I hardly know what to say. It may be that the fact that I did not *know* Roosevelt *personally* counts against saying that I personally remember him: that is, personally remembering a *person* perhaps requires a feature which personally remembering the Spanish-American War, say, does not, namely, that one should have known him *personally*. (It would not make sense to speak of having known that War personally.) On the other hand, it is not absolutely clear that this feature is required.

Personal memory is not a completely vague concept, however,

and it is of some interest to pay attention to it since some philosophers have assumed that *anything* which can properly be called "memory" must be personal memory. For example, W. von Leyden, in his recent book, *Remembering*, says: "Everyone would agree that what we can remember is not just any past event or fact, but a certain kind of past events or facts, namely those that form part of one's own previous experience." [18] In the next sentence he speaks of memory as being limited "to what one has personally witnessed in the past." He thinks, therefore, that all memory is personal memory. This is certainly wrong. A reader of European history can remember that the French won the First Battle of the Marne, even if it was fought before he was born. It will not do to say that "strictly speaking" he remembers reading about the battle and reading that the French won, and does not really remember that the French won. On the contrary, a person who was born after that battle was fought can properly say "I remember that the French won." And his statement is not equivalent to the statement "I remember reading that the French won," for he may not remember reading it, or even that he read it.

What is the logical relation between personal and perceptual memory? Could one's memory of something be perceptual if it was not personal? Perceptual memory requires mental imagery of what is remembered. But if a person remembered something and on the same occasion had a mental image of it, would it follow that he had perceptual memory of it? Suppose that someone, B, has not seen the Eiffel Tower, nor any pictures, drawings, photographs, or other representations of it. Yet the structure has been described to him in detail and he can form a visual image of it. (Perhaps this is unlikely, but one could hardly be justified in thinking it to be a logical impossibility.) B belongs to a group of people who are being taught about the architecture of some famous buildings. The instructor has described several buildings during the course, and now wishes to test his students' knowledge. He says to B: "Do you remember the Eiffel Tower? Can you tell me the nature of its construction?" B replies: "Yes, I remember it. Its construction is. . . ." He proceeds to give an

[18] *Remembering* (London: Gerald Duckworth & Co., Ltd., 1961), p. 60.

accurate account. Let us further suppose that as he describes the Tower he has a visual image of it.

In this example, B has much factual memory about the Tower, and it is correct to say that he remembers it. It is also the case that he sees the Tower in his mind as he talks about it. Let us ask whether he *personally* remembers the Tower. He has not seen it, nor any representations of it. He heard and understood an oral description of it. Has he "experienced" the Tower? The vagueness of this word becomes very evident here. I imagine, however, that our strongest inclination will be to say that hearing and understanding a description of it would *not* be "experiencing" it.[19] If we decide the matter in this way, and a *decision* is called for, we shall be ruling that B's memory of the Eiffel Tower is not personal memory.

Shall we say that B's memory of the Tower is *perceptual* memory? He remembers it and he sees it in his mind. Is this enough? I believe our strongest inclination would be to say that it is not perceptual memory because it is not personal memory.[20] If B had seen the Tower in movies or photographs, we should have a much stronger inclination to say that he has both personal and perceptual memory of it. In the present case our inclination is so indefinite that it is fair to say that another decision is required.

Let us rule that in the case described, B has neither personal nor perceptual memory of the Eiffel Tower. The reason for this decision is not that B lacks some experience or "mental content" on the occasion of his remembering the Tower. The reason is solely a fact about his previous history, namely, that he did not ever see the Tower or any representations of it. It is logically possible that the sensations, feelings, imagery, or thoughts that B has when he says "I remember the Tower," and proceeds to describe it, should be exactly the same as those of another person, C, who previously saw the Tower and has both personal and perceptual memory of it. The force of saying that C has, and B

---

[19] It strikes me as odd that, apparently, we are willing to say that a man who never participated in the Spanish-American War could personally remember that War, but we are disinclined to say that a man who never perceived the Eiffel Tower could personally remember the Tower.

[20] I touched upon this point on p. 208.

has not, personal and perceptual memory of the Tower is not that C has some "memory experience" that B does not have.[21]

The decision to say, in respect to our hypothetical case, that B does not perceptually remember the Eiffel Tower, really amounts to the general ruling that perceptual memory requires personal memory. We are ruling that a person cannot perceptually remember something that he has not perceived or experienced. Broad says, "We can remember only the things and events which *we* have perceived. . . ." [22] Since this remark occurs during his discussion of perceptual memory, its scope is probably limited to the latter. If so, there is in the background of his remark (although not explicitly) the same decision we have made, namely, to say that a proposition of the form "B perceptually remembers x" logically implies a proposition of the form "B personally remembers x."

We are now in a position to give a definition of *perceptual* memory. Imagery and personal memory are each necessary conditions. Is their conjunction a sufficient condition? It would appear so. The definition is the following: "B perceptually remembers x if and only if B personally remembers x *and* B can form a mental image of x." Let me make some comments about this definition. First, it is not a definition of *remembering* but only of the adverb "perceptually," as it modifies the verb "remember." [23] Second, what is defined is the notion of a perceptual memory *ability*, not the notion of a perceptual memory occurrence.[24]

I argued previously that perceptual memory requires factual memory. Let us ask whether personal memory requires factual memory. Is it possible that a man should personally remember something of which he had no factual memory?

---

[21] B and C might have the same mental image of the Tower: but C's image would be a memory image and B's an "imagination image."

[22] *Mind and Its Place in Nature,* p. 228.

[23] I define "perceptual memory" as follows: "B has a perceptual memory of x if and only if B perceptually remembers x."

[24] I will not go into this distinction here, but will only remark that normally when we use "remember" in the third person, present tense ("He remembers") we are speaking of an ability, and normally when we use it in the past tense, in all persons ("I (you, he) remembered") we are speaking of an occurrence. The first person, present tense ("I remember") is used in both ways.

Let us recall that factual memory necessarily is *correct* memory, i.e., one cannot remember that p if p is false. It does not follow that correct memory is identical with factual memory. And it seems that it is not. A man could correctly remember a melody he had heard, in the sense that he could play, hum, or whistle it correctly, from memory. I cannot think of any statement, expressed in terms of "remembering that," which would be *equivalent*. Still, the proposition that a man correctly remembers a certain thing *entails* that he has some factual memory of that thing. For example, the man who correctly remembers a certain melody remembers that it goes like *this* (here one could exhibit the correct musical sequence) and not like *that*. I will not give further examples, but I believe it is true that correctly remembering something will entail remembering that p, where p is some true proposition about the remembered thing.

My next step is to argue that personal memory of something cannot be totally incorrect. This really follows from our definition of personal memory. A man personally remembers something, x, only if he previously perceived or experienced x. This requirement *could* be interpreted to mean that personal memory cannot be incorrect at all. But we may take it less strictly. For example, a man might claim to personally remember the launching of the *Queen Mary*. If this *is* personal memory there must be something right about his claim, e.g., that he once saw a launching or that he once saw the *Queen Mary*. He might be right about one of these claims and wrong about the other. But if there was nothing right at all in his claims then it could not be *personal* memory, because he would not be referring to anything that he had previously perceived or experienced. That personal memory of something must be at least partly correct is, therefore, a logical consequence of the way we have defined it. (This point is independent of my argument, in the first lecture, to prove that not all memory could be incorrect.)

Putting together the two results that, first, correct memory of something entails some factual memory of the remembered thing and, second, that personal memory of something must be at least partly correct, we obtain the consequence that personal memory of something entails some factual memory of it. Since perceptual memory of something entails personal memory of it, and since this latter entails factual memory of it, it follows that perceptual memory of something entails factual memory of it. This confirms a result that we had come to previously in our discussion of perceptual memory.

Does personal memory entail perceptual memory? This question comes to the following: If a man personally remembers something does it follow that he can form mental imagery of it? No. A man who had not seen his grandfather for many years could say: "I remember him well. He always wore his Confederate uniform, chewed tobacco, and told jokes; but I can't any longer see him in my mind as I formerly could." This man's memory of his grandfather is personal memory, since it is based on his personal encounters with his grandfather. But it is no longer perceptual memory. This imaginary case is a possibility and something like it probably occurs in fact.

Previously we decided to hold that a person cannot have perceptual memory of something unless he personally remembers it. Is personal memory required, in the same sense, for factual memory? No. In a previous example we imagined a man who could not be said to personally remember the Eiffel Tower, but who remembered, from his instruction, that q, that r, and so on, these being facts about the Tower. But though there can be factual memory of something without personal memory of it, a vast amount of our factual memory pertains to things which we personally remember, and if we had no personal memory of those things we should have no factual memory of them.

I argued that all mankind could have existed without perceptual memory. Is the same true of personal memory? Could creatures who never remembered anything they perceived or experienced, have anything like human powers? Surely not. For one thing, these creatures would not be able to *recognize* any particular person or object. This alone would imply that they could not have many of the concepts that human beings have, and could not do many of the things that human beings do.

Unlike perceptual memory, both factual and personal memory are essential to mankind. They are so thoroughly entwined with one another that it would be impossible to say which is *more* essential.

A Definition of Factual Memory

Enough has been said in the previous two lectures to show that factual memory (remembering that p) holds an important position in the family of concepts of memory. Some forms of memory can be defined in terms of factual memory plus the purely logical notion of existential quantification. Other forms are related to factual memory as *species* to *genus*.[1] Still other forms, not related to factual memory in either of these two ways, *imply* it.[2] I have not been able to discover any form of memory which does not have at least this latter relation to factual memory. I will not undertake to provide an account of the exact position that factual memory occupies among the concepts of memory, but it has sufficient importance to make it worthwhile to attempt to *define* it.

In my second lecture I produced definitions of perceptual and personal memory. As we noted they are not definitions of *memory,* but only of the adverbs "personally" and "perceptually," as these modify the verb "remember." That they are not definitions of *memory* is shown by the fact that the verb "remember"

---

[1] For example, if a man "remembered to" water his horse it follows that he remembered that he should water his horse and also that he watered it. Remembering *to* do something appears to consist of remembering that one should do it plus doing it.

[2] Both personal and perceptual memory imply factual memory.

occurs in the *definiens* of each of those definitions. The definition of factual memory which I shall propose will really be a definition of *memory*—not of memory in general, but of one use of the verb "remembers." In this definition that verb will not occur in the *definiens*.

The definition is very simple. It is the following: A person, B, remembers that *p* if and only if B knows that *p* because he knew that *p*. It will be convenient to say that this definition is composed of three elements: the present knowledge that *p*, the previous knowledge that *p*, and the relationship between the present and the previous knowledge expressed by saying that B knows that *p because* he previously knew that *p*. Each element is a logically necessary condition and the conjunction of them a logically sufficient condition of factual memory.

I wish to discuss each of these three elements in turn. But before I do so I want to anticipate one objection to the definition. Let us suppose that a man saw a bird of striking appearance in his bird feeder last week, but did not know what bird it was. While looking through a book about birds he comes upon a picture of a cardinal and now knows it was a cardinal he saw. He might naturally say "I remember that I saw a cardinal in the feeder last week." But it is false that *previously* he knew that he saw a cardinal. It might be concluded that the element of *previous* knowledge is shown not to be a necessary condition of factual memory.

I deal with this kind of case by distinguishing between what I call "elliptical" and "nonelliptical" uses of the expression "remembers that *p*." I believe that the man in our example would agree to substitute for his sentence "I remember that I saw a cardinal" the *conjunctive* sentence "I remember that I saw this bird (or: a bird of this kind) *and* now I know it was a cardinal." The sentence he originally uttered was an ellipsis, in the grammarian's sense, the meaning of which is given by the conjunctive sentence. In this conjunction the first conjunct expresses factual memory, the second conjunct expresses the new information. Another way of putting the distinction is to say that the original sentence did not express "pure" factual memory. In the conjunctive sentence substituted for it, the first conjunct expresses pure factual memory, the second conjunct expresses something other than memory. The whole conjunction expresses "impure" memory.

There could be many different kinds of impure factual memory. For example, suppose that someone had often noticed, as a boy, that the house in which he lived faced the setting sun. Years later, when conversing with someone, he suddenly realizes, for the first time, that this implied that his house faced the west, and he says "I remember that our house faced the west." This sentence of his expresses impure factual memory, which is a compound of pure factual memory and present inference or realization. The definition I am presenting is intended solely to be a definition of *pure* factual memory, with no admixture of inference or present realization.

I turn now to a consideration of the three elements in the definition. The first two elements are present and previous knowledge, and so whatever is true of knowledge will apply equally to both. In the history of the philosophy of memory there has been a considerable amount of puzzlement and confusion about the relation of memory to knowledge. First, if memory involves knowledge what *kind* of knowledge is it? Second, if a person remembers that p just *how certain* is it that p? Third, when a person remembers that p does he have *grounds* for saying that p? These are some of the questions that puzzle us, and I hope that this discussion will help to answer them.

Obviously one necessary condition for the knowledge that p is that p should be *true*. If p is false then B does not know, and did not know, that p; and also B does not remember that p.

A second necessary condition for someone's knowing that p may be expressed, roughly, as the condition that he should be *sure* that p. Being unsure whether p is true counts both against knowing that p and against remembering that p. If a man previously knew that p and now not only is not sure but does not even believe that p, we are sometimes ready to say "He really remembers it": but what we mean would also be expressed by saying "He *will* remember it" or "His forgetting it is only *temporary*." We should have to admit that at present he does not remember it.

Of course there are many differences of degree in the confidence with which one believes or is sure of something. A person can be *inclined* to believe something and at the same time be quite unsure about it. Sometimes we should say he knows the thing in question and sometimes that he does not, depending on what contrasts we were making. Suppose some pupils were being tested on their knowledge of Roman history. They are supposed to tell who killed Caesar. Suppose that one of them, A, is inclined to think it was Brutus, but has little confidence in this answer. Should we say A *knows* that Brutus killed Caesar? If we were comparing him with B, who believes that Cassius was the assassin, we should say that A knows the answer but B does not. If we were comparing A with C, who is *certain* that Brutus slew Caesar, we should say that C knows the answer but A does not "really *know*" it, or does not know it "very well." The same considerations apply to the question of whether A *remembers* that Brutus killed Caesar. Thus we can say, in summary, that if someone has *no* inclination to believe that *p*, this counts absolutely against either his knowing or remembering that *p*. If he has some inclination to believe that *p* but is unsure about it, whether we say he does or does not know, or remember, that *p* depends on the comparisons we are making. In short, if one is unsure about something this *can serve*, in some circumstances, to justify the claim that one does not know, and does not remember, the something.

The considerations about truth and certainty, so far adduced, apply equally to knowledge and memory. A third consideration is that of *grounds* for being sure that *p*.[3] It has often been supposed that, in addition to being right and being sure, a further thing necessary for knowledge is the possession of grounds, or adequate grounds, or conclusive grounds. I am not convinced that this third feature is a requirement for knowledge, although I admit that not just any true belief is knowledge. My discussion of this difficult point will necessarily be skimpy.

In the first place, I call attention to the knowledge that human beings normally have of their own voluntary actions, both of what they are doing and what they are going to do. Suppose a

[3] It is worth noting that we do not speak of a person's grounds for *knowing* something, but of his grounds for believing it, being sure of it, asserting it, denying it, saying it, or doubting it. On the other hand, we ask *how* he knew it.

man was for a while undecided as to whether he would quit his job, but now *knows* he will quit it. Should we expect him to have *grounds* for being sure he will quit it? It is hard to see what this could mean.[4] Could one say that his grounds for being sure he will quit is his *decision* to quit? But in the case, which is common enough, where a person is trying to make up his mind whether or not he will quit his job, not through the consideration of evidence that he will or will not quit it, but of reasons for and against quitting it—in this case, what *is* his deciding to quit other than the transition from his being unsure about it to his being sure that he will quit? In this example, his deciding what he will do is the same thing as his becoming sure what he will do, and is not his grounds for being sure. Nothing can be put forward as his grounds for being sure he will quit: yet it is correct to say "He knows now that he will quit his job."

In the second place, sometimes people know in advance about things they do *in*voluntarily. A nervous amateur actor, about to make his first appearance on the stage, might say with conviction, "I know I shall forget my lines." Sure enough, he does forget them. This use of "know" is entirely natural. Did he have grounds? He could have been relying on some statistics—but that would not be the normal case. We are willing to say that he knew he would forget his lines, yet we do not expect him to have had evidence or grounds.[5]

In the third place, I can imagine a man who has unusual knowledge of the whereabouts of various persons, of what they are engaged in, what will happen to them, and so on. The man I am imagining (let us call him "the seer") is sure about these things and apparently is always right, but he does not have *grounds* for being sure. He has no special sources of information, he does not make use of tips or hints, and he does not guess. But he can tell someone the whereabouts of the son who left home

[4] Of course we might expect him to have grounds or reasons *for* quitting his job—a different matter.

[5] A friend of mine died after an illness of several weeks. Those who were with him reported to me that *he knew* he would die on the night he did die. Am I supposed to think that either they were wrong, or else that he had grounds for his conviction? "He felt his life ebbing away." What does this mean, except that he knew he was dying?

five years ago and has not since been heard from. As his powers became known, people would come to him to inquire about their relatives and friends. I am supposing that in a large number of cases his answers have proven true and in no cases have they proven false. It is unquestionable that people would regard the seer as a source of *information*. "He informed me of the whereabouts of my son" would be a natural thing to say about him: and also "He knew the whereabouts of my son." The seer, as said, does not have grounds for being sure of the things he is sure of. He might even admit that he does not know *how* he knows the things in question. Sometimes when a question is put to him he has to wait a bit until the answer comes to him, like an inspiration; and sometimes he knows the answer immediately. But never is it a matter of grounds, evidence, or reasoning.

It is sometimes held that a person cannot properly be said to know something unless he is *in a position* to know it. But one might say that what is extraordinary about the seer is that he knows things which he is *not in a position to know*. A. J. Ayer says that "the necessary and sufficient conditions for knowing that something is the case are first that what one is said to know be true, secondly that one be sure of it, and thirdly that one should have the right to be sure." [6] I question the third condition. I believe Ayer would agree with me that the seer *knows* the things he reports, for Ayer says that if someone "were repeatedly successful in a given domain" although "without appearing to have any adequate basis for it," then "we should grant him the right to be sure, simply on the basis of his success." [7] But I think it is odd to say that the seer has a right to be sure of what he is sure of. The rest of us would have a right to be sure of something because the seer told us so, and because (to the best of our knowledge) he is invariably right. *We* have grounds for being sure. But the seer does not have our grounds, or any other grounds. As said, he is not, in the ordinary meaning of the phrase, *in a position to know* what he tells us. I cannot understand, therefore, the expression "has a right to be sure"

[6] *The Problem of Knowledge* (London: Macmillan & Co., Ltd., 1956), p. 34.
[7] *Ibid.*, p. 32.

when it is applied to the seer, unless it merely means "*knows* what he is sure of," in which case it cannot express an element in the *analysis* of knowledge.

I have argued, from several different kinds of cases, that having grounds for being certain of something is not a necessary condition of knowing it. I imagine there are still other kinds of cases. I suspect that a stronger candidate than grounds or evidence, for being a necessary condition of knowledge, is the negative requirement that to know something one should not be certain of it because of a *mistake*, e.g., because of mishearing what someone said or because of fallacious reasoning.

The connection of this discussion of grounds with the definition of factual memory is that if having grounds is not a necessary condition of knowing something there is then no reason to suppose it is a necessary condition of remembering something.

When people do have grounds for being sure of something the grounds can differ in strength. If an American living in England converts his dollar holdings into pounds because he is sure that the American government is going to devalue the dollar, his grounds for being sure could be of many sorts. Let us suppose there are three people, A, B, and C, each of whom converts from dollars to pounds because he is sure the dollar will be devalued. A's grounds for being sure of this are that several of his friends, who are "generally well-informed about developments in international finance," are convinced it will happen. B's grounds are that a friend of his was told in confidence by an American Treasury official that it was "bound to happen." C's grounds are that the Secretary of the Treasury himself, in his last news conference, said he "did not see how this step could be avoided." All three are right; the dollar is devalued.

A person commenting on the matter afterwards could correctly say that all three *knew* the devaluation would occur (in contrast, for example, with D, whom the devaluation took by surprise). The person commenting on the matter would allow that B's grounds for being sure of it were stronger than A's, and that C's grounds were stronger still. Indeed, he would think that C's grounds were "just about as strong (or conclusive) as one could have in a matter of that sort." As he might put it, A's grounds were pretty good, B's grounds were even better, and C's grounds were as good as one could have. Another way to express the difference would be to say that on A's grounds it was "reasonably certain" it would happen; on B's grounds it was still more certain; and on C's grounds it was as certain as could be. Finally, another way to express it would be to say that although A knew it would happen his knowledge of it *was less certain* than B's, and B's knowledge was more certain than A's although not as certain as C's, and C's knowledge of it was as certain as knowledge can be in such matters. The interesting point here, if I am right, is that in ordinary discourse we conceive of *knowledge* as being *more or less certain*. We *grade* knowledge in terms of certainty. This grading of knowledge is solely in terms of the strength of the grounds. Grading *knowledge* as more or less certain is *equivalent* to grading *grounds* as more or less conclusive. If this is right, the assumption we are often tempted to make in philosophy, that if someone really knows that *p* then he must have grounds which make it perfectly certain or perfectly conclusive that *p,* is shown to be false. Knowledge is not all wool and a yard wide.

Our definition of factual memory requires the elements of present and previous knowledge. Let us raise again the questions that we put before: First, what *kind* of knowledge is involved in memory? Second, when someone remembers that *p* does he have *grounds* for being sure that *p*? Third, when someone remembers that *p,* just *how certain* is it that *p*?

Let us consider the first question, keeping in mind that memory involves both previous and present knowledge. The element of *previous* knowledge involved in memory can be any kind of knowledge at all. It might be the knowledge that a person has of his own voluntary or involuntary actions; it might be knowledge based on a newspaper report, or on a mathematical demonstration, or on an inference from what someone said; it might be the kind of knowledge that the seer has. Of what kind is the *present* knowledge involved in memory? Of exactly the *same* kind that the previous knowledge was. I think that here it may be misleading to speak of *two* elements of knowledge in memory, previous and present knowledge. There are not two pieces of knowledge but one piece. Memory is the *retention* of knowledge. One knew something and still knows it. The present knowledge in memory is the *same* as the previous knowledge.

Let us go to the second question: When someone remembers that p does he have grounds for being sure that p? The answer is that he has the same grounds, if any, that he previously had.[8] If B remembers that his friend, Robinson, was ill last year, then B previously knew of the illness. His previous knowledge may have been based on perception (He saw Robinson when the latter was ill); or on testimony (Jones told him about Robinson's illness); or on inference (B inferred that Robinson was ill from his absence from work). B's *present* knowledge that Robinson was ill, if it is solely memory, has the *same* grounds. If the ground of his previous knowledge was testimony then the ground of his present knowledge is that same previous testimony. And so on. If what made him sure, previously, that Robinson was ill was that Jones told him so, his present ground for being sure is that Jones told him so previously. If a man's previous knowledge that p had *no* grounds, then in remembering that p his present knowledge has *no* grounds.

There is an interesting problem that arises here. If a man previously had grounds for being sure that p, and now remembers that p, but does not remember what his grounds were, does he *have* grounds for being sure that p? I will not go into this point, but I am inclined to say that he *has* the *same* grounds he previously had. In some cases if a man cannot give any grounds for believing something it follows that he has no grounds. But I think this does not hold for the special case of his *forgetting* what his grounds were. I should say it does not follow that he *has* no grounds for being certain that p, any *more* than it follows that he *had* no grounds. But by hypothesis he had grounds.

Our third question was: When someone remembers that p, how *certain* is it that p? The answer I give is that his present knowledge that p has the *same* degree of certainty that his previous knowledge that p had. Of course, if he has forgotten what his grounds were, *he* may be less certain than he was—but that is a different matter.

One thing which is obvious is that no matter how well a person

[8] This is true insofar as his present knowledge that p is solely *memory*. I am not dealing with the case in which it is partly memory and partly present evidence.

remembers something, his present knowledge cannot be *superior* to his previous knowledge. His present knowledge that *p*, if it is solely memory, cannot be *more* certain than was his previous knowledge that *p*. This fact provides one clear sense for the claim that memory is not a *source* of knowledge.

When I remember that *p*, does my *remembering* it have grounds? If we are not merely asking again whether my certainty that *p* has grounds, then this seems a nonsensical question. If by "my remembering it" is meant the *relation* between my present and my previous knowledge that *p*, then my remembering it cannot be said to have or to lack grounds. This is reflected in the definition of factual memory—knowing that *p* because one previously knew that *p*. It would be unintelligible as well as ungrammatical to ask whether one had grounds for *that*.

Let us try to summarize briefly the place of knowledge in factual memory. If a person remembers that *p* then he knows that *p* and he knew it before. Knowing implies being sure, save for the qualification noted. There can be and are cases in which people know things without having *grounds* for being sure. If the previous knowledge was without grounds then the present knowledge is without grounds (if the present knowledge is solely memory). When a man had grounds for his previous knowledge that *p*, his previous knowledge was more or less certain, depending on the strength of his grounds; and his present knowledge (if it is solely memory) has this same degree of certainty regardless of whether he *remembers* his grounds.

I turn now to the third element in the definition of factual memory. What does it mean to say that someone knows that *p* *because* he previously knew that *p*? Could it mean that the past knowledge *caused* the present knowledge? W. von Leyden says that "it is part of the meaning of memory that, when it is correct, it is causally dependent upon a previous perception." [9] He is saying, for example, that someone's memory of having seen the *Queen Mary* in drydock is causally dependent on his having seen the *Queen Mary* in drydock. One might object to the idea that the supposed effect is *causally* dependent on the supposed cause,

---

[9] *Remembering* (London: Gerald Duckworth & Co., Ltd., 1961), p. 31.

for the reason that the "effect" is *logically* dependent on the "cause." It is logically impossible that one should remember having seen *x* unless one saw it.

But we are concerned now with factual memory and whether it is a possibility that the present *knowledge* that *p* is causally dependent on the previous *knowledge* that *p*. Here it is not true that there is logical implication, in either direction, between supposed effect and supposed cause. Furthermore, one might think that we must be justified in speaking of a "causal dependence" here, simply because it is a natural use of language to say that someone knows that *p* "because" he knew it before, or to say that his present knowledge is "due to" his previous knowledge.

Granting this to be so, it does not tell us what this "causal dependence" *means*. There is an important sense of "cause" in which a singular causal statement of the form "*x* caused *y*" implies a general proposition of the form "In like circumstances, whenever *x* then *y*." But *this* meaning of "cause" cannot be involved in factual memory, since in saying that someone remembers that *p*, we are certainly not committing ourselves to the truth of the general proposition that "In like circumstances, whenever a person has previously known that *p* then he knows that *p*," even if we could give any clear meaning to it.

To come back to von Leyden, he holds that recollecting something implies that there is "a memory process or causal chain stretching continuously from the occurrence of *x* and the original experience of *x* up to the present recollection of *x*." [10] Another way he puts it is to say that there is a "continuous connexion" between a remembered fact and a present memory of it. [11] Sometimes he calls it an *unbroken* connection. [12] But this requirement, he holds, creates a problem about knowing whether *anyone* remembers *anything!* For, "the process of retention," says von Leyden, is "unobservable." [13] The "causal chain" implied by memory is "elusive." [14] It is difficult if not impossible, he says, to prove that an unbroken connection or persisting process intervened between a past experience and one's present recollection

---

[10] *Ibid.*, p. 42.   [11] *Ibid.*, p. 45.   [12] E.g., *ibid.*, p. 40.   [13] *Ibid.*, p. 55.
[14] *Ibid.*, p. 46.

of it.[15] The conclusion drawn by him is that "no memory statement is, strictly speaking, verifiable." [16] I think he means by this remark that it is *never* verifiable that someone remembers something!

I should have thought a more reasonable conclusion would be that the concept of memory carries *no* implication of a continuous process of retention or of an unbroken causal connection. The imagery suggested by what von Leyden says is fairly definite. Remembering consists in a certain *process* which begins at the time a person witnesses or learns something. What the process is *in its own nature* is not known. But it is there, going on, and the person's occasional recollection of what he witnessed or learned is a *manifestation* of this underlying process.

This picture gives rise to two sorts of skeptical reflection. First, perhaps the underlying process is not *always* in operation during the intervals between the manifestations of it, and consequently we are sometimes mistaken in thinking that we remember certain things even though we give the right answers. Second, perhaps the required process is *never* there, and occurrences of so-called "recollection" are *never* manifestations of a process of remembering, and we are *always* deceived in thinking we remember something. It merely *looks as if* people remember!

Rather than to dwell on the absurdity of this conclusion, I want to try to explain the third element in the definition of factual memory. What does it mean to say that A knows that *p because* he previously knew that *p*? It does not mean that there is a "continuous" or "unbroken" connection between the previous and the present knowledge, even if this were an intelligible notion. I am afraid my explanation of the meaning of the "because" will be disappointing. I believe its meaning is essentially *negative*. This will be brought out by reflecting on one sort of consideration which would *disprove* the claim that A remembers that *p*. Suppose we know that A had known at a previous time that Robinson walked across Cayuga Lake when it was frozen. Suppose we also know that A knows it now. Could it turn out that A's present knowledge is not memory? Yes. If A were to

[15] *Ibid.*, p. 53.
[16] *Ibid.*, p. 43.

tell us that he would not have had his present knowledge of the incident had not someone informed him of it *just now,* or had he not read about it in his diary a moment ago, or had he not inferred it from some remarks he overheard just now, then we should know that A's present knowledge that Robinson walked across the lake is not memory.

In this example, A had *forgotten* that *p.* But his having previously forgotten it is not a sufficient condition of his not remembering it. He might have forgotten it and then later remembered it, just as it often happens that one is for a time unable to remember a name and then finally does remember it. What keeps it from being true that A remembered the incident is not that he had previously forgotten it, but that he had just now *learned about it over again.* To say that A knows that *p because* he previously knew that *p* implies that A has *not* just now learned over again that *p.* This brings out, in part, the negative sense of the "because."

Another expression we can use here is "source," i.e., the *source* of A's present knowledge that *p* is his previous knowledge of it. This word carries a certain physical imagery. A river has a source and stretches continuously from its source to its mouth. The imagery of this word might play some part in producing von Leyden's inclination to postulate a "continuous connexion." But when the word "source" is used in the analysis of memory it must, like "because," be understood in a negative sense. To say "His previous knowledge is the source of his present knowledge" implies that he has not just now learned over again that *p.*

The meaning of "just now" is, however, pretty indefinite. If I was told something two hours ago would that be "just now"? Or would "just now" have to be ten minutes or ten seconds ago? I believe this is an artificial problem. I think that when we say "A remembers that *p,*" we refer, more or less vaguely, to a more or less definite previous time when A knew that *p.* We are asserting that A remembers that *p from that time.* This will imply that A has not learned over again that *p* since that time. If this is correct we can get rid of the phrase "just now" in stating our analysis of factual memory. The statement "He remembers that *p*" will imply: "He knows that *p, and* at a previous time, *t,* he

knew that p, *and* he has not learned over again that p since t."
It would be up to the person who made the original statement
to specify the time, t, to which he refers.

There is another objection to this analysis of factual memory.
Let us imagine the following case: A man, B, learned that p.
B then suffered an injury to a certain part of his brain, as a
result of which he no longer knew that p. Later an operation was
performed on his brain which had the effect that again he knew
that p. At this later time it would be true that B knows that
p and also that he knew that p at a previous time, t, and that he
had not learned over again that p since t. (The operation on his
brain, or the effect of it, cannot be called "*learning* over again"
that p.) Our proposed definition of factual memory is satisfied:
yet should we really wish to say that B remembers that p?

Whether we should say this or not may depend on what we
suppose to be the efficacy of the brain surgery.[17] If we supposed
that what was done to B's brain would cause him to know that
p, *regardless of what his previous knowledge had been*[18] (i.e.,
he would know that p even if he had not ever previously known
that p) then we should be disinclined to say that the operation
had "restored his memory," and also disinclined to say, "Now
he remembers that p." If, on the other hand, this operation could
cause a person to know that p *only if* he had previously known
that p, then we should be inclined to say those things.

It appears, therefore, that in this described case we should call
B's present knowledge that p *memory*, only if we supposed that
he would not now know that p had he not previously known that
p. This fits in with the general feature of knowing something
on the basis of memory, namely, that the present knowledge
must be dependent on previous knowledge. As suggested before,
when we claim that someone remembers a certain thing, we refer
(more or less tacitly) to a previous time, t_1, when he knew the
thing, and we are claiming that he remembers it *from* that time.

---

[17] In my discussion of this point, I am indebted to John Rawls and David
Sachs.

[18] I do not assume that this is, or ever will be, a factual possibility. I am
not entirely sure that it even makes sense. But it is not clear to me that it
does not, and so my analysis of factual memory should take account of it.

Our claim implies that he has not learned the thing over again since t_1.[19] More generally, our claim implies that nothing whatever has occurred at some later time, t_2, such that his knowledge "dates" from t_2 instead of from t_1. This general requirement eliminates the possibility that, for example, a brain operation at t_2 should have been a sufficient condition of B's present knowledge.

The most concise and accurate formulation of this requirement which I have been able to think of is this: A person, B, remembers that p from t, only if it is the case that had B not known that p at t, he would not now know that p. The negative counterfactual conditional statement "If B had not known at t that p, he would not now know that p" does not express a *law*. It is similar in meaning to such a statement as the following: "If you had not given me a cigar I should not have one now." This would simply mean that, in fact, no other opportunity of my obtaining a cigar presented itself. Similarly, our negative counterfactual conditional about B's knowledge means that, as a matter of fact, if he had not obtained this knowledge at t he would not have it now. This is a kind of thing we often know to be true, just as we often know it to be true that this man would not have a cigar now if someone had not given him the one he has. Nothing is implied, in either case, about the existence of a causal chain or of a continuous process.

I have been trying to explain the meaning of the third element in our definition of factual memory, namely, the meaning of saying that someone now knows that p *because* he previously knew it. Our definition of factual memory can now be stated in full as follows: A person, B, remembers that p from a time, t, if and only if B knows that p, *and* B knew that p at t, *and* if B had not known at t that p he would not now know that p.

One point should be mentioned here. Something may *remind* one of some fact. You remember the latter *because* of something you saw or heard or thought. This meaning of "because" is dif-

---

[19] It is worth remarking that if I have forgotten something temporarily, and then suddenly remember it, it cannot be said that I have *learned* the thing over again. This is because my present knowledge of it is "due" to my previous knowledge of it.

ferent from the meaning it has in the definition of factual memory. Without going further into the matter, I will say that these two meanings of "because" are quite compatible. It can be true both that a man should now remember that p (which implies that he now knows that p *because* he previously knew it) and also that something made him remember that p (i.e., he remembered it *because* of something he perceived or thought). I think that this second "because" has a genuine *causal* meaning.

It must be admitted that one feels some mystification about my negative interpretation of the words "because" or "source" in our definition of factual memory. It seems mysterious that a man should know that p, having previously known it, unless there is something that comes *between* his previous and present knowledge and *ties them together*. It is probably this feeling that chiefly contributes to von Leyden's view of memory. We feel that there is a *gap* between the previous and the present knowledge, but at the same time we do not know how to fill in the gap. Should we say that what fills it is some persisting state of the brain or neural process? Whether or not it makes sense to postulate a specific brain-state or neural process persisting between the previous and the present knowledge that p, such a postulation is obviously not required by an analysis of the *concept* of remembering. Our everyday verifications of whether some person does or does not remember that p are not bound up with any questions about what is and has been going on in his brain. Our use of the language of memory carries no implications about inner physiology. Nor can we fill the gap with a continuous process of thinking about what is remembered. People could not think, continuously and simultaneously, of all the things they remember. If we resorted to *unconscious* thoughts in order to bridge the gap, we should then be in a difficulty about the *criterion* we should use for the existence of those unconscious thoughts. If we had no criterion our "solution" would, in a sense, be unintelligible. If we used the existence of the gap itself as our criterion for the existence of the unconscious thoughts that bridge the gap, then our solution would solve nothing.

This feeling of the mysteriousness of memory, unless we assume a persisting state or process between the previous and the present knowledge, provides one *metaphysical* aspect of the topic of memory. I believe this feeling explains why it is so commonly taken for granted, by philosophers, psychologists, and physiologists, that there is a "*process* of retention." It would be a valuable piece of philosophical work to explain why we have this feeling —what comparisons, what analogies, give rise to it. My own guess would be that our strong desire for a mechanism (either physical or mental) of memory arises from an abhorrence of the notion of action at a distance-in-time.

Leaving aside the question of why we have it, the idea of there being a gap between the previous and the present knowledge in memory is certainly a confusion. There is a gap only if there is something *missing*. But what is missing? We have no idea.

What *could* fill the gap? I have mentioned three candidates: a persisting physiological state or process; continuous thinking about what is remembered; continuous unconscious thinking about what is remembered. We see that for different reasons none of these candidates can be included in the truth conditions for statements of the form "A remembers that *p*." I believe we do not have the conception of anything else that might fill the gap. In a sense, therefore, we do not know what it means to speak of a *gap* here.

All of us (myself too) tend to have a piece of imagery, namely, of a *physical* gap. I can express that imagery with gestures. With a wave of the hand I can say, "Over *there* is the previous knowledge that *p*, and over *here* is the present knowledge that *p*: but what *connects* the two?" Yet if someone were to take seriously my pointing gestures and my expressions "Over there" and "Over here," I should be embarrassed. I have the imagery, together with the feeling that it illustrates something significant; but at the same time I cannot take it seriously. This is a frequent predicament in philosophy.

Two additional objections to our definition of factual memory must be considered. The first one is the following: Bodily sensations are among the objects of memory. A person can remember that he had an earache and that the pain was excruciating. But it is senseless, it may be said, to speak of someone's *knowing* that he is in pain.[20] Our definition cannot be satisfied, therefore, since it requires that a person who remembers that he had an earache should have previously known that he had one. The time at which he had this previous knowledge would have to be the very time at which he had the earache. For if it were at a later time, his knowledge at this later time would itself be memory and, by our definition, would require a previous knowledge. And so on. Our definition really requires that a person who remembers that he had a certain sensation (solely on the basis of having had it) must have shown that he was having it at the time he was having it. But since this latter is nonsense, it would follow that one could not remember a sensation. We can and do remember sensations, and so the definition is wrong.

My reply to this objection is to point out that *a* sense can be given to saying that a person knows that he has a sensation at the time he has it. He knows it in the sense that *he can tell you* that he has it. This is a significant thing to say, because a dog or a human baby *cannot* tell you that he has a painful ear, although it could be determined that he has one. In this sense, there are various sensations that lower animals and human infants have without knowing it, whereas human adults both have them and know it. As a human being learns language he acquires the capacity to know that he has those sensations. Therefore he can subsequently remember that he had them. Our definition of factual memory in terms of knowledge does not presuppose that knowledge is always the *same kind* of thing. Any legitimate sense of "know" yields a legitimate sense of "remember." [21]

The second and final objection to our definition, which I am going to consider, is the following: A person can remember that

[20] "It can't be said of me at all (except perhaps as a joke) that I *know* I am in pain" (Ludwig Wittgenstein, *Philosophical Investigations,* tr. G. E. M. Anscombe [New York: The Macmillan Company, 1953], sec. 246. See p. 110).

[21] I do not believe there is any sense in which a dog or infant can be said to know that it has some sensation. I accept the consequence that a dog cannot be said to remember that he had a painful ear, and also the more interesting consequence that a human being cannot be said to remember that he had one, if he had it at a time before he knew enough language to be able to tell anyone that he had it. This point is connected with what Wittgenstein says about William James's Ballard (*Investigations,* sec. 342).

he had a dream and what it was. But a person cannot know that he is dreaming *while* he is dreaming. Remembering that one had a dream cannot be analyzed, therefore, into knowing that one had a dream because one previously knew it.

I believe this argument is sound. In my monograph on dreams I argue that the sentence "I am asleep" cannot be used to express a judgment about one's own condition, i.e., one cannot judge that oneself is asleep.[22] If this is correct then there cannot be such a thing as knowing that oneself is asleep, and from this it follows that one cannot know that one is dreaming. One can know that one *dreamt* but not that one *is* dreaming.

Is this knowledge that one dreamt *memory,* and if so, does our definition of factual memory fit it? There is no doubt that often the knowledge that one had a dream is memory, e.g., when one knows that one had a dream last week or last month. But if a person awakened suddenly from sleep and immediately declared that he had a dream, should we call this *remembering* that he had a dream? I am not sure: but if so then this use of "He remembers that *p*" does not fall under our analysis of factual memory. We cannot hold that here "He remembers that he dreamt" is equivalent to "He knows that he dreamt because he knew that he dreamt," since we should not know how to determine a previous time at which he knew that he dreamt. It would not be satisfactory to hold that "At some previous time he knew that he dreamt" means the same as "If he had been awakened at some previous time he would have said that he dreamt," since, in our example, the latter might be false.

The conclusion I draw is, not that our definition of factual memory is wrong, but that this special sense of remembering that one dreamt differs sharply from the central use of the factual memory locution.[23] Our definition gives a correct account of the central use, but perhaps not of absolutely every use of this locution.

---

[22] Norman Malcolm, *Dreaming,* second impression (New York: Humanities Press and London: Routledge & Kegan Paul, Ltd., 1962). See especially Chapters 3 and 9.

[23] See *Dreaming,* pp. 56-59, for a discussion of the notion of remembering dreams.

Index

Abelson, R., 162n.
After-images
  errors of perception, 77, 86
  mistakes, 82, 85
  numerical identity, 73-77
  unnoticed features, 79
Agreement
  in judgments, 194-196
  and truth, 196
Allen, R. E., 162n.
Ambrose, A., 181n.
Analogy
  argument from, 130-138
Anselm, St., 141-162
Aristotle, 204n.
Armstrong, D. M., 196n.
Attitude
  toward a person, 118
  toward a soul, 118
  toward statements, 68
Augustine, St., 146
Austin, J. L., 83n., 91n., 178n.,
    182n.
Ayer, A. J., 3, 65, 83, 187, 227

Baier, K. E. M., 154
Behaviorism, 138
Berg, J., 162n.

Bergson, H., 209, 210
Belief
  mistaken for knowledge, 60
Berkeley, 87, 88
Broad, C. D., 205, 207n., 219
Brown, T. P., 162n.

Calhoun, R., 146n.
Carnap, R., 3, 8, 9, 24, 53, 54, 55
Caterus, 157, 158
Certainty, 69-70
  absolute, 5, 6, 43, 48, 55, 56,
    70
  and doubt, 116
  highest degree, 57, 70
  metaphysical, 56, 64, 70
  perfect, 56, 64, 70
  philosophical, 57n.
  practical, 55
  and risk, 56-57n.
  theoretical, 45-46, 55-56
Chappell, V. C., 180n.
Common belief, 169, 181, 182
Common sense, 169-170, 173,
    181, 182
Common sense view, 170, 182
Confidence, 59
Confirmation, 3

241

Consequences
  of empirical statements, 6-14,
    25, 38
  infinite, 11, 51, 52
Criterion
  of another's pain, 117
  of another's sensation, 117
  and certainty, 115, 116
  and circumstances, 113-114
  of identity, 129
  and logical implication, 113-
    115
  of mental phenomena, 136-137,
    138, 140
  of others' thoughts and feelings,
    131-132
  outward, 123, 138
  of pain, 112
  of same, 112
  of understanding, 102
Crombie, I. M., 153

Descartes, 64, 70, 142, 143, 149,
  151, 157, 159
Direct perception, 73-95
  of after-images, 72-75, 86
  excludes doubt, 87
  excludes error, 94
  excludes inference, 88
  of physical realities, 73, 75, 86,
    87
Direct seeing, 73
  definition, 95
Doubt, 70, 87
  lacking, 119
Dreaming, 67, 240

Existence
  contingent, 49
  perfection, 143-144, 146
  predicate, 144
Existential propositions, 153-155

Findlay, J. N., 152n. 154-155
Form of life, 119-120

Frankfurt, H. G., 23n., 36n., 56-
  57n.
Frege, G., 64n.

Gassendi, 145, 151
Gaunilo, 143, 149n.
Geach, P., 23n.
Gilson, E., 158n.
God
  self-contradictory concept, 159-
    160
Grounds, 59
  conclusive, 52
  degrees of strength, 228-229
  not entailing, 49
  required for knowledge, 225-
    228, 230

Hallucination, 48, 67, 93
Hampshire, S., 132-133
Henle, P., 162n.
Hintikka, J., vi, 72n., 189
Huggett, W. J., 162n.
Hume, 43-44, 154, 156, 174, 175,
  202

Impossibility
  logical, 201
  of perceiving material things,
    174
  of seeing bodies, 175-178, 180,
    182
Incorrigibility, 91-93, 95
  of after-image descriptions, 83-
    86
  of dream reports, 110
  of identification, 127-129
  of pain-behavior, 112
  of psychological sentences, 110
Incorrigible statements, 4
Infinite being, 160

James, W., 239n.

Kant, 144, 145, 151-153, 156-
  158
Kierkegaard, 161, 162

Knowledge
  and being mistaken, 61
  degrees of certainty, 231
  strong, 62, 64, 67, 70-72, 90
  weak, 63

Lazerowitz, M., 181n.
Language-game, 119-120, 123, 156
  private, 123
Leibniz, 63n., 159
Lewis, C. I., 1-56, 89
Lichtenberg, 96
Locke, 64, 65, 70

Making sure, 69
Masters and slaves, 118
Matthews, G. B., 162n.
Memory
  by acquaintance, 208, 209
  behavior, 197-198
  being sure, 224-225
  and brain, 235
  causal connection, 232, 233
  and certainty, 229, 230
  correct, 191, 220
  delusive, 190-191, 193, 198
  of dreams, 240
  factual, 204-205, 208, 209, 210, 212, 213, 214, 220, 221, 222-240
  forms, 203
  grounds, 224, 225, 229, 230
  habit, 209, 210
  images, 197, 206, 208, 219n.
  impression, 100-101
  impure, 224
  incorrect, 188-192, 220
  inner physiology, 237, 238
  and knowledge, 191, 192, 193, 223, 224, 229
  perceptual, 205-210, 212, 213, 214, 217, 218, 219, 220, 221
  personal, 214-221
  process of retention, 238
  pure, 223-224

requiring imagery, 212n.
  true, 209, 210
  verification, 199
Mental imagery, 211, 212, 213, 217
Mill, J. S., 88, 130-131
Mistake
  about after-image, 82, 83, 84
  impossible, 57, 67-69, 70, 72, 89, 90, 91-92, 93, 94, 129
  possible, 66
Moore, G. E., v, 16, 73-76, 86-87, 89-90, 91, 93-95, 163-183, 189, 214

Necessary existence
  perfection, 146
  property of God, 150, 156
Normal reaction, 195

Ordinary language
  defence, 180-183

Paradigm, 179
  of one's own pain, 139-140
  of others' sensations, 117
  of seeing a body, 179
Penelhum, T., 162n.
Perfection, 159
Plantinga, A., 162n.
Popper, K., 3n.
Possibility
  and certainty, 34-35
  degrees, 30
  of error, 57
  logical, 28
Prediction, 8, 68
Price, H. H., 87, 133-134
Prichard, H. A., 58, 60, 61, 71, 72, 175-183
Private definition, 98
Private identification, 137-138
Private language, 97, 105, 123-124, 125
Private object, 127, 128
Private rules, 100, 103-104

Rawls, J., 235n.
Reid, T., 169
Remembering
  the future, 204, 208
  incorrectly, 187
  to do something, 222n.
Russell, B., 39, 165, 187-202, 208-210
Ryle, G., 153, 207

Sachs, D., 235n.
Same, 101-103
  after-image, 175-178
  assertion, 173
Seeing
  after-images, 73-86, 91-95
  direct, 73
  in one's mind, 205, 207, 208, 209, 211, 218
  material things, 177
Seeing bodies
  logically impossible, 178-180, 182
Self-observation, 138-139
Sensations
  descriptions, 121
  expressions, 106-111
  identifying, 125-129
  naming, 121, 122, 126
  of others, 105-106
  recognizing, 125, 138
Sense-data, 70-71, 73-74

Shaffer, J., 162n.
Sight
  illusion, 175-176, 178n.
Simple qualities, 159
Smart, J. J. C., 153, 155n.
Solipsism, 106, 136-138
Spinoza, 148
Strawson, P., 120-129

Taylor, R., 71n.

Understanding
  requires human behavior, 135-136

Verification
  complete, 2, 53
  ends, 54
  infinite, 56
  partial, 2
Verification argument
  finished, 25-26
  original, 21
  revised, 22
Von Leyden, W., 217, 232, 233, 234, 237
Von Wright, G. H., vi, 181n.

White, A. R., 180n.
Wittgenstein, L., v, 57, 72, 96-129, 132, 136-140, 156, 159, 165, 171, 182, 183, 194-196, 199, 200, 239n.